The Promise of
World Order

Written under the auspices of the
Center of International Studies,
Princeton University

Also by Richard Falk

Law, War and Morality in the Contemporary World, Praeger, 1963, 120 pp.

The Role of Domestic Courts in the International Legal Order, Syracuse University Press, 1964, 184 pp.

Security in Disarmanent, ed. with Richard J. Barnet, Princeton University Press, 1965.

The Strategy of World Order, ed. with Saul Mendlovitz, 4 vols., New York, World Law Fund, 1966.

International Law and Organisation: An Introductory Reader, ed. with Wolfram Hanrieder, Philadelphia, J. B. Lippincott Co., 1968, 346 pp.

Legal Order in a Violent World, Princeton University Press, 1968, 610 pp.

Neutralisation and World Politics, with C. E. Black, Klaus Knorr and Oran R. Young, Princeton University Press, 1968.

The New States and International Legal Order, Leyden, A. W. Sijthoff, 1968, 102 pp.

The Vietnam War and International Law, ed., Princeton University Press, Vol. I, 1968; Vol. II, 1969; Vol. III, 1972; Vol. IV, 1976.

The Future of the International Legal Order, ed., with C. E. Black, Princeton University Press, Vol. I, 1969; Vol. II, 1970; Vol. III, 1971; Vol. IV, 1972.

The Status of Law in International Society, Princeton University Press, 1970.

This Endangered Planet, New York, Random House, 1971.

Crimes of War, ed. with R. J. Lifton and G. Kolko, New York, Random House, 1971.

The International Law of Civil War, ed., Baltimore, Johns Hopkins University Press, 1971.

Regional Politics and World Order, ed. with Saul H. Mendlovitz, San Francisco, Freeman, 1973.

A Study of Future Worlds, New York, Free Press, 1975, 506 pp.

A Global Approach to National Policy, Cambridge, Mass., Harvard University Press, 1975.

The War System: An Interdisciplinary Approach, ed. with Samuel S. Kim, Boulder, Col., Westview Press, 1980, 659 pp.

International Law and World Order: A Problem-Oriented Coursebook, ed. with Burns H. Weston and Anthony A. D'Amato, St. Paul, Minn., West Publishing Co., 1980, 1195 pp.

Basic Documents in International Law and World Order, ed. with Burns H. Weston and Anthony A. D'Amato, St. Paul, Minn., West Publishing Co., 1980, 447 pp.

Human Rights and State Sovereignty, New York, Holmes and Meier Publishers, 1981, 261 pp.

Toward a Just World Order, ed. with Samuel S. Kim and Saul H. Mendlovitz, Boulder, Col., Westview Press, 1982, 652 pp. (Studies on a Just World Order, No. 1).

Indefensible Weapons: The Political and Psychological Case Against Nuclearism, with Robert Jay Lifton, New York, Basic Books, 1982, 314 pp.

The End of World Order, New York, Holmes and Meier Publishers, 1983, 368 pp.

International Law: A Contemporary Perspective, ed. with Fredrich Kratochwil and Saul H. Mendlovitz, Boulder, Col., Westview Press, 1985, 715 pp. (Studies on a Just World Order, No. 2).

Reviving the World Court, Charlottesville, VA, University Press of Virginia, 1986, 215 pp.

The Promise of World Order
Essays in Normative International Relations

Richard Falk

TEMPLE UNIVERSITY PRESS
PHILADELPHIA

First published in the United States in 1987 by
TEMPLE UNIVERSITY PRESS,
Philadelphia, 19122

Library of Congress Cataloging-in-Publication Data

Falk, Richard A.
  The promise of world order.

  Bibliography: p.
  Includes index.
  1. International relations.
  2. International organization.
  I. Title.
  JX1395.F296   1987   327   87–10164
  ISBN 0–87722–517–6

Typeset in Linotron Times 11 on 12pt by
Input Typesetting Ltd, London SW19 8DR

Printed in Great Britain

For Mary
With praise
joy
love

Contents

Acknowledgements

I wish to acknowledge with gratitude permission to reprint in revised form articles and essays from the following journals and books:

'Lifting the Curse of Bipartisanship', *World Policy Journal*, Vol. I, No. 1, Fall 1983 (Chapter 2); 'Nuclear Weapons and the End of Democracy', *PRAXIS International*, Vol. 2, No. 1, April 1982 (Chapter 3); 'Nuclear Weapons and the Renewal of Democracy', *PRAXIS International*, Vol. 4, No. 2, July 1984 (Chapter 4); 'The Global Setting and Transition to Democracy', *Alternatives*, Vol. VIII, No. 2, Fall 1982 (Chapter 5); 'Rethinking Neutrality in the Nuclear Age', *Journal of World Peace*, Vol. II, No. 1, Spring 1985 (Chapter 6); 'Beyond Deterrence: The Essential Political Challenge', in Peter C. Sederberg (ed.), *Nuclear Winter, Deterrence and the Prevention of Nuclear War*, New York, Praeger, 1986 (Chapter 7); 'Can Decency Guide the Quest for Peace?', *Alternatives*, Vol. X, No. 3, Winter 1984–85 (Chapter 8); 'Normative Initiatives and Demilitarisation: A Third System Approach', World Order Models Project Working Paper No. 13, 1982 (Chapter 9); 'Towards Security for the People', *UNESCO Yearbook on Peace and Conflict Studies 1982*, Westport, Ct., Greenwood Press, 1983 (Chapter 10); 'The Future of World Order', in Gabriel M. Wilner and others (eds.), *Jus et Societas: Essays in Tribute to Wolfgang Friedmann*, The Hague, Martinus Nijoff Publishers, 1979 (Chapter 4); 'Technology and Politics: Shifting Balances', *Alternative Futures*, Vol. 3, No. 2,

Spring 1980 (Chapter 12); 'The Spirit of Thoreau in the Age of Trident', *Agni Review*, 23, 1986 (Chapter 13).

A part of Chapter 1 was presented as a paper at a conference on 'Pathways: A Dialogue on Alternatives for a Time of Transition', held in Lucerne, Switzerland during Spring 1985.

During the preparation of this volume I was greatly assisted by the overall facilities and congenial atmosphere provided by the Center of International Studies, and wish to express thanks to both Cyril Black and Henry Bienen who served successively as Director of the Center. I also want to thank Gladys Starkey for her impressively efficient and gracious administrative leadership of the Center staff.

My research assistant of the past two years, Philomena Fischer, has been a great help, always cheerfully, often beyond the call of formal duties, expressing her sense of solidarity with scholarly work that seems dedicated to the promotion of peace and justice in our political life.

My greatest debt is to June Garson who with characteristic intelligence and skill did all that was necessary to prepare this manuscript for publication. Her help and support over the years are a great source of strength.

This book represents a stage in a transnational scholarly effort to develop a world order approach to international studies. In particular, two collaborative undertakings have exerted a considerable influence: The Peace and Global Transformation Programme of the United Nations University and The Committee for a Just World Peace of the World Order Models Project. Colleagues in both these settings have been stimulating and suggestive over the years, especially when most sharply in disagreement.

Mary Morris, to whom the book is dedicated, has been supportive in countless ways, not least of which has been her unsparing editorial eye. And my two younger sons, Dimitri and Noah, have been there to remind me in the most tangible manner, that it is vital not to relinquish the future to starry-eyed political realists or wild-eyed militarists, technocrats, terrorists, arrayed in the ranks of various fanaticisms.

1 The World Order Approach: Issues of Perspective, Academic Discipline and Political Commitment*

Throughout these essays there is a unifying theme arising from an insistence on my part that thought without action equals zero, and that thought without a bedrock of acknowledged values to provide direction is a minus quantity. I proceed in this introductory essay to provide a sketch of this orientation, thereby disclosing, in part, 'the hidden agenda' implicit in subsequent chapters.

I A PERSONAL POINT OF DEPARTURE

The Vietnam War was a formative political experience for me, as it was for many other Americans. By professional accident – or fate – my first invited academic paper was on the topic of foreign intervention. I was thrilled to deliver the paper at Brussels, at a sort of academic sideshow during the world's fair being held in that city during the Summer of 1958, but startled to be attacked while on the podium by a Hungarian participant who denounced me because I had criticised the Soviet intervention in Hungary in 1956, and as such, was acting as a US propagandist. I pointed out in response that while I did indeed criticise Soviet interventionary behaviour, most of the paper was devoted to a criticism of the American intervention in Lebanon that had occurred only months earlier. After the session my Hunga-

---

* Some of the material in this chapter is drawn from an essay entitled 'Finding Light: If Politics Recaptures Hope'.

rian critic came and apologised, informing me sheepishly
that he had been instructed to denounce the paper back in
Budapest where his superior evidently assumed from the
title that any US citizen discussing foreign intervention in
the late 1950s would surely be delivering an anti-Soviet
tirade. Such reflexes of the mind disclose the dreadful
humiliations imposed upon bureaucrats in the employ of
governments with an aversion to democracy.

Opposing US intervention in Vietnam came to me
naturally. Somehow, the American ideals of self-determination and anti-colonialism were embedded in my political
consciousness. I identified quite automatically with the
underdog in the United States and overseas, although
without at the same time being drawn to embrace any of
the obvious solutions, intuitively believing that the world
would neither be safe nor pleasant until the causes of misery
associated with oppression and exploitation were substantially removed. The rationalisations and sheer lies told by
'the best and the brightest' to keep the war in Vietnam
going made me convinced that the problem was less one of
foreign policy than constitutionalism at home and world
order abroad, and that, at any rate, liberals had little more
than conservatives to offer on these matters of underlying
importance.

So long as powerful states waged war at their discretion
it would be difficult to secure the peace. Further, more and
more governments, also, turned in various ways against
their own peoples. The fiction of 'national interests' seemed
a cruel deception. It even became evident that powerful
governments were not serving their own peoples' well-being
when they built up huge armaments, intervened in distant
lands, ignored human rights at home and abroad, insisted
that large non-accountable intelligence agencies were essential for national security, and failed to exert demographic
and ecological self-discipline and generally adopted a
paternalistic stance toward their own citizenry.

It was a more extended process to realize that the kind
of outlook that fed the arms race and the militarisation of
the world was deeply embedded, indeed, so much so, that
traditional democratic methods (elections, political parties,

legislative initiative) to achieve change were losing much of their potency in the war/peace area even for those countries that adhered to the forms and spirit of democratic procedure, especially through the tolerance of opposition politics, rights of dissent, and freedom of assembly for anti-governmental activists. The rituals of elections remain important, but political parties and representative institutions (legislature) have become virtual creatures of the state when it comes to national security policy, largely unresponsive to shifts in popular mood, opposing parties and tendencies being preoccupied with little more than quibbles within an agreed consensus covering the fundamentals of foreign policy. As a consequence, liberal trust in the dynamics of gradual reform, in the persuasive force of reason and education, and in the problem-solving capacities of governmental process in a formally democratic society have lost much of their credibility in the face of statist encroachment upon civil society over the course of the last several decades.

But this mood of disillusionment rests on additional factors as well. As corporate growth proceeds it promotes the ideology of technological inevitability, and exerts an influence on the state apparatus to adapt governing policies to the open-ended logic of continuous innovation and expanding scale. Despite declining real security arising from military moderisation ever since 1945, this dynamic of modernisation acts to suppress the political imagination. Not only weaponry, but life–style patterns, especially consumerism, reflect the wider impact of technological determinism. Uncritical enthusiasm, reinforced by profit-maximising advertising campaigns and political lobbying, robots, computers, video education, adopted without ever pausing to weigh its dysutopian consequences, or acting to prevent them. We cheerfully devote billions to space exploration while our cities and their inhabitants rot away, and a virtual epidemic of teenage suicide takes place beneath our dazed eyes. There is no overall governmental effort to balance priorities, make principled choices, and provide leadership commensurate to the problems.

What is more, the main liberating energies of the political

left, as a pressure for societal improvement, have evidently been spent, temporarily at least. Socialism as a creed remains attractive, but as an orientation toward the acquisition and exercise of power its record of performance is disappointing, or worse. Either the violence relied upon to prevail in a struggle for power has carried over into the governing process to reproduce oppression in some new form, as in the Soviet Union and its East European protégé states, or socialism has prematurely and amateurishly given effect to a radical vision of social justice while playing the constitutional game, rendering the process vulnerable to a bloody and regressive backlash, as happened most conspicuously in the transition from Allende to Pinochet in the Chile of the 1970s. Neither reliance on violence, nor its disavowal, seems convincingly sustainable in the pursuit of a just and peaceful society, and by extension, a just and peaceful world. This immobilising dilemma is also a disturbing element in liberation struggles. Albert Camus shared his anguish over such a moral dilemma by withdrawing from participation in the Algerian War of Independence. What conclusions are we to draw from the growing practice by black militants in South African townships of 'executing' suspected collaborators with *apartheid* by such arbitrary and cruel method as 'the necklace', supposedly, to inhibit cooperation with the regime? Does such behaviour contaminate the anti-apartheid struggle, or merely make us pessimistic about human nature and the likely political sequel to *apartheid* in South Africa? But withdrawing from history is no solution either, although in specific situations it may at least spare individuals a sense of active complicity in immorality, but at the cost of turning the field over entirely to the anti-apartheid absolutists.

With such knowledge, then, how can we act politically in a manner that is at once constructive and effective? My emphasis is increasingly upon the grassroots/interpersonal nexus of opportunities to revitalise democracy and politics by embodying values and visions in the relationships, commitments, and enactments of everyday life. In the remainder of this chapter, I will consider the most plausible scenarios that arise out of the mainstream, dominant politics of our times and then depict a counter-politics that is in the process of formation in the minds and hearts and souls of citizen pilgrims variously situated throughout the planet.

II FOREBODINGS

When we consider to whom the future belongs there are a variety of sensible answers each of which seems compelling without being comprehensive. Our Western sensibilities tend to be reductionist (seeking always the single, grand leverage-point upon history, as Marx insisted class owner-ship of the means of production to be, or Freud claimed for the suppression of desire on behalf of the rational ordering compulsions of civilization), and resist the more durable, if less spectacular, understanding that flows from plural truths. Our either/or occidental orientation needs to be enriched by the appreciation that many, but not all, interpretations of what is happening can be simultaneously valid and useful.

A Sufi tale expresses a preferred style of wisdom. Two persons cannot settle an argument, and approach the village mullah, venerated for his judgment and fairness. He listens to the first party expressing his grievance and responds 'Yes, I have heard you, and you are right'. The second party is then invited to state his position, after which the mullah responds as before, 'Having heard you, I am persuaded you are right also'. The mullah's wife placed by the culture in the background asserts herself at this stage to cut through an apparent Gordian Knot of confusion: 'You fool, how can they both be right'. The mullah responds quietly, not displaced from his serenity by this challenge, 'Don't worry dear one, you too are right!'. To live with this lack of closure requires that we acknowledge contradictory features in the complexity that composes the reality we confront. Yet to intervene at all with the power of an interpretation entailing action is to deny complexity the possibility of overwhelming us with uncertainty and formlessness.

Surveying the implications of present tendencies now shaping our political existence, discloses the potency of some dark visions. Let us consider these as establishing a setting for more positive action. Without this setting, positive visions seem mere expressions of desire, easily dismissible as without relevance, lacking in realism.

The Future Belongs to the Technocrats

There is a strong disposition to give up on the world, but to rely on technology to do the hard work of the civilization. As matters get worse on the planet, technocrats shed their scientific pretensions, and claim for their solutions a kind of transcendence that fills the normative vacuum left by the death of mainstream religion. Ronald Reagan's espousal of the Strategic Defense Initiative (SDI, or 'Star Wars') is a chilling illustration of this hold that technocrats have achieved over the political imagination of the culture.

What is remarkable here is not the fantastic claim on resources for a new line of innovational weaponry in space, but the receptivity of society to a utopian approach to the challenge of nuclear war. Without any sensible expectation that a defensive shield can ever protect society from the threat of such weapons, the espousal of SDI as national policy has proceeded with relatively little mass resistance.

What does this tell about ourselves? That we cannot find an acceptable rational solution to the problem of peace in the nuclear age. But more than this, that an escape route must assume a specific form. To advocate total disarmament, as have the more rationalistic Soviets in the Gorbachev era, is to appear propagandistic. To call for world government is to invite derision as naive. Yet SDI is promoted effectively as an exciting voyage to the future that offers hope.

Ronald Reagan with his charismatic capacity to express the unconscious strivings of American society, has packaged his utopia in saleable form. He has drawn upon the technocratic idolatry that suggests that anything can be done if the resources are put at the disposal of the makers of things and the manipulators of information. As such, the divine energy of our civilization is capital plus human ingenuity.

What is more, many powerful individuals are generally receptive despite their inner rejection of the overarching claims made to achieve popular, public justification. Militarists welcome SDI because it provides a way to build up enough defence capabilities to increase the disposition by leaders in the United States to threaten or use nuclear weapons, whether in a time of crisis or when dealing with challenges other than those coming from Moscow. And the research establishment associated with big science and the military is supportive, finding ample mandate for proceeding fully funded in a variety of directions of inquiry for years and years.

SDI takes on a great significance when we consider that it revives the whole 'faith' of the Enlightenment that science and technology would eventually deliver human society from the torments of scarcity and even mortality. Genetic engineering holds out the promise of abundance of resources and even of everlasting life. And so while we confront the possibility of Armageddon (often a dark vision that co-exists, in Reagan's case, with such technocratic delusions of emancipation as that of SDI), we also suppose that perseverance on the path of modernisation can produce the sort of miracles for humankind that were rejected as mere superstitution in the early modern period centuries ago. Another variant of aberrant technological imagination is the literal supposition that the crowding of the planet can be handled by mass migrations to space colonies established in the geosynchronous orbit between earth and sun, or that population expansion can always be accommodated by technological ingenuity. These compulsively optimistic outlooks even dismiss as illusionary any inhibiting limits on human endeavour and reject notions of fixed quantity in relation to arable land or forest as defeatist.[1]

Even some sensitive students of human evolution can subscribe to this sort of technocratic ideology. The anthropologist, Peter Farb, grounds his optimism about the future in such faith. He writes that 'The sweep of hominid history provides a basis for believing that the modernised human will invent new techniques to meet new needs, as they always have in the past.'[2] And even more declaratively, 'If we can survive a few great hazards that face us in the coming decades, then I forecast the ushering in of a new era expressive as never before of the human potential.'[3] Farb's confidence rests on the past record of human ingenuity in overcoming, or circumventing, adversity, as well as a sense that human problem-solving gifts will enable adaptation in the future as well.

This faith in modernisation arises out of the West, but it has spread elsewhere, to those who seek a rapid ascent to power and affluence. In the West itself, confidence in the future is closely associated with the quest for new forms of imperial order to overcome the threats and losses of control and resources associated with the collapse of colonialism in the decades after World War II. More profoundly, this technocratic outlook is a continuation of that grave mistake of supposing that human society could successfully separate itself from nature and sacred power. It represents a failure of balance, a loss of the capacity to distinguish adequately limits and dangers, as well as opportunities, at the technological frontier. If the future belongs to the technologists, we face a permanent prospect of regimentation and catastrophic adjustment, that is, if all goes well!

The Future Belongs to the Traditionalists
As if in defiance to the excessive claims arising from the modernising energies of the West, one discerns some disruptive reactions that threaten perfect chaos as our planetary destiny, 'the Beirutisation of the world'. There is a great surge of fundamentalist claims to restore human society to a simple clear path of traditional virtue sanctified by revealed truth that assures literal guidance to the faithful in their life struggles. In this conception, perhaps most vividly exemplified in the Islamic Republic of Ayatollah Khomeini, techology and modernism in all forms is harshly repudiated as authority (although selectively relied upon for tactical purposes) and blamed for corruption of the spirit and exploitation of the body.

In these regards, fundamentalism summons the latent energies of society to throw off alien forms of rule and behaviour. The Iranian results are quite spectacular on this level. Without weapons or assistance, the fundamentalists banished foreigners and toppled a millennial experience of dynastic rule. These are achievements that build credibility among those dispossessed throughout the Third World, especially where Islam is strong. There is a fundamentalist resonance visible in many different settings, even in the belly of the modernist monster. The success of the Rev. Moon's Unification Church, Jerry Falwell's Moral Majority, or even such Eastern cults as those associated with Hare Krishna or Rajneesh, display disturbing societal vulnerabilities and cravings that create a surprising range of openings for fundamentalist politics.

To return to such constraining pre-modern visions of social order with this vehemence and venom inevitably involves a revival of the inquisitorial methods of the past. Those who hold out for greater freedom and a more plural view of human destiny are branded 'infidels', and rendered fit for an exterminating crusade. Violence is put at the service of dogmatic truth, and human society is imprisoned in traditionalist chains.

The Future Belongs to the Terrorists
Closely connected with both technocrats and traditionalists are those who would gain their ends of order or chaos by means of violence directed at the innocent. Because the West controls information technology, there is a disposition to reserve the opprobrium of terrorism for the weak who strike with viciousness at the rich and strong, most symbolically at such cathedrals of technocracy as modern airports.

Deep confusions beset our understanding of terrorism. While we castigate Qadaffi and Palestinian groups for their endorsement of terroristic methods, leaders in the West adopt nuclear strategies that could eventuate in total destruction of civilisation. On a lesser scale, governments under the cover of 'intelligence' hire and train terrorists to carry out secret missions that have all the features of a terrorist enterprise. Consider the official French willingness to send several teams of their agents to Auckland, New Zealand to destroy the Greenpeace vessel, *The Rainbow Warrior*, on 10 July 1985 while it was peacefully docked at Marsden Wharf. The motive here seems to have been partly vindictive, partly deterrent, evidently seeking to discourage, if not to preclude any further interference by Greenpeace with French nuclear testing at its Pacific island of Moruroa.[4] Or, consider the efforts by President Reagan to mobilise counter-terrorist righteous indignation while simultaneously calling on Congress to provide funds enabling the *contras* to go on terrorising the Nicaraguan countryside at great loss of peasant life.

The spread of terrorism *in all forms* is very dangerous to the spirit of compromise and diversity that makes politics and conflict tolerable. Endorsement of terrorism for *any purpose* lends credibility to violence, to denials of normal freedom, and to the vesting of still more authority in the militarised portions of governments. As we proceed into a world of encounter between technocrats and traditionalists, the political dialogue on *both sides* becomes dominated by the outlook and methods of terrorism. Nothing else seems to get headlines and results.

As a consequence, political actors free themselves to varying degrees from the limiting influence of moral or legal norms. Political struggle acquires an unconditional quality that includes the collapse of authority systems, and a remorselessness toward 'the enemy'. Lebanon since 1975 offers as much a warning about the precariousness of our world as did Hiroshima and Nagasaki. And again, this is a double warning, not only about recourse to violence by the disenfranchised but also about violence unleashed from modern aircraft and naval vessels raining down bombs, rockets, and artillery shells on refugee camps and residential urban areas.

It is worth pondering the degree to which variants of claims to be a chosen people produce terroristic politics, either to sustain positions of undue advantage or to challenge them. In this regard, it is worth reflecting upon the correlation in the early 1980s between the use by Americans of 30–35 per cent of the annual consumption of world resources while providing targets for 30 per cent of the incidents officially classified as terrorism. Could there be important, if obscure, connections between taking more than its share of resources and becoming a prime target for those who are desperate about their circumstances of poverty and denial?

The Future Belongs to the Ecological Fanatics

It is not only the technocrats, traditionalists, and terrorists that cast their shadow across the future. It is also those who in one way or another believe that it is essential to get rid of the human surplus now consuming resources and occupying space on the planet. Such a disposition whether filtered through a belief in the invisible hand of the market, the wisdom of Malthus and Darwin, or the ecological implications of 'the tragedy of the commons' tends toward the same kinds of relentless social policies that vindicates coldness about the misery and suffering of the poor.

The most articulate advocate of ecological adjustment at the expense of the poor is Garrett Hardin, a biologist with an unflinching willingness to follow through on what is implied by a human population that cannot be contained within the carrying capacity of the earth. While explicitly resisting a clear endorsement of a human liquidation programme (not for intrinsic reasons but because it might prove 'infectious and addictive', and thereby 'bring into existence a positive feedback system that . . . can destabilize society, bringing on a new Dark Age') Hardin does call for 'a posture of attrition'.[5] Attrition is meant to encourage a clear-headed realisation that letting famines and disease take their course is in the overall human interest.

Hardin, accordingly, repudiates the view that this strain in carrying capacity can be corrected by aid to the disadvantaged or a more egalitarian approach to resource use. He believes that aid only defers coming to terms with ecological limits and is counterproductive, while asking or requiring the rich to reduce their consumptive patterns only results in making everyone poor without addressing the issue of surpluses directly. In effect, this kind of ecological fanaticism is both a rationalisation for the existing hierarchy of society and classes, and for hardheartedness toward the most helpless victims of current societal and international arrangements. Hardin's 'ecolate view' is convinced that the planet would be far better off if it could shed its nonproductive poor, and in the process, achieve diminished fertility rates. In practical terms, this implies a gigantic race war, including resistance by the poor through whatever weapons are at their disposal. Once again, terrorism beckons.

No longer can the poor and weak be counted upon to be meek, awaiting deliverance in the afterlife or through the cycle of rebirth. While 11,000 French police and troops could subdue the Vietnamese during the height of colonial submission in the 1930s, more than 500,000 American troops backed by over 1,000,000 South Vietnamese soldiers and by a vast array of modern weaponry were defeated by the mobilised resistance of the Vietnamese populace in the 1970s. Hardin acknowledges that his outlook is likely to give rise to a massive increase in 'terrorism and sabotage'. To address the causes of terrorism is for Hardin futile and fatuous. He is convinced that any accommodation of grievances from below will lead victims to escalate their demands indefinitely until the old oppressors are reduced to the level of victim and themselves resort to terrorism in 'a reversal of roles'. The ecologist joins forces with the most extreme apologists for state power as Hardin italicises his final solution – *the only rational response to terrorism is police action*: it is not perfect but it is the best there is'.[6]

As with other modes of coping, this ecolate view rests on undirected violence, and on a racially-charged structure of conflict between the white enclaves of post-industrial development and the rest of the world. Even the supposed beneficiaries cannot hopefully contemplate such a future given their own vulnerabilities to disruptive violence. It is, in my view, a perversion of the ecolate outlook, which fails to take values and spiritual identity into account as vital elements of any acceptable human ecology. There is an ecological challenge, of course, but it can be met, if at all, by enlarging our sense of human community and by all of us living within the limits of the life systems of earth on *some* sustainable basis, not one that is necessarily austere or rigidly egalitarian.

There is an equally disturbing fanaticism associated with the dogmatic insistence that resource scarcity is an illusion, that human ingenunity and technology can devise solutions indefinitely for expanding populations, and that concerns about environmental protection are alarmist.[7] This ecological euphoria is associated with an absurdly positive orientation toward science and technology, as well as about the problem-solving capacities of the human brain. In effect, this refusal to acknowledge limits in relation to human activity on the planet is best understood as anti-ecological fanaticism.

III TOWARD FOCUS: THE PROCESS OF ACADEMIC INQUIRY

My recent academic preoccupations, as reflected in this volume, is the outcome of an ongoing concern about the appropriate ways to study the agenda of world problems and prospects. Retracing some of the main steps along the path may help to provide a context for assessing the more recent work. Throughout a spirit of tentativeness has prevailed, a continous sense that it is always desirable to move on, that it is possible to find better ways to express and understand the complex substance of politics on a global scale, as well as a depressing realisation that the world situation is not improving despite all those past efforts to mobilise opinion in support of various images of global reform. The emphasis on process is at the core, then, of the overall intellectual stance.

It should not be assumed that comparable flexibility pertains to critical commentary on the world order approach. On the contrary, it has been exceedingly difficult to get a fair hearing from prevailing realist and neo-realist intellectual pundits. There has been a tendency all along toward dismissive labelling of world order studies as 'utopian', 'idealist', 'legalist', and as advocate of 'world government'.[8] The approach is viewed by the realist mainstream as fixed, monolithic, dogmatic, whereas, I think, the more accurate observation is that the critical reception in mainstream circles has been fixed, monolithic, and dogmatic. That is, world order adherents have been pigeonholed, often in defiance of their actual views, making it easier for critics to justify a negative assessment. I want to argue here that not only is the corpus of world order studies by now rather complex and diverse, but that the intellectual history of its adherents is often one of search rather than of mechanical promotion of a given pattern of normative solution.[9] I will illustrate this generalised claim by reference to the evolution of my own outlook.

Phase One: Comprehensive Humanist Reform

Myres McDougal and Harold Lasswell exerted a strong influence during my period as a law student. I was persuaded by their attempt to perceive law as a value-realising instrument for those in positions of authority. The academic task was to evolve and apply a framework that would encourage decision-makers to reach enlightened choices based on relevant knowledge, systematically assessed, that embodied value preferences and also took account of how to assure effectiveness of decision (i.e., enforceability in its broad meaning).

In this period, also, I became convinced that there tends to be a kind of nationalistic and ideological bias that creeps into scholarly inquiry no matter how objective and evidence-oriented it *appears* to be. The 1950s and 1960s were in the United States a time when Cold War thinking shaped and constrained intellectual discourse on global policy. As such, academic work was often quite partisan, effusively endorsing the merits of Free World positions, or the importance of defending the West against the menace of Soviet expansionism. My own earliest publications incorporated this bias, although some effort was made to assert a normative framework of law and morality that could sort out conflicting claims in international conflict from a more neutral or global standpoint.[10] The denationalising of scholarship remains an important critical focus for world order inquiry.

More evidently related to world order studies, is the search for global solutions, a confidence that the problems of international life can be solved by a blend of education, ingenuity, and good will. Here, diagnosis has tended to concentrate on matters of organisation and governance. In this regard, the problem is territorial sovereignty and the solution is world government in some form. Such a linkage is particularly natural in the West among those with idealistic outlooks or who regard the federalist formation of the United States as a percursor to the restructuring of the world as a whole. The Clark–Sohn proposals as evolved in successive editions of *World Peace Through Law* are illustrative of this approach at its most careful and rigorous.

As a normative theorist, I resisted the advocacy of world government on political and ethical grounds. Politically such centralisation of authority seemed utterly infeasible for the foreseeable future. Nationalism was too strong a force in the lives and imaginations of the peoples of the world. Interests and identities were too fragmented among leading political actors to enable any kind of coordinated assault on the dominance of the state in both the internal and external politics of civil societies. Also, the imperial dimensions of world politics intruded upon any feasible undertaking to reform, let alone transform, the state system. Both super-powers claimed not only sovereign rights, but projected their power and influence upon weaker states situated within so-called spheres of influence. Other states exerted this hegemonic control on a regional basis. In effect, a strong hierarchical dimension shapes the character of international political life in any given historic time period.

Ethically, the fusion of separate polities seemed quite dangerous, even if it were a feasible project, almost inviting a choice between a disillusioning impotence and tyranny. Without the prior emergence of a positive global identity for the peoples of the world, it would require considerable coercion and hierarchical ordering arrangements, to sustain any kind of effective planetary scale management of political life. Even within the state, subordinate nationalities and minority peoples, are often victims of acute forms of oppression. There is a need for a new world order, but it is neither practicable nor desirable that it take the form of world government at this stage of social and cultural development.

This rejection of world government as a policy goal of world order studies has rarely been assimilated by realist critics. In part, this is understandable. The world order approach did seem to evolve out of concerns that have been frequently expressed as advocacy of a world organised around a central constitutional arrangement that appears governmental in character. A further source of confusion arises because world federalist perspectives have in recent years sought to coopt world order approaches, even if anti-federalist, because of shared concerns about global reform. Perhaps, a deeper part of the explanation for misapprehension lies within the structure and manifestations of political imagination. If world order theorists reject the state and power politics as providing the basis for peace and justice in human affairs, then what do they offer in its place? From such an outlook, the inference of 'government' follows, as there is a correct view that world order advocacy is not comfortable with an endorsement of anarchy as a replacement for geopolitics as we know it. If world order theorists make their own real positions known more generally it might help steer the dialogue about drastic global reform in helpful directions.

In fact, in this early phase of work, roughly 1955–1965, no overall design emerged. Rather, a process of normative assessment evolved that relied heavily upon legal and moral criteria. In this regard, two sets of studies predominate. First, those that view various claims by states to use military force as incompatible with international law. This concern concentrated upon First World interventions in the Third World, and in my own case, climaxed with a preoccupation over the various dimensions of the international law critique of deep US involvement in Vietnam starting in the 1950s and continuing until the mid-1970s.[11] Apart from the substantive aspects of controversy, this set of issues has normative importance for at least two other reasons: it rested on a premise that a citizen can demand adherence by his or her own government to the constraints of international law without disloyalty; and secondly, that the serious implementation of international law is a beneficial rule of the game that should be extended to all states, whether powerful or weak. As can be imagined, such argumentation produced intense controversy, as to both facts and law, especially on the home front.[12]

The other set of concerns involved the status of nuclear

weapons. Again, as an American, raising questions of legal and moral propriety meant challenging the entrenched security policies of my own government by appealing to higher principles of general application. Here, the initial reaction was neglect rather than controversy. In this period critical discussion was limited to academic commentary upon the *Shimoda* case involving a reasoned analysis of the international law status of the atomic attacks on Hiroshima and Nagasaki by a Tokyo district court. These judicial proceedings provided critics with a fundamental normative text.[13] In addition, debates with other scholars around the issue of renouncing first use options for nuclear weapons helped to shape an abiding personal concern about this overriding menace of weapons of mass destruction.[14]

In the 1960s my collaborative work with Saul Mendlovitz in the area of world order studies got its start. We shared most of the normative premises discussed above, but differed, at times sharply, as to whether or not to put forward proposals for centralised solutions for the problems of international life. I was uneasy with such proposals for the reasons indicated in the discussion of world government; also, I felt that the serious criticism of existing policies on global issues could be evaded more easily if it were possible for power-wielders and their apologists to dismiss our work as utopian. In this early period, this effort to reconcile our views is evident in the four-volume series *The Strategy of World Order*.[15] In these volumes, focus is placed upon encouraging a process of global reform that elevates law and world order values (peace, economic well-being, social and political justice, and ecological balance) above geopolitical calculations of state advantage. It does not posit any overall organisational alternative to the state system. In this regard, a central aim is to demilitarise international relations within the existing framework of states and empires, as well as to promote reformist policies of a functional (management of interdependence) and humanistic (human rights, developmental assistance) character. There is, also, an openness to a variety of structural reforms by way of an augmented United Nations, stronger regional institutions, and the evolution of a variety of specialised regimes to handle growing complexity and interdependence.

On reflection, the preoccupations and perspectives of this early phase of world order studies, despite cosmopolitan pretensions, was an expression of its US base of operations. Many of the issues of practical relevance to the current world involved controversies over the drift of the policies and overseas behaviour of the US Government; that is, although the world emphasis led to a critical stance toward US foreign policy, the agenda of concerns was set in Washington. In scholarly settings, as well, the boundaries of debate were provincial, and incorporated even European views only in superficial fashion. Marxist and non-Western orientations were virtually neglected. For these reasons, it is not surprising that the world order approach has often been criticised abroad as an ideological export of imperial United States, and has rarely found a sympathetic reception in Marxist and neo-Marxist circles. At best, it is perceived as an effort by left liberals to delineate an internationalist position that may have some importance in the internal United States debate, but is of little interest to those polities around the world in which development strategies occupy centre stage, and political struggle is perceived in relation to contending social forces and their supportive ideologies.

Phase Two: Transnational Collaboration
To move intellectually beyond provincialism was the immediate *academic* and political challenge. The World Order Models Project (WOMP) provided that opportunity, a consequence of the organising energy of the Institute for World Order (later renamed World Policy Institute) and the leadership of Saul Mendlovitz. A group of scholars were solicited to take part from most of the major world regions and meetings were held once or twice a year for almost a decade starting in 1968 at New Delhi. An intellectual biography of WOMP as an undertaking has not yet been written, and I will not attempt it here.[16]

Suffice it to say that its main participants were selected and induced to take part because of their intellectual credentials and generally progressive orientation, not because they shared a particular stance on global reform. Any careful reader would, I think, be struck by the diversity of outlook among these authors, not by their commonality. What held the group together was its shared commitment to political democracy, human rights, and anti-imperial geopolitics in contemporary affairs and the willingness of participants to subscribe to some variant of a world order future based on peace, economic well-being, social and political justice, and ecological balance.[17] Even as to this consensus there was some tension among participants, arising mainly from a certain reluctance to reject realist thinking altogether.[18]

Among the diversities that caused disagreements at meetings were issues of priority and agenda. The Third World participants insisted upon an anti-imperial orientation that depicted the consequences of post-colonial forms of exploitation. Their priorities were associated with finding a positive strategy for economic and political development at state and regional levels, as well as finding a way to safeguard the independence of Third World states against First World intervention and dominance in political, economic, and cultural spheres. As such, it contrasted with the characteristically Western liberal features and concerns of my work as embodied in my principal contribution to the WOMP process.[19] My concerns were to state the case for and depict the possibilities of global-scale reform in a manner that did not reject altogether the canons of Anglo-American notions of social science, as well as to put issues of war prevention and denuclearisation at the top of the policy agenda. Beyond this, while writing *This Endangered Planet*, I became substantively worried by the mounting array of ecological threats to the biosphere and to the quality of planetary life.[20]

As the WOMP discussions proceeded, an interesting process of convergence occurred on most issues, although Mendlovitz held out for a focus of inquiry on centralised planetary management (humane governance on a global scale) and the need to provide a vision of constitutional order that could replace balance of power mechanisms associated with a world of states. But overall, the First World participants shifted their concerns to wider questions of oppression and struggle, thereby encompassing issues of war, human rights, poverty, conservation of natural resources, and environmental quality, adopting a more balanced and variegated emphasis on the conditions for human survival. On the Third World side there was a complementary 'opening' to issues of war/peace, environment, and resource policy.

There was also an emerging consensus on the importance of translating ideas into programme for social action. Such an emphasis was a reaction against the failure of preferential thinking to exert much influence directly on élites. Only by activating counter-élites and by identifying agents of change in settings of ongoing struggle could there be much hope for global reform.

What set WOMP apart was its sustained collaborative character on a transnational basis, and its repudiation of geopolitics *as conceived* by realists in the West. Almost no attention was given to the East/West rivalry as such, or to such related notions as 'containment'. Also implicit was an utter lack of confidence in a capitalist world economy guided by market factors, especially profit opportunities and the transmission of capital and technology by way of multinational corporations and banks. The rejection of this kind of high-technology growth-oriented capitalism was a negative consensus. It did not give rise to a clear positive alternative, although the sympathies of WOMP participants were definitely with generalised ideas of humanistic socialism resting on forms of national and regional self-reliance. Also, there was strong sympathy for the movement during the early 1970s for a new international economic order, and with the assertiveness of the Third World in such arenas as the General Assembly, the Non-Aligned Movement, UNCTAD, and even OPEC. Yet, there was also some scepticism. These initiatives seemed overly statist in their orientation and it was never clear that the Third World possessed the geopolitical weight or political will to persevere when it encountered resistance.

Also evident within this collaborative process was an altered view of the state, more nuanced, and far less rejectionist than in the early work. The WOMP perspective

started off with a sharp internal controversy on the normative consequences of the strong state. The participants from
the North tended to regard the strong state as an unconditional liability from the perspective of global reform, the
chief obstacle, as well as the storm-centre of arms races,
nuclearism, and militarism. The participants from the South
tended to be worried by the adverse effects of weak states
that could be penetrated from without and were unable to
sustain tolerable forms of order within territorial boundaries. In this regard the contrast was between a country like
Israel and one like Sihanouk's Cambodia. In the former
case, regardless of other considerations, Israel was appreciated as a state able to act effectively internally and externally
in light of its goals as an actor, whereas Cambodia, or in
the 1970s, Lebanon, were countries that were acted upon,
without any autonomy, and victimised in the most extreme
respects by wider conflict formations of the region and the
world that generated highly destructive patterns of domestic
political decay leading to human agony for the people.

But as Third World governments became militarised and
acted in brutal ways against their own peoples, or came
under the command of leaders that squandered and plun-
dered resources, a new emphasis on human rights and
democracy emerged. No longer were issues of internal
constitutionalism derided by Third World intellectuals as
luxuries of the industralised West that could only be
indulged once the basic needs of the poor were satisfied.
The experience of the Emergency in India during 1976–77
and the militarisation of sub-Saharan African republics and
of the Southern Cone countries in South America during
the 1960s and 1970s made a particularly strong impression.
In this regard, the transformation of the state as a prime
goal of struggle by contending forces within civil society
became a world order priority by the end of the 1970s.

WOMP slowed down in the 1980s. It became difficult to
fund a project that lacked official backing of any sort
anywhere and that depended on expensive transnational
conferences and research programmes. The main participants were pulled towards more activist roles within their
own countries. It became difficult to find a mechanism for

collaboration as the areas of consensus did not lend themselves to a coherent vision of the future. And some disagreements remained – was it useful to set forth visions of global-scale reform? did such visions go beyond a new round of reformist constitutionalism, even if in the mild form of a strengthened United Nations? was centralisation feasible and desirable at a regional level? at a global level? what were the economic features of a positive ideology of global reform?

WOMP has not disappeared, or been suspended. Its activities include the journal *Alternatives* and support for educational materials in the world order area. In a sense, these activities enable a continuing and, even expanded, dialogue across boundaries of states and disciplines. Several WOMP participants, including myself, are intimately involved in two follow-on collaborative undertakings: The Peace and Global Transformation Project of the United Nations University and the Committee for a Just World Peace. These initiatives will be discussed as part of Phase Three.

Phase Three: Social Movements and the Struggle for Peace and Democracy
Perhaps the shaping element in this latest phase of world order activity is the realisation by world order adherents that their capacity to exert influence on the drift of policy is quite marginal, whether their locale is North or South, East or West. With rare and honourable exceptions, governments and centres of economic power are not looking for ideas that will improve the prospects of the poor and the oppressed. Intellectuals with these normative identifications are kept at arms length from most arenas of authority. Governments, in particular, have dropped in many cases the pretence of doing anything more than to manage existing arrangements. In some prominent instances, the 1980s has been a decade of declining expectations, of cutting back on promises. There is a renewal of more individualist forms of capitalism in many Western countries, with a frontal assault on the welfare state as an impediment to aggregate well-being. And on the socialist side, there is either the kind of

drab life style associated with the Soviet-type economy or a deliberate abandonment of socialist practice as in the Chinese move toward the development of a more mixed economy.

What has happened in civil society is a loss of confidence in existing structures coupled with intense doubts about the promises of crusading religious and political ideologies. In such a setting, there is a natural inclination to abandon politics altogether, and many have done just that in many parts of the world. To find a helpful path to the future under these conditions is not an easy or simple matter.[21]

In this period the disposition of world order intellectuals is to identify with ongoing social movements active in struggles for value-oriented change. There is also a strong interest in assessing the wider implications of local activism and militancy. The rise of local movements at odds with the state, or with intermediate-scale institutions of governance, discloses grassroots dissatisfaction with the discharge of custodial roles by governments in relation to their own citizens.[22] Controversies over nuclear safety, toxic waste disposal, acid rain, siting of hazardous activity (chemical plant, biogenetic research facility, and so forth) are illustrative.

Also important are social movements that want to restructure society in fundamental respects: the women's movement, the peace movement, the movement for the rights of indigenous peoples, the movement for democracy, the anti-apartheid movement. The Committee for a Just World Peace, under the joint leadership of two WOMP principals – Saul Mendlovitz and Yoshikazu Sakamoto – strongly reflects this new emphasis. The Committee seeks to explain this movement orientation and to limit its policy ambitions to the task of providing social activists with an understanding of 'global implications' (think globally, act locally).

What is noteworthy here is a new insistence that the main target audience is made up of social activists, not of officials or élites, not even of educators or of 'people like ourselves'. Such a pedagogical switch, if it is to be successful, will require a different style of expression than that which has dominated the world order literature to date – more direct and earthy writing, less scholarly apparatus of footnotes and documentation, and a closer linkage to groups engaged in 'illegal' activities, often of a resistance character. The line between action and criminality is even becoming blurred. I have supported this reorientation both as scholar and as citizen.[23]

The Peace and Global Transformation Project (PGT) of the United Nations University follows a similar path, but one that is more ambitious in its undertaking. PGT seeks to produce a series of 'composite documents' that address anew the global problematique from the standpoint of the late 1980s. Unlike WOMP, PGT has a rather like-minded view of the world situation. Its main collaborative effort to date, *A Liberating Peace*, seeks to show the complex linkages between the main sectors of international political life, and to identify the open political space where movements and other social actors can take initiatives. The main hope is to provide constructive support and guidance for movements that are engaged in various struggles for human betterment. Whether such a perspective is itself 'a pipe dream' cannot be answered without some feedback from activists and further output.

Perhaps the shift in intellectual energy can be clarified. In the 1960s my own writing was designed to get a hearing in Washington at least among the doves, and secondarily, to open a debate among academics. These goals have not been discarded as much as lightly regarded in the 1980s. Now my emphasis is upon writing that responds to, or supports, movements of resistance, especially in relation to war/peace, human rights, and environment. For instance, I have written and lectured extensively in this period on issues of personal accountability of all citizens, including especially leaders and occupants of public roles, of a free society that flows from a reinterpretation of the Nuremberg and Tokyo War Crimes Tribunals. I express this support also by appearing frequently as a *pro bono* expert witness in cases involving claims that international law is being violated by the government, as well as by lecturing and writing in these settings, and generally, by serving as a resource person.

IV FINDING LIGHT

There are various responses to the grim encounter of contending dark images of the future. One type of response is to interpret the ascendency of dark tendencies as inevitably culminating in collective disaster, throwing the force of one's imagination into the work of surviving in some post-apocalyptic world of survivors. Among the artistic instances of such post-apocalyptic imagining are Denis Johnson's *Fiskadoro*, the Mad Max series of films, several works of Karlheinz Stockhausen's music, and some of Doris Lessing's late fiction including *Shikasta* and *Memoirs of a Survivor*.

The idea of citizenship is closely connected with opportunities for participation and feelings of allegiance to a specific political community. In modern times, governments of states have tried to appropriate the notion of citizenship to themselves, and establish monopolistic control over mind, heart, and spirit when it comes to matters of participation and allegiance. The acme of this kind of citizenship is an unreflective patriotism put at the disposal of militarism, inducing a citizen to sacrifice even his/her life, if necessary, for the sake of the state.

All along this sort of blind allegiance encountered islands of opposition, and in times of stress, resistance. Individuals insisted that their conscience should take unconditional precedence over the injunction to obey a government edict. Socrates and Jesus are prominent among exemplary practitioners in the West. For modern sensibilities Thoreau's formulations of civil disobedience in the form of an oration at the Concord Lyceum on 26 January 1848 (and first published the following year) exerted a major influence upon such other historic personalities as Leo Tolstoy, Mahatma Gandhi, and Martin Luther King, Jr.

The victorious powers in World War II took another step. They prosecuted leaders of the defeated countries of Germany and Japan, including generals, judges, and businessmen, for their wartime role in the commission of crimes of state.[24] The Nuremberg Judgment, whose conclusions were later formulated as general duties for all circumstances in the form of the Nuremberg Principles, and were endorsed unanimously by governments at an early session of the United Nations General Assembly. The Nuremberg Principles, above all else, insist that an individual owes a higher obligation to the rules and principles of international law in the area of war and peace, than to the superior orders handed down by officials of the state, including its foremost leader.

Also, the ecological and security systems of our world ever more remind, and even warn, us of the unity of life and death on the planet. Explorations of space have given us for the first time widely shared, photographic images of the earth as an exquisite island spinning in space, an overarching unity. From these images a new human identity is gradually, although in many diverse and confusing forms, emerging. With this experience, we can speak of global identity without being sentimental, or calling into question any of the more specific identities of self, family, community, nation that together compose our sense of self. This newer and wider pattern of allegiance is an expansion of earlier feelings of identity.

The idea of pilgrim is primarily associated with a religious or spiritual journey. The pilgrim goes somewhere to express and manifest a commitment to the ultimate meaning of life. At this historical moment, one form of pilgrimage is to journey towards the uncreated future of humankind. It is a journey in time, given narrative shape by the acts and activities of committed individuals at various places in space, especially by their courageous witness and by their solidarity with oppressed people regardless of class, racial, or geographical factors.

Connecting the words citizen and pilgrim is intended to convey a distinct and new kind of orientation toward reality – a sense of allegiance to and participation in the struggle to build a future that realises some of our potential as a species. The concept is itself new and evolving, without dogma, or even clear specification. It will be given new shape and content by the words and deeds of its adherents, by those who proclaim themselves as citizen pilgrims and dedicate some part of their life to the great common task of making dreams about the human future come true.

The citizen pilgrim is unwilling to relinquish the future, and also unwilling to escape the pain of the present by some form of mind/spirit killing expedient, whether drugs, materialist excess, political subservience, or psychic withdrawal. Instead the citizen pilgrim in diverse ways commits his/her mind/spirit to the imagining and realising of a desirable future. Yet not as phantasy, but as a project that can be achieved eventually in space/time. As such it must, at least, seem consistent with the apparent boundaries of human nature, seem grounded in some careful rendering of historical tendencies, and take seriously emergent constellations of social forces that might act as bearers of new values and innovative political possibilities.[25]

From many different sources, a citizen pilgrim can take bearings for the journey into the future from the double tendency in the recent past to discover both the unity of the planet and the grassroots and local opportunities for action (often of resistance) on behalf of humane possibilities. Whether it is a matter of the reflections of earth from space or the growing effort to construct a variety of planetary information technologies there is a serious realisation now that the destiny of life on earth is shared across boundaries of race, class, nation, and gender. Such a cumulative experience of unity and even solidarity, including its interdependent aspects, establishes the ground for the strengthening of global unity. Such cultural conjecture is further reinforced by scientific support for 'the Gaia Hypothesis', the sense of earth as a resilient and adaptive living system that has extraordinary built-in adjustment capabilities.[26]

While at the same time, the refusal of many of the most extreme victims of the existing structures to accept as fate their misery, creates an array of concrete possibilities for action, both locally and transnationally. Whether it be a matter of rock musicians raising 'live aid' to relieve famine in Ethiopia or Japanese Buddhists beating their peace drums at the courthouses of America when nuclear resisters are put on trial, there is an evolving series of peace networks that dramatise various types of transnational and local bonding. These connections sustained by dynamic activity gradually *recentres* our understanding and experience of political loyalty and patriotism. The citizen pilgrim, above all else, gives allegiance to a country in the future whose contours can only be barely discerned upon the horizons of his/her imagination. This country has no *physical* presence in the world of today, yet it already enjoys a powerful psychological status that shapes, serves, and satisfies.

To grasp these possibilities more firmly some specific sources of inspiration can be identified, and explored. There is awaiting our attention a rich tapestry of experience and wisdom contained in the torments and fulfilments associated with the many narrative histories of indigenous peoples all over the planet. These peoples have been swept aside and generally brutalised to make way for 'civilization' and 'progress', their forms of knowledge scorned and disregarded, their remnants often assigned to concentration camps called reservations and their public image sustained as something quaint or, at most, as an origin that has been superseded.

Only recently have we discovered that the ecological sensitivity of indigenous peoples was a kind of wisdom lost and abandoned during the century-and-a-half of industrialism that has recently brought the human experience to the brink of its own destruction. Post-industrial survival and positive development depends on recovering, if in transmuted form, pre-industrial capabilities for the generally harmonious co-evolution of the human and natural environment. Chief Seattle in 1854, already sensing the doomed destiny of his people, expressed the ecological imperative with striking, assured clarity: 'This we know. All things are connected like the blood which unites one family. Whatever befalls the earth, befalls the children of the earth. We did not weave the web of life, we are merely a strand in it. Whatever we do to the web, we do to ourselves.'

In our infatuation with materialist and technological conceptions of progress, with their linear imagery, we lost the most fundamental cyclical understanding of recurrence that is associated with sustaining life on the planet. Preserving even now what remains of indigenous peoples, and restoring their position as legitimate presences on earth, is one way of creating post-industrial ecological awareness, as well as preserving the kind of diversity that adds to the strength of the earth as an ecosystem seeking the forms and practices that will assure survival and positive development.

A further source of orienting wisdom arises from the complex realisation that the torments of our present circumstance may express above all else a loss of balance between masculine and feminine energies as embodied in societal forms.[27] The secular expression of this new cultural rearrangement is a movement by women for various types of equality and dignity, and there is no doubt that masculine ascendency entailed cruel and varied types of oppression directed at women. Yet for our purposes, more significant than the redressing of past wrongs, is the potentiality implicit in this realisation that women, as prime bearers and guardians of the feminine, can help enlarge our sense of political possibility, especially with respect to the achievement of order, the exertion of authority, and the handling of conflict.

It should not be supposed that these explorations are only taking place in the West. Not long ago the current President of the Islamic Republic of Iran, while on a state visit to Zimbabwe, insisted that no women be seated at the head table during an official dinner. The leader of Zimbabwe, Robert Mugabe, recalling the heroic role of women during the country's liberation struggle, sent the Iranian visitor home rather than accede to such fundamentalist demands. And in the Philippines, the aged dictator Fernando Marcos insisted that Corazon Aquino, his female opponent in the 1986 presidential elections was not a proper rival for political leadership because 'a woman's place is in the bedroom' (note that such regressive patriarchy does not even give the woman the freedom of the home, but confines her figuratively, at least, to the bedroom).[28] It is worth observing that such recent incidents reveal the linkage between the patriarchical view of order and regressive responses to the present challenges by way of traditionalism and statist oppression.

A third, more problematic, source of inspiration for the

citizen pilgrim arises from the gropings of religious institutions and traditions for a renewal of their spiritual authority. Above all else, this move toward renewal involves an entry onto the terrain of human struggle on the side of victims of the present arrangements of power and authority. As such it breaks those culturally diverse relationships of partnership that had been built up between church and state in recent centuries. Whether it is liberation theology in Latin America, the underpinnings of *Solidarnse* in Poland, providing 'illegal' sanctuary to Central American immigrants in US churches, or the drafting and dissemination of Pastoral Letters and church statements on nuclear weapons and poverty there is evident a sense that the integrity of the religious path increasingly depends on directly challenging statism and secularism, even if this means entering into arenas of turmoil and struggle. This same process of religious awakening has also produced a surge of fundamentalist challenges to secular authority that are regressive in their overall impact.

In this regard the efforts by the Sandinistas to bring Marxism and progressive Christianity together in a new type of socialist polity was a daring experiment, although one that seems now largely spoiled by the United States effort to destroy such a threatening type of politics, an effort that has induced the Nicaraguan government to defend its right to exist by shifting resources and energies from economic and cultural to military activities. A resulting dynamic of militarisation has for the present, at least, compromised the revolutionary achievements of the Sandinistas. It is to be expected, of course, that resistance will work both ways, and that the custodians of the old order will use the means at their disposal, often violent and destructive, to eliminate any impression that it is possible to build a different kind of future, especially a future that rejects their primacy.

The citizen pilgrim is not easily diverted, nor is he/she impatient. We cannot know how close to the horizon of desire we now find ourselves, but we do realise that the self-vindicating possibilities for acting in deference to that future exist in the here-and-now. The more we take seriously our own patriotism to the future we aspire to achieve, the more likely it is to happen, and sooner, possibly sooner than we can now believe credible. To what extent the cultures of the world have been incubating such possibilities of positive adjustment is almost impossible to assess as a factor. We do have considerable evidence that revolutionary possibilities beyond the wildest expectations of spectators often lie latent within a given constellation of social forces. William Irwin Thompson locates our situation in the dynamics of transition cautiously, yet confidently:

I can see that we seem a long way off from a new political Enlightenment. It would appear we are more in a period like the Renaissance than like the eighteenth century; a period of new intuitions in poetry, art, and philosophy more than a period of consolidation into political form.[29]

Perhaps a leader with a particular feeling for these concealed possibilities or some illuminating incident that discloses the oppressive and vulnerable character of the dominant forms will emerge to confound those who suppose the future is determined by the dominant trend-lines of the present. It might be helpful to consider such lives as that of Buddha or Jesus, or Gandhi or Martin Luther King, or social movements that succeeded against the perceived odds of the day, whether the movement to abolish slavery or to challenge royal prerogatives or to overthrow the colonial order or to rid a given society of oppressive political and economic arrangements.

The citizen pilgrim finds hope by considering the past as well as by peering ahead. But even more so, the exhilaration of acting in solidarity with others, on behalf of a future that unifies and preserves on all levels of our being, validates and vindicates this questing outlook.

NOTES

1. The quintessential formulation of this economistic outlook is that of Julian L. Simon, *The Ultimate Resource* (Princeton, N.J.: Princeton University Press, 1981).
2. *Humankind* (Boston, Mass.: Houghton, Mifflin, 1978), p. 442.
3. Ibid., p. 443.

4. For early helpful accounts see David Robie, *Eyes of Fire: The Last Voyage of the Rainbow Warrior* (Auckland, New Zealand; Lindon Publishing, 1986); *Rainbow Warrior: The French Attempt to Sink Greenpeace, The Sunday Times* Insight Team (London: Arrow Books, 1986).

5. 'An Ecolate View of the Human Predicament', *Alternatives* VII: 242–262 (1981).

6. Ibid., p. 260.

7. See Simon, note 1; also Julian L. Simon and Herman Kahn (eds), *The Resourceful Earth* (London: Basil Blackwell, 1984); for a helpful overview, with special emphasis on population, see Jonathan Lieberson, 'Too Many People?' *The New York Review of Books*, 26 June 1986, pp. 36–42.

8. E.g. Hedley Bull, *The Anarchical Society: A Study of Order in World Politics* (New York: Columbia University Press, 1977); Stanley Hoffmann, *Duties Beyond Borders: On the Limits and Possibilities of Ethical International Politics* (Syracuse, N.Y.: Syracuse University Press, 1981).

9. Falk and Samuel S. Kim, 'An Approach to World Order Studies and the World System', World Order Models Project, Working Paper No. 22, 1982.

10. E.g. Falk, *Law, Morality and War in the Contemporary World* (New York: Praeger, 1963).

11. Cf. four volume series sponsored by the American Society of International Law. Falk (ed.), *The Vietnam War and International Law* (Princeton, N.J.: Princeton University Press, 1968, 1969, 1972, and 1976).

12. See especially debate with Professor John Norton Moore that appeared originally in the *Yale Law Journal* and is republished in Vol. I of work cited note 11, pp. 362–508.

13. For text of *Shimoda* decision see Falk and Saul H. Mendlovitz, *The Strategy of World Order* (New York: World Law Fund), Vol. 1, pp. 314–54, 1966; for commentary see Falk, *Legal Order in a Violent World* (Princeton, N.J.: Princeton University Press, 1968), pp. 374–413.

14. For earliest formulations on nuclear weapons policy see ibid., pp. 414–40.

15. Falk and Saul H. Mendlovitz (eds), *The Strategy of World Order*, (New York: World Law Fund), 4 vol., 1966.

16. For one interim assessment see Falk and Kim, note 9.

17. For general overview see Saul H. Mendlovitz (ed.), *On the Creation of a Just World Order* (New York: The Free Press, 1975); more elaborated perspectives are contained in book-length manuscripts by the main WOMP participants.

18. See von Weizsacker and Lin contribution to Mendlovitz volume of essays, ibid., pp. 111–50, 259–94. Also, the orientation of the Soviet participation, as expressed by a sequence of representatives, was generally realist and anti-cosmopolitan in character.

19. Falk, *A Study of Future Worlds*, (New York: The Free Press, 1975).
20. Falk, *This Endangered Planet: Prospects and Proposals for Human Survival* (New York: Random House, 1971).
21. For one attempt see Falk, 'Solving the Puzzles of Global Reform', *Alternatives*, Vol. XI, No. 1 (January 1986), pp. 45–81.
22. See Chadwick F. Alger and Saul Mendlovitz, 'Grass-Roots Activism in the United States: Global Implications', *Alternatives*, IX: 447–474 (1984).
23. See Falk, 'Government Accountability 40 Years After Nuremberg', *Journal of World Peace*, Vol. III, No. 1 (Spring 1986), pp. 11–15.
24. The story of the thinking and diplomacy that eventuated in these trials is well recounted in two books by Bradley F. Smith, *Reaching Judgment at Nuremberg* (New York: Basic Books, 1977); *The American Road to Nuremberg* (Stanford, Calif.: Hoover Institution Press, 1982); for texts of the main cases associated with these World War II prosecutions see Leon Friedman (ed.), *The Law of War* (New York: Random House), Vol. II, 1972.
25. For a recent exploration along these lines see William Irwin Thompson, *Pacific Shift* (San Francisco: Sierra Club Books, 1986).
26. See J. E. Lovelock, *Gaia: A New Look at Life on Earth* (Oxford: Oxford University Press, 1979).
27. Cf. e.g. Edward C. Whitmont, *The Return of the Goddess*, New York: Crossroads, 1981.
28. It is worth noticing that Marcos 'won' the election by fraud and 'lost' the government by an extraordinary movement of protest at the popular level. As a consequence, the housewife is now running the government and the old patriarch is languishing in exile.
29. Thompson, note 25, p. 181.

2 Lifting the Curse of Bipartisanship

American foreign policy remains compulsively bipartisan on the most basic issues of principle and practice. Whether the issue is the controversial deployment of Pershing II and cruise missiles in Europe, the application of the War Powers Act to American military operations in Lebanon, the exclusion of the PLO from the Middle East peace process, or even the costly pursuit of interventionary goals in Central America, disputes between leading Democrats and Republicans are generally restricted to tactics and nuances. Underlying assumptions are rarely questioned, and genuine alternatives of policy are almost never advocated when representatives of the two main political parties debate foreign policy. As a result, US foreign policy is essentially frozen at a time when the pressures for fundamental adjustments are becoming ever more intense.

In important respects, bipartisanship in foreign policy is normal and, many would argue, even beneficial. An effective foreign policy requires continuity and leadership, and this means making foreign policy relatively immune to partisan politics. The American foreign policy process itself reinforces bipartisanship. Intelligence services process vital information through the White House and national security bureaucracies, which are staffed by large and influential corps of civil servants whose careers have been shaped by the bipartisan consensus regarding the proper role of the United States in the world. This consensus is informally 'enforced' by the media and by special interests. Political

34

figures believed to challenge the consensus or even to raise fundamental doubts about it are discredited.

The bipartisan consensus on foreign policy can be challenged from the Right far more easily than it can be from the Left, as Ronald Reagan's election to the presidency, and as the careers of Barry Goldwater and George Wallace, amply demonstrate. There are many reasons for this, the most important of which is the enormous resources the Right wields by virtue of its representation in the upper reaches of government, business and media. The Right also possesses an ideological plausibility and a mass appeal that arise from its straightforward, unwavering emphasis on the Soviet Union as the evil enemy. No comparably simple or unifying outlook exists on the Left.

There are other factors at work. The monolithic character of the Soviet Union, especially its ability to speak with a single, unwavering voice on world issues, exerts pressure on Americans to sustain a consistent foreign policy. America's role as Alliance leader imposes additional pressures for policy continuity; even as it is, the United States is criticised abroad for its frequent subtle shifts of tone and emphasis. Experts in and out of government often are able to use supposedly dispassionate knowledge to make the public believe that genuine alternatives to current policies are 'unreasonable' or 'extreme' and lie outside the orbit of 'responsible discussion'. And, perhaps, underlying all of these considerations is a deep cultural bias, stemming from Aristotle, that associates virtue and prudence with a position of moderation, the golden mean between extremes. This bias is confirmed for many by the bloody excesses of revolutionary breaks with the past, starting with the French Revolution and continuing through the Russian Revolution, and further confirmed by the Islamic Revolution in Iran.

Against such formidable obstacles, it may seem foolhardy to question the current bipartisan foundations of American foreign policy. Yet, unless this consensus is challenged, American foreign policy will be unable to bridge the widening gap between the content of the bipartisan consensus and the world situations to which it is being applied. Bipartisanship has virtually nullified the electoral process as a means of reforming foreign policy. We proceed from Vietnam to El Salvador without any serious debate as to whether it is necessary or serves American interests to intervene in foreign societies to control the outcome of largely internal struggles. We continue to build nuclear weapons systems without pausing to question the postulates of the arms race, or even to inquire whether there might be cheaper and saner forms of deterrence. A decade ago there was unquestioning support at the top echelons of the political process for placing multiple warheads (MIRVing) on missile systems. Now there is comparable bipartisan enthusiasm for the alleged stabilising virtues of single-warhead missiles. Aside from keeping weapons-makers happy, such policy gyrations reveal more about the bipartisan strictures on the political process than they do about the merits of the various weapons choices.

The current bipartisanship is an outgrowth of America's dominance in the non-communist world after World War II. This leadership role rested firmly on American military and economic power, but even more so on the diplomatic and ideological pre-eminence the United States enjoyed in the years after 1945. The initial bipartisan consensus in this country envisioned a peaceful world sustained by the collective security mechanisms of the United Nations. American political leaders, however, soon became preoccupied with the contradictory task of forming a Western Alliance pledged to meet the Soviet challenge and to limit the opportunities for the spread of communist influence in the Third World occasioned by the impending collapse of colonialism. Bipartisan convictions also extended to international economic policy. A broad spectrum of American leaders believed it crucial to establish a cooperative framework of trade and capital flows to be administered from Washington. Economic conflict in the form of protectionism and hostile trading blocs was widely regarded by American policy-makers as responsible in part for the tensions of the 1930s that led to World War II. In essence, US postwar foreign policy was based on 'the bomb' and on a dollar strong enough to build a mutually beneficial trading and monetary system.

American postwar foreign policy could have been bipartisan and yet could have proceeded along different lines. The bipartisan consensus might have been dedicated, for example, to the avoidance of a Cold War or to disentangling responses to Third World nationalism from the dynamics of East–West rivalries. Whether such alternative lines of foreign policy could have succeeded and been sustained is a subject of endless discussion. What is important to realise is that it was not bipartisanship as such, but a particular type of bipartisanship that was essentially conflict-oriented and expansionist, that led to the current course of failure.

However one regards these alternative possibilities, the postwar consensus that emerged did represent a reasonable fit between means and ends, and was seemingly vindicated for at least the first fifteen years by an impressive record of accomplishments: Europe and Japan staged remarkable economic recoveries and built their futures around American-style political institutions; the world economic system entered a period of rapid and sustained growth; and, outside of Eastern Europe, the Soviet Union was confined to its borders and substantially isolated as an ideological force without provoking World War III. At critical points, Washington was able to mobilise widespread international support, as it did when it obtained United Nations support for its defence of South Korea in 1950–52. It was also able to use its position of nuclear predominance to force a humiliating Soviet retreat in the Cuban missile crisis of 1962.

All along, contradictory forces were at work eroding the effectiveness of the postwar consensus. The decolonisation process produced new outlooks among the nations of Asia, Africa and Latin America that challenged the premises of US diplomatic leadership. The success of the economic recovery facilitated by the United States, especially the performance of Germany and Japan, the main losers in World War II, produced a more plural and competitive world economic order that reshaped the hierarchy of relations upon which Washington's control had earlier rested. US resistance to political radicalism in the Third World often aligned the United States with reactionary forces which often proved to be 'losers' in the competition for state power, perhaps most notably in the case of China. In the 1970s, these difficulties reached a dramatic climax with the American defeat in Vietnam, the rapid rise of oil prices, the militancy of Third World diplomacy, an Indian nuclear explosion, a series of anti-Western national revolutions, the end of easy economic growth, the emergence of high unemployment and inflation in the West, and the deteriorating position of the United States economically.

The postwar consensus, while challenged by these shifts, failed to make suitable basic adjustments. Instead, the United States insisted on proceeding as if its overall dominance remained undiminished. This insistence inevitably led to a further militarisation of US foreign policy, because only in the military domain could the illusion of dominance be maintained. US leadership in world affairs had to this point been based on a mixture of economic, military, diplomatic and ideological strengths, but by the early 1970s its non-military capabilities had been substantially undermined.

The United States, and indeed the rest of the world, is tasting the bitter fruit of this inability to acknowledge the waning of US dominance. The Cold War atmosphere, and its resulting tensions, have been revived, giving rise to an accelerating arms race, heightened risks of nuclear war, and expensive and wasteful uses of resources. The United States has adopted policies unpopular at home and unsuccessful abroad in a vain effort to stem radical nationalist movements in the Third World; these policies create the impression that the United States is, at once, reactionary and ineffectual. In Central America there is the spectacle of 'aircraft-carrier diplomacy' (gunboats no longer suffice, nor is it clear that even aircraft-carrier-led task forces can impose the imperial will) trying to beat down Nicaraguan assertions of its sovereign rights. In the last decade, the United States has found itself isolated and beleaguered in the United Nations on such symbolic issues as the Arab–Israeli conflict and the anti-apartheid struggle in southern Africa. Even NATO allies take pains to stake out positions different from those of the US government on many controversial issues and generally, edge closer to that of the global consensus.

Bipartisanship has persisted despite substantial indications by the American people that they would be receptive to major changes in foreign policy, provided these were explained and endorsed by respected national leaders and backed by a leading political party. Substantial support exists, for instance, to end the arms race and to get out of the intervention business. But the government and the two political parties remain wedded to past assumptions about foreign policy goals. As a result, national policy discussion tends to focus on tactical disputes over narrow choices and controversies over styles of leadership. When it comes to fundamental foreign policy choices, the 1984 presidential elections are likely to be a farce.

The persistence of this unsuccessful and increasingly unpopular bipartisan stance on foreign policy poses a serious challenge for political democracy. How can the United States adapt to a new global setting if the American people are not given a genuine choice and if the governing process is resolved to cling to old policies, however discredited by experience? The stakes could not be higher – peace, economic vitality, a participatory democracy, and the possibility that international tensions can be handled without courting disaster. The failure of the current bipartisan foreign policy is partly a reflection of how the two-party system operates. If opposition is not mounted by the party out of power, then it does not enter into the formal political process. Only a far more intense popular campaign for foreign policy reform can lessen the constraints of bipartisanship and allow the electoral process and the institutions of representative government to be revitalised.

ADJUSTING TO THE END OF THE POSTWAR WORLD

During the 1970s the dominance the United States enjoyed for approximately 25 years began to erode. The evidence of this erosion necessarily is impressionistic, and it has been largely ignored by those who wield the power of the state. None the less, the erosion is most clearly evident in the economic and diplomatic domains. The United States now

controls a far smaller percentage of world trade, manufac-
turing, monetary reserves and gross product than it did in
the late 1940s and 1950s. Its growth has lagged behind that
of Japan and West Germany, revealing that the United
States has failed to keep pace in productivity increases and
in sectors such as automobiles and electronics in which it
once enjoyed a commanding position. Unlike in the security
context where the loss of US dominance can be blamed on
the Soviet Union, in the economic context the reality of
economic rivalry is scarcely admitted. The effects of the
relative economic decline of the United States have been
largely suppressed to avoid undue strains on the alliance.
The declining diplomatic dominance of the United States
has been similarly dramatic. The United States is no longer
perceived as invincible in world affairs; it has been beaten
in war and humiliated by a series of incidents, such as Iran's
holding of American diplomats hostage during 1979–81 in
the embassy compound in Teheran. Nor has the United
States retained its reputation as a champion of peace and
justice in world affairs. It is widely held primarily responsible for the growing anxieties about nuclear war. Moreover,
the role of the CIA in numerous armed interventions in
Third World countries has disillusioned many earlier
admirers of American diplomacy. Instead of being viewed
as the natural leader of orderly progress toward a better
world, the United States now is seen as the main bastion of
defence for the status quo.

What has remained far more intact is the postwar structure of US military dominance. True, the Soviet Union has
challenged this dominance in a number of key respects,
notably in strategic weaponry and maritime supremacy. Yet
the lure of technological innovation appears to sustain
American hopes that even in superpower relations the
United States can regain a decisive upper hand. US dominance is increasingly seen to rest on its military prowess,
whether this means its capacity to intervene on short notice
anywhere in the world or its perceived superiority as an
arms supplier, recently enhanced by Israel's victories over
Syria's Soviet-supplied forces in the early days of the 1982
Lebanon war.

So far, the efforts by American leaders to adjust to the loss of American dominance have proved insufficient. Two phases of response can be distinguished, each of which attempted to reclaim global leadership without adjusting the expectations of Americans to the realities of the international situation. In the first instance the management of complexity was seen as the new challenge ('the soft phase'), while in the second instance, directly engendered by the disappointment about 'American decline', militarised geopolitics was emphasised as the necessary means to guard against the cardinal menace of Soviet aggressiveness ('the hard phase').

THE SOFT PHASE (1968–1979): MANAGING INTERDEPENDENCE IN A CHAOTIC WORLD

Commencing with the presidencies of Nixon and Ford and ending in the Carter administration at the moment of the Soviet invasion of Afghanistan, the soft phase enjoyed bipartisan sponsorship and support. The historical logic of this response was decisively shaped by the failure of American policy in Vietnam. This failure led to a wider disillusionment with military approaches to the defence of American interests and to a realisation that an array of economic issues involving trade and money required serious managerial attention. The soft phase seemed sensitive to the great complexity of international life that had resulted in part from the participation of many more states as independent actors with a weight and outlook of their own, and from the emergence of the Third World as an active political force. Insisting that their independence dictated a stance of non-alignment, developing states in Asia, Africa and Latin America posed a challenge to the economic and political primacy of the West.

Reacting to these circumstances, the Nixon–Kissinger–Ford leadership, despite impeccable Cold War credentials, attempted to redirect US foreign policy. In response to the frustration of defeat in Vietnam, this leadership proposed a partial abandonment of interventionary diplomacy in the form of the Nixon doctrine. As enunciated by Nixon at Guam in 1969, this doctrine asserted that henceforth the United States would help foreign governments by training and equipping them to fight their own internal battles, but that it would not get involved in the fighting. This 'withdrawal' was to be compensated for by a great reliance on Western-oriented 'regional influentials', such as Iran, Nigeria, Indonesia and Brazil, to contain radical political tendencies within their regions.

The major accomplishment of the soft phase was to establish a different mood in international society. The normalisation of relations with China and an abatement of the Cold War by way of détente were the centrepieces of this effort. East–West trade, SALT negotiations, and a general relaxation of tensions ensued. Nixon and Kissinger even floated the idea of reorganising international politics around a five-power world concert to be composed of the United States, the Soviet Union, China, Japan and Western Europe.

Beginning in 1976, these emphases were extended, by the Carter administration, to problems of managing the international economy. Here the response was fashioned by the new militancy of the Third World, culminating in the crisis of 1973–74, the time of the OPEC oil embargo, the initial wave of oil price rises, and the American ordeal of gas lines and consumer distress. The Carter administration came to Washington with a mandate influenced by the heavy emphasis of the Trilateral Commission on more coherent and cooperative relations among the advanced industrial democracies, as well as by its moderate conviction that the way to handle the Third World was through accommodation and co-option (letting economically dynamic countries into the rich man's club). At the beginning of his presidency, Carter had also added human rights to the foreign policy agenda, temporarily reclaiming America's moral leadership.

But the soft phase foundered on many shoals. The SALT process did little to arrest the arms race, especially qualitative improvements in strategic weaponry that brought the spectre of nuclear war closer. During this era of arms control negotiations, strategic doctrines emphasising war-fighting surfaced, and a continuous flow of new weapons systems made a mockery of claims on behalf of negotiated agreements between the superpowers. The partial renunciation of intervention implicit in the Nixon doctrine was not accompanied, even on the part of liberals, by an acceptance of the dynamics of self-determination. Each successful national revolution was perceived as a setback for US foreign policy and as a confirmation of conservative contentions that American leaders had lost their nerve and that the country was in decline. In fact, as with arms control, the renunciation of intervention was partial and half-hearted. It was during this period that innovations in interventionary capability and doctrine were given dramatic emphasis, especially the 'rapid deployment force' designed as a hedge against future uncertainties in the Persian Gulf region.

The domestic controversy over the Panama Canal treaties also revealed the shortcomings of the soft-phase response. Carter pushed ahead with these treaties, despite vitriolic attacks from the Right, but in an atmosphere that required selling their virtues to old-style nationalists. In reality, the Panama Canal treaties were not very satisfactory from any viewpoint, a classic example of a centrist mish-mash that neither clearly renounced nor firmly retained the earlier colonialist regime. The negotiated agreements were in the end made acceptable to the American people and to two-thirds of the Senate, quite unconvincingly, on the pragmatic grounds that they retained the substance of the American presence in the Canal Zone while giving way on its form. Yet this qualification of American sovereignty seemed to confirm the fear of the resurgent Right that the United States was losing out in the global struggle against the Soviet Union.

The Right mobilised a cleverly orchestrated counter-offensive against this soft phase of adjustment. Its campaign to influence public opinion was greatly reinforced by that substantial portion of the governmental bureaucracy (especially in the military and intelligence sectors) that had always opposed and resisted the soft phase. The Soviet Union, by continuing its strategic build-up as if détente had never been established, by provocatively intervening in several African countries, and by acting with brutal disregard of the sovereign rights of its neighbours in Poland and Afghanistan, did little to encourage US moderation.

A mixture of cynicism and scorn was heaped on the idealistic elements of Carter's foreign policy. Although presented as 'flexible' and 'selective', an American espousal of human rights did not seem to mix well with geopolitical hardball. First, it struck progressive Americans as hypocritical to make 'exceptions' of strategically important countries such as South Korea, Iran and the Philippines. At the same time, conservatives regarded it as detrimental to American interests in the struggle against Soviet power and communism to raise tensions with geopolitical friends such as Argentina, Brazil and even South Africa, especially because it was morally repugnant to equate their political shortcomings with the far greater failings of communist countries. Third, it struck many moderates as inconsistent with maintaining world peace and promoting world trade to allow human rights criticisms of the Soviet Union to obstruct the path of détente. In many respects, human rights diplomacy was at odds with the managerial imperatives of the soft approach to post-Vietnam adjustment, which aimed to improve the efficiency of the world economy and to diminish ideological rivalries.

The soft phase failed, in effect, because it did not go far enough to find either appropriate policy instruments or convincing public explanations for the new international situation. The Right successfully put all mainstream political leaders on the defensive. Gerald Ford, while still president, was so embarrassed by the word 'détente' that he ordered it expunged from the political vocabulary of his administration. Moreover, the architects of a moderate geopolitics had no clear conception of its implications for American foreign policy. In the Carter period, Henry Kissinger, always a weather vane, abandoned the moderate orientation he had earlier espoused, and shamelessly jumped on the bandwagon of Cold War revivalists. Brzezinski, uncomfortable with the moderate style yet owing his prominence to its espousal, helped persuade Carter to shift course rightwards during the last two years of the Carter presidency.

Perhaps most central to the demise of moderation was its

failure to appreciate that the most dangerous loss of US influence was not along an East–West axis (China's shifting alignment was by far the most momentous geopolitical event of this period and could have been taken as evidence of Soviet 'decline'), but in the struggle for shares of the world market. Here, the real adversary was not the Soviet Union, but Japan and Germany, and to a lesser extent, the Newly Industrialised Countries (NICs) of the Third World, many of whom were US 'clients' when it came to national security. To make the American economy competitive was and remains the prime security challenge to US foreign policy, an assertion that national leaders are fond of making, but only in a rhetorical spirit. To avoid the full domestic impact of this challenge, the United States has resorted to direct and indirect forms of protectionism, even using its role as alliance leader to insist that its economic rivals, especially Japan, 'waste' more resources on weapons. Underneath declarations of alliance solidarity are profound differences: the main economic rivals of the United States think in a less ideological vein and seek to strengthen East–West trade links, to accommodate national revolutions, and to extend a truly competitive international economic order.

In short, the expectations associated with postwar dominance were never convincingly renounced by American leadership during the soft phase. The spread of national revolutions and the decline of US economic power were thus perceived as US foreign policy failures. Centrists were hopelessly ambivalent in explaining away these failures, and Rightists alone made coherent sense by their insistence on calling a failure a failure. The soft phase ended with a pathetic whimper.

THE HARD PHASE (1979–198?): A MILITARY FIX FOR AMERICAN DECLINE

When Carter jumped on the militarist bandwagon halfway through his administration, he did so without the backing of either the resurgent Right or the hawkish sectors of the national bureaucracy. It was natural, then, for the discrediting of the soft phase to be completed by the electoral repudiation of Carter, and of the liberal tradition he continued to represent.

As one high-level White House adviser put it in a recent private discussion, 'the Reagan people came to Washington convinced they had to scare the American people'. Neoconservatives believed that military prowess and assertiveness were the keys to overcoming the decline of America. Even during the 1973–74 OPEC oil embargo and price rise, neo-conservatives called for military responses, seeking to whip up nationalistic fervour by devising scenarios of paratroopers floating out of the skies to occupy the Arab oil fields on behalf of Western interests. A strategic arms build-up and interventionary diplomacy were the main planks of a revamped American foreign policy that aimed indirectly to expose the weakness of the Soviet economy under the stress of an all-out American effort. The early reinstatement of the B-1 bomber and an upgrading of development activities for the neutron bomb were emblematic of the pro-defence outlook of the Reagan administration. At the same time, global negotiations on SALT II, the Law of the Seas, and North–South relations were scorned as liberal giveaways detrimental to US national interests. The US contribution to world order was viewed as completely incidental to the unilateral pursuit of its own interests through military strength and a strong dollar, the principal pillars of US dominance in the postwar period. In one sense, Adam Smith's invisible hand was reaffirmed and extended to the domain of national security – an explosive formula for stability in the nuclear age.

The Reagan administration's efforts to reacquire dominance were much less benign than had been similar efforts in the late 1940s and 1950s. The decision to rest US foreign economic policy on a strengthened dollar at a time of deep global recession required adopting the austere strictures of monetarism. This meant high interest rates which squeezed the poor at home and slowed economic recovery in other countries. Rapid increases in the defence budget and a desire to reduce federal deficits made it inevitable that welfare spending would be curtailed. In the early 1980s, these policies gave birth to a peace movement in Western Europe, North America and Japan, whose strength and durability have not yet been fully tested. Although the Reagan leadership has softened its rhetoric about nuclear confrontation, it has proceeded undaunted with its dangerous arms build-up.

The most serious drawback of the hard phase has been its overemphasis on the military dimension of foreign policy. It exaggerates the military character of the Soviet threat to justify draining scarce resources for an adequate military response, thereby further weakening the strength of the US economy. Yet the loss of US dominance has little to do with military power for the difficulty of translating military superiority into political results seems greater than ever. The hard phase, rigidly committed to retaining dominance, presides over a misguided adjustment in which largely non-military challenges (economic, diplomatic and political, including Third World nationalism) are met with increasingly militarist responses, with the perverse consequence of spreading the danger. For instance, a few years ago a political response to Central American turbulence might have produced mutual accommodation; today, a military response is leading to regional warfare, a much greater prospect of prolonged confrontation, and the possibility that the domino theory will be vindicated – but in reverse. Similarly, high-frontier weaponry to defend against the possibility of nuclear war further fuels the arms race and makes a future breakdown in deterrence much more likely. The general picture, then, is an ironic and dangerous one: as the emphasis on military power increases, its utility as an instrument of foreign policy declines.

The soft phase flirted half-heartedly with a demilitarised foreign policy and then was blamed for its failure to take military steps to safeguard American interests. This critique was misguided because these interests were incapable of military protection. The best available response required a flexible diplomacy, not hung up by ideological blinkers. The bipartisan imperative makes advocates of the soft phase bend quickly, rather than defend their claim that American foreign policy in the late 1970s rested upon managerial ingenuity, not military capabilities. In contrast, the hard phase has readily remilitarised US foreign policy and revived the Cold War, but without the political payoffs associated with the postwar years. Its persistence under adverse international conditions poses horrifying risks that the hard phase could end with a final bang.

CHANGING SOME BASIC GUIDELINES

A proper adjustment to the erosion of American dominance requires several fundamental shifts in US foreign policy. Even apart from the practical need to reshape US foreign policy around the international realities of the 1980s, these shifts seem desirable on their merits. Adjusting to the loss of dominance requires, in the first instance, giving up certain outmoded claims and prerogatives. But it is not, in reality, all negative. A renunciation of outmoded assumptions would open up new possibilities for US foreign policy. The United States remains the most formidable economic, cultural and political force in the world, and if its capabilities are used to address geopolitical realities, not deny them, then it is likely that American citizens, foreign leaders, and international public opinion will be favourably disposed to new foreign policy directions.

Renouncing the Nuclear Option

After the bombings of Hiroshima and Nagasaki, American leaders became ambivalent about the atomic bomb. They realised the apocalyptic dangers of a possible nuclear war, yet they believed that this most powerful of all weapons provided the United States with a decisive tool for exerting international influence. By the late 1940s, these inhibitions had virtually disappeared, primarily because of Soviet resolve to acquire nuclear weapons and because of the impossibility of negotiating a reliable disarmament arrangement that did not seriously abridge sovereign rights.

Nuclear weapons, especially after the Soviet Union acquired them in the 1950s, have had two contradictory meanings for American foreign policy: they have increased the importance of avoiding *direct* military encounters with the Soviet Union that might spark a mutually suicidal war, yet at the same time they have tempted US policy-makers to cash in politically on the enormous US investment in nuclear weaponry. As current US foreign policy reveals, the United States has not been able to resist the lure of the nuclear option. This option involves more than a willingness to use nuclear weapons as the ultimate deterrent against nuclear attack; it also entails a willingness under certain conditions to *initiate* the use of nuclear weapons to defend threatened interests.

At times the US nuclear option has been more pronounced than at others. The Cuban missile crisis of 1962 may have been its most dramatic expression, but on more than this one occasion the United States has resorted to the threatened use of nuclear weapons. Its war plans consistently have envisaged an array of first-use options. Desmond Ball, a researcher on nuclear strategy, counts 20 instances in which American leaders have threatened, primarily through secret diplomatic channels, to introduce nuclear weapons into a combat situation.[1] The reliance on nuclear weapons has been justified in part on fiscal grounds, particularly during the Eisenhower–Dulles years. Nuclear weapons were then seen as the only way to keep federal deficits down while upholding the farflung network of US commitments. The temptation to use distinctive American 'assets' explains the periodic surfacing in public debate of ideas such as 'limited nuclear war' and 'flexible response'.

The extent to which American foreign policy relies on the nuclear threat is most explicit in relation to the defence of Europe. American leaders have insisted, and continue to insist, that a NATO 'first-use' doctrine is necessary to deter the Soviet Union from taking advantage of its alleged superiority in conventional forces. US nuclear weapons are deployed in several other places in the world to threaten their use in some future local or regional crisis. For instance, several hundred American nuclear weapons are kept in South Korea, apparently to discourage a possible North Korean *non-nuclear* attack.

Revealingly, the Harvard Nuclear Weapons Study, a

quintessential consensus document for the 1980s, published under the title *Living with Nuclear Weapons*,[2] endorses the nuclear option under the heading of maintaining our nuclear guarantee to our allies'.[3] It envisages using nuclear weapons in response to a Soviet non-nuclear attack on US allies or to Soviet military intervention in the Third World. The Harvard authors conclude that 'the risks' of withdrawing 'our nuclear guarantee . . . would in the long run probably be far worse than the risk the US faces today.'[4] In the end, they seem to suggest – the writing is less than clear – that a US willingness to threaten the use of nuclear weapons is needed to maintain influence over its allies and to discourage possible adversaries from challenging American-supported positions in the world. Such views almost always presuppose a benign role for the United States: America is assumed to be the defender, the other side is treated as the aggressor. Hence, supporters of the nuclear option claim it is necessary for the defence of free societies against aggression, whereas such a posture, if adopted by the Soviet Union or by the other enemies of humanity, would be said to constitute an unacceptable risk to peace.

One of the most serious consequences of the nuclear option is that it works against stabilising the nuclear environment. In essence, the United States seeks to stay ahead of the Soviet Union, while the Soviets seek to catch up. In foreign policy terms, the US government wants to maintain its nuclear option, while the Soviet government wants to neutralise it. This competition, in an atmosphere of secrecy and distrust, provides a rationale for the arms race that allows it to persist under virtually all conditions. It is a rationale that is reinforced by bureaucratic and industrial forces in both societies that have built up vested interests in a research-directed arms industry, especially with respect to nuclear weaponry.

By the 1970s the Soviet Union had reached essential parity with the United States with respect to strategic nuclear weapons, as the SALT negotiations and other agreements of the 1970s acknowledged. At the same time, pressures mounted on the United States to rely more directly on nuclear threats to uphold its overseas commitments, especially in the aftermath of the Vietnam defeat. In fact, statements by former Secretary of Defence, James Schlesinger, in the mid-1970s, later supplemented by Presidential Directive 59 (on flexible response) and the Carter doctrine (understood to threaten a US nuclear response to any Soviet military challenge in the Persian Gulf region), caused American foreign policy to rely more overtly than ever before on its nuclear option.

The current arms race, then, is not just an outgrowth of the Reagan presidency. It was on the books of the Carter administration, reflected in its advocacy of such components of a first-strike strategy as the MX and Trident II weapons systems, efforts to achieve breakthroughs in anti-submarine warfare, and open commitments to retain the nuclear option to meet challenges in Europe, the Persian Gulf, Korea, and possibly elsewhere. Reagan merely accelerated the bipartisan pursuit of these goals.

It should be evident by now that there is no reliable way for the United States to regain the nuclear upper hand, yet the very effort to do so has grave costs. Obviously the Soviet Union will not acquiesce in an American attempt to subordinate its nuclear capabilities, but will merely strain harder to keep abreast and to make certain that US officials harbour no illusions about the feasibility of an American nuclear option. This rivalry inevitably raises tensions as each side must justify to its own public the devotion of additional resources to defence by pointing to the evil intentions of the other. Such accusations inevitably deepen international tensions and, with US and Societ naval and air forces spread out around the globe, make incidents of confrontation and frightening tendencies toward escalation more likely to occur, particularly if one side resorts to a violent response or suffers a local defeat. At the very least, the US nuclear option can intensify existing crises, a pattern vividly illustrated by the Soviet downing of the Korean Airlines commercial plane in September 1983.

The nuclear option, although it continues to enjoy bipartisan support, has drawn increasing criticism from a variety of sources. Four prominent national security officials (McGeorge Bundy, George Kennan, Robert McNamara and Gerard Smith) published in 1982 a widely discussed article urging the United States to consider adopting a no first-use stance in Europe. Moreover, there is a rising tide of public doubt about the propriety of any reliance on nuclear weapons beyond the barest minimum possession, and that solely as protection against blackmail and for ultimate retaliatory purposes. This doubt has been nurtured by various groups like the Physicians for Social Responsibility who have demonstrated the absurdity of the proposition that the medical profession would be able to treat the survivors of a nuclear attack. Even more, the Catholic Bishops of the United States overwhelmingly endorsed a *Pastoral Letter* that concluded that *any* contemplated use of nuclear weapons for foreign policy goals or against civilian populations was profoundly immoral and at odds with the values of civilisation and its leading religious traditions. In a parallel analysis, the Lawyers' Committee on Nuclear Policy argues that existing US strategic policy flagrantly violates international law and compromises the constitutional legitimacy of the US government. Together these developments suggest the emergence of a *societal consensus* in favour of the unconditional repudiation of the nuclear option. To the extent that bipartisanship blocks the translation of this consensus into official policy, it renders inconsequential the electoral process and representative institutions.

What would a renunciation of the US nuclear option entail? In practical terms, it would require a series of coordinated denuclearisation steps: a freeze on further deployment and development activities; efforts to achieve a comprehensive test ban; a no first-use posture that would consign nuclear weapons to the sole function of deterring nuclear attack; a withdrawal of forward-based tactical nuclear weapons and the elimination of dual-purpose theatre forces; the maintenance of survivable retaliatory capabilities to avoid first-strike pressures in times of crisis and to minimise the risk of miscalculation through misinformation or computer malfunction; the elimination of all nuclear weapons with a first-strike potential; a firm decision not to build non-nuclear weapons of mass destruction such as biological, chemical, radiological and near-nuclear conventional weapons; and efforts to prevent the further militarisation of space, the oceans and the polar regions. Some of these steps can be taken unilaterally, others depend on agreement and mutuality. Because of the extraordinary monitoring capabilities of existing long-range sensing and surveillance technologies, what Daniel Deudney has aptly called 'the transparency revolution',[5] the United States can proceed confidently with these steps knowing that verification can be achieved without trusting the Soviets.

Soviet foreign policy has never been based on the nuclear option, but rather on neutralising ours. Of course, one of the dangers is that at this stage Soviet efforts to neutralise our nuclear option can plausibly be interpreted as an effort to establish a nuclear option of its own. None the less, Soviet policy still seems preoccupied with removing nuclear weapons from an active role in superpower diplomacy. Brezhnev's June 1982 unconditional pledge to renounce the first-use of nuclear weapons, a pledge renewed by Andropov, confirms the impression that the Soviet Union perceives its self-interests to require the elimination of the nuclear option. Gorbachev has greatly intensified Soviet efforts to encourage an arms control process that aims at total denuclearization.

In most contexts, including Europe and the Middle East, a Soviet military challenge is exceedingly remote. If the challenge to American interests arose as a result of other, more probable, developments, for instance, a radical Saudi uprising, it is difficult to imagine any possible utility of nuclear weapons, especially because considerable non-nuclear military capabilities exist to deter military attack. Moreover, both superpowers realise that any serious outbreak of conventional warfare could easily escalate beyond the nuclear threshold, particularly if one side is faced with defeat.

More important, perhaps, is the realisation that the end of the postwar world *necessarily* means a loss of American control over the process of change in the world. This control never fully existed, and in any event, cannot be reacquired by a feverish effort to restore US nuclear predominance. The *best* that can be done is to allow the play of forces to proceed without interference. If the United States were willing to adjust to new international realities, it might suffer some geopolitical setbacks, but this would be far less likely than it is at present.

The tension between the loss of US nuclear predominance and an apparently heightened dependence on the nuclear option captures the central failure of US foreign policy to move actively beyond the end of the postwar world. To maintain the nuclear option under the altered conditions of the 1980s is not only increasingly dangerous and expensive, it also causes public anxiety and places the United States in a posture of permanent moral impropriety. Although the renunciation of the nuclear option does not question the propriety of the possession of nuclear weapons as such, it would immediately narrow the widening gap between the wishes of the US public and the direction of US policies. Moreover, it would greatly reduce the risk of nuclear war and would eliminate one of the main driving forces sustaining the nuclear arms race.

Renouncing the Interventionary Option
In the postwar world, US foreign policy was overtly centred around the idea of the containment of Soviet expansion. This priority led to an interventionary foreign policy for several reasons. In the first place, American policy-makers accepted the view that the collapse of colonial power following the upheavals of World War II created a 'vacuum' in the ex-colonies that inevitably would be filled by one superpower or the other. In fact, because both the Soviet Union and the United States realised that a world war might arise from armed encounters in the First World, they increasingly channelled their rivalry into Third World settings. Although many of the conflicts that developed were *internal* power struggles, they were none the less waged in ideological terms that made a victory for radical nationalism appear to be a victory for the Soviet Union. Thus as strong *nationalist* movements emerged in many countries throughout Asia and Africa, the United States generally found itself committed to the defence of particular governments within these countries. Such considerations induced American policy-makers, starting with the enunciation of the Truman Doctrine in 1947, to develop capabilities and

doctrinal justifications for an interventionary diplomacy that would be reinforced as needed by the US nuclear option.

Because intervention is always at odds with such fundamental notions of international law as respect for the sovereign rights and self-determination of foreign societies, its nature must be disguised. The United States, in particular, must camouflage its interventionary projects because they so blatantly conflict with the American revolutionary heritage and with its professed support for international diversity. Nevertheless, the geopolitical pressures of 'extended containment' have consistently prevailed, and the United States has intervened in many foreign countries on numerous occasions since 1945. At times intervention has been more or less covert with the CIA playing a prominent role. At other times, it has been justified openly as undertaken on behalf of established governments under attack by allegedly Soviet-supported insurgents. Until the defeat in Vietnam, US interventionary policies enjoyed a string of successes – in Iran (1953), Guatemala (1954) and the Philippines (1950s) – with the notable exception of China. Nuclear deterrence seemed to have made the world safe for interventionary diplomacy. At the same time, revolutionary nationalism, with its potential for mobilisation, made it evident that intervention was an increasingly costly enterprise for the United States, especially as exercised on behalf of corrupt and brutal elites isolated from their own peoples.

The Vietnam War made American leaders temporarily reluctant to practice intervention on a large scale, but the pressures generated by OPEC oil policies and by a series of revolutionary victories in Iran, Nicaragua, Angola and Ethiopia in the 1970s soon revived the interventionary option. New interventionary methods were developed and new justifications put forward. The Rapid Deployment Force and regional command centres were created to prepare the way for US intervention if required in the Persian Gulf – for instance, in Saudi Arabia – and possibly also in the Caribbean, southern Africa, and within the Pacific Command Zone. Bipartisan support for a military response to threatening Persian Gulf contingencies, including possible reliance on nuclear weapons, is particularly strong.

Since Vietnam, resistance to the interventionary option has also increased. The Third World increasingly perceives such American diplomacy as a violation of sovereign rights; even reactionary governments frequently reject US justifications for intervention. At home, interventionary policies towards the Third World are no longer supported. This influences US political leaders to deny their underlying purpose, as is evident in US policy toward Central America. Above all, the American people do not want another Vietnam; they do not want Americans to die on behalf of a dubious cause in a Third World country.

In his 27 April 1983 address on Central America to a Joint Session of Congress, President Reagan asserted, 'Every President since this country assumed global responsibilities has known that those responsibilities could only be met if we pursued a bipartisan foreign policy'. Senator Christopher Dodd, selected by the Democratic Party leadership to respond to the President on this occasion, strongly endorsed this essential feature of bipartisanship – 'on some very important things all Americans stand in agreement.' 'All patriotic Americans', Dodd went on to say, agree that 'we will oppose the establishment of Marxist states in Central America.' Reagan's major premise had been conceded. As columnist George Will skilfully argued, Dodd's criticism of Reagan's approach reduces to 'a narrow and empirical question' of the choice of means to achieve a *shared* goal of 'preventing the spread of Sandinista-style regimes in Central America'. Once prevention becomes the accepted goal, intervention is implicit, and militarists almost unavoidably prevail in policy settings. As Will points out, with apt irony, it is difficult to remember many wars 'that have been ended by social reforms [rather] than military victory'.[6]

And, in fact, once there is bipartisan support for interventionary goals, tactical criticism of a President engaged in carrying out his role as commander in chief does often sound both irrelevant and irresponsible. The cult of bipartisanship was manifest in Henry Kissinger's remark about hearings conducted before the presidential commission on long-range policy toward Central America: 'If there was unanimity on any point, it was that we emerge out of these discussions with a consensus: that we can't really afford to be divided on an issue that is important to the future of our country.'[7] The 'we' in Kissinger's comment cannot possibly refer to the American people, who will certainly remain divided on such questions. It refers instead to the political leaders of both parties, as well as to Congressional–Executive relations and to the national security bureaucracy. As a result, it is not likely that Washington will seriously consider whether the United States should renounce the business of intervention altogether and pursue accommodation with whichever government prevails in the internal struggle. Even though the United States has developed an acceptable relationship with Marxist-Leninists, for example, in Yugoslavia, and more recently in China, the bipartisan interventionary syndrome persists.

Growing official pressures to support US intervention in Central America illustrate both the dangers and opportunities for American foreign policy in this period. With the ending of the postwar world, the struggle against communism, especially in Third World settings, seems clearly less central to the overall international position of the United States. Furthermore, the United States, as Alliance leader, is under pressure to refrain from interventionary diplomacy. Both western hemisphere allies (for instance, the Contadora group) and West European allies have plainly indicated their disagreements with the ideological assumptions underlying the US response and have expressed their preference for accommodation to intervention. The loss of international support for the extension of 'containment geopolitics' to internal struggles in the Third World contrasts sharply with the widespread international support the United States enjoyed for its involvement in the Korean War and in the early years of the Vietnam War. This is reflective of an overall erosion of US diplomatic leadership and is underscored by the fact that virtually only Israel and (pre-Falklands) Argentina have unconditionally supported US interventionary policies in Central America.

Likewise, public opinion polls demonstrate that the American people oppose current levels of involvement in Central America and fear that the policies being pursued may lead in a Vietnam direction. Young Americans have resisted draft registration laws in numbers incomparably greater than during the early stages of the Vietnam era. Religious institutions, especially the Catholic Church, oppose US intervention and perceive the struggle in the region much more as a mass quest for economic and human dignity than as an ideological or strategic challenge posed by Moscow-directed forces of atheistic communism. Such perceptions are similar to those professed by non-communist intellectual opinion in Latin America, succinctly summarised by Mexican author Carlos Fuentes when he wrote that Reagan's policies are 'causing incalculable political stress throughout the Latin continent, where considerations about Marxism come after consideration of nationalism and cultural identity'.[8] Of course, the American position ends up giving real life to its propaganda campaign – by threatening the autonomy of Nicaragua and by siding with right-wing military repression in the region, Washington leaves the popular forces of the Left little choice but to depend for their survival on their only allies. Economic and diplomatic dependence on the Soviet Union, even in the case of Cuba, was not an initial goal of the Castro leadership, but was largely a product of a variety of pressures exerted on Cuban independence by the American promotion of counter-revolution.

As with nuclearism, the return to interventionary diplomacy reveals an increasing gap between what official US policies propose and what most citizens appear to prefer. In this sense, US intervention in Central America is proceeding anti-democratically – in defiance of popular will; by secret and, seemingly, unconstitutional means; in flagrant violation of international law, including riding roughshod over even formally declared Congressional policy. In the face of these realities, it is astonishing that the Democratic Party has not mounted a principled opposition built on an anti-interventionist vision of US interests and how to protect them. Instead, the opposition is content to snipe at the quantities and types of effort. Seemingly afraid of being blamed for 'losing' Central America, it has not been prepared to challenge the interventionary undertaking itself. But if the public rejects intervention, who is to do 'the blaming'? Politicians, whatever else, are not fools, and Democratic leaders are probably prudently wary that the militarised bureaucracy and its neo-conservative allies can make serious opposition to intervention appear to verge on anti-Americanism. As an unnamed White House official recently commented, 'Intervention doesn't have a serious political downside until American soldiers and airmen get shot at or killed.'[9] And so, despite a sceptical public, a shaky bipartisan consensus persists and actually is in the process of being strengthened despite the likely dreadful consequences. The Korean Airline incident appears to have further intimidated liberals and moderates, making opposition to presidential policy even tamer than it has been to date.

If the United States were to abandon intervention, it would not become vulnerable to Soviet exploitation. The analysis presented here of why intervention no longer works for the United States applies to the Soviet Union as well. In fact, the Soviet Union has been forced out of a variety of countries including Ghana, Egypt, Somalia and Indonesia. Should the Soviet Union seek to extend its influence through intervention, it is likely to be self-defeating. Of course, if the intervenor is prepared to pay a high enough cost in blood, resources, and prestige, intervention can *in certain instances* succeed, at least for a time. Generally speaking, however, Soviet interventionism would actually help restore American leadership on a global level. American interventionism in the past has, in fact, eroded the moral and even the legal force of international condemnations of Soviet interventionary practice. The costs of Soviet intervention in Afghanistan are evidently high for Kremlin planners and likely to encourage future caution. If the United States renounced the interventionary option, it would, of course, strengthen international pressures and procedures against Soviet intervention.

The United States does not need the interventionary

option to uphold its vital national interests in the Third World. US access to Third World markets and resources and positive relations with foreign governments cannot be assured by the interventionary option. In fact, the effect of US military intervention in the Third World has been a net geopolitical loss; it has created sharp tensions between a professed respect for self-determination and the bloody realities of interventionary diplomacy. National revolutions could well jeoparadise short-run relations and damage certain vested U.S. economic interests, but such outcomes would not necessarily harm national interests as a whole. The adjustment to reduced control seems historically inevitable, but whether this adjustment is prolonged and made more costly by sustained violence is a serious question for American foreign policy, just as it earlier was for the European colonial powers.

Naturally, the transition to a non-interventionary diplomacy, admittedly a vast challenge, would need to be handled with wisdom and tact to avoid immediately 'destabilising' effects. As a first step, the United States should adopt a firm non-interventionary diplomatic posture and should give immediate substance to it by negotiating a rapid withdrawal from Central America. Furthermore, a comprehensive re-evaluation of the vast panoply of US interventionary capabilities, ranging from foreign bases to CIA covert action programmes, should be undertaken. The abandonment of interventionary politics would imply reduction, and finally the elimination, of such capabilities. This would involve a complicated task of distinguishing between capabilities needed for collective self-defence and those designed to serve interventionary goals.

Admittedly, such distinctions are sometimes next to impossible to make. Take South Korea, for example. American troops stationed there arguably make some contribution to preventing the renewal of warfare between North and South Korea. Yet, as evidenced by the role of the American military commander in authorising the use of a key South Korean regiment for the brutal repression of the Kwangju demonstrations in 1980, an interventionary dimension exists. In the Persian Gulf, the linkage is more explicit. From the outset, the RDF has been justified both in terms of collective self-defence and in terms of preventing 'a second Iran' in the region. This is not to suggest that collective self-defence arrangements, even aside from their potential role in intervention, should not also be transformed. After many years, the continued stationing of large detachments of American troops in Germany and Japan seems anachronistic, an outmoded legacy of the postwar world. Unlike intervention, however, this issue is more ambiguous and requires separate treatment. It can be argued, for instance, that despite the ending of the postwar world, the removal of American troops from Germany and Japan might well pave the way for a resurgence of militarism in these two countries, including the acquisition of nuclear weapons, a process which could greatly destabilise East–West relations.

In the end, a diplomacy of non-intervention requires a change of heart and a deepened respect for both the collective procedures of international institutions and for the dynamics of self-determination in foreign societies. Given the possibility of intervention by others and a variety of interdependencies, there may well be divergent interpretations of the requirements of non-intervention. These ambiguities can be resolved only by recognised international institutions, and even then some uncertainties will remain. In the interim, the United States should seek to establish an informal US–Soviet code of conduct to remove some areas from the domain of competitive intervention and reduce the severity of intervention elsewhere. In this regard, restrictions on arms sales to the Third World and the establishment of 'zones of peace' such as have been proposed by Moscow for the Indian Ocean, could be explored. Non-intervention, to be implemented worldwide, requires collective procedures for administering the rules of the game in international life, including peacekeeping forces to protect states against external attacks. Given an insistence on the exercise of sovereign rights and the character of self-serving ideological perceptions of foreign policy choices, it is unlikely that international institutions will soon be entrusted with such a central administrative role. Hence, the most that can be achieved in the years ahead, and this mainly on the basis of a reassessment of national self-interest, is a renunciation by the United States of grosser forms of military intervention in the Third World.

Achieving Collective Management for the World Economy
Bipartisanship is perhaps most pronounced when it comes to foreign economic policy. Aside from sectional special interests that press for or against free trade, the pro-capitalist, anti-socialist bias has prevailed since 1945, along with the shared conviction that US economic power should be used to shape a market-oriented non-communist framework for maximising trade and investment opportunities. Relative to the rest of the developed world at the end of World War II, the United States was at least as strong economically as it was militarily. Not only did US productive capacity dominate the world economy, but American innovative prowess and research and development seemed to assure its continuing dominance. This dominance was symbolised, of course, by US custodianship over nuclear technology, and underscored by the battered condition of all other leading national economies.

American economic leadership seemed benign, and many specialists believed that the world economy could function successfully as a mutually beneficial trading system only if organised and maintained by some single powerful actor. The economist Charles Kindleberger, among others, has argued that the erosion of British economic dominance in the 1930s led directly to the formation of hostile trading blocs and to mutually detrimental forms of protectionism. In effect, only a dominant actor with a larger conception of its role than national economic interests, narrowly conceived, is capable of providing international society with the confidence required for a robust trading system.

The postwar bipartisan consensus in America sought to facilitate and maintain control over an expansion of world trade on the basis of substantially free capital flows, stable currency and financial arrangements, restored economies in Europe and Japan, and the modernisation of the Third World under Western, particularly American, auspices. The international arrangements created to carry out this design were the General Agreement on Tariffs and Trade, the World Bank, and the International Monetary Fund. The stability of this system and its global character all were underwritten by the dollar. There were unilateral initiatives as well. Most notable were the Marshall Plan for the restoration of the European economy and foreign aid of various sorts to Third World countries to provide them with incentives to resist Marxist-Leninist solutions and the capabilities to make the transition to the allegedly self-sustaining growth characteristic of a modern society. These policies were closely tied to the anti-Soviet containment doctrine that was the centrepiece of US postwar foreign policy.

The American design was a great success in the postwar world, speeding economic recovery and producing sustained economic growth for virtually all parts of the world. The United States, as the architect and leading actor, seemed to have created an economic framework that genuinely served the common good, even if it gained somewhat more than others. Of course, objections were voiced in various settings. Foreign governments resented generally the loss of control over their participation in the world economy, even though they benefitted from it. Europeans worried about 'the American challenge', fearing that their national sovereignty was endangered by capital penetration of such magnitudes. The Third World viewed the leading multinational corporations, overwhelmingly American until the 1970s, as 'neo-colonial' bearers of alien values and as uncontrollable and non-accountable presences closely aligned with foreign political forces. The type of development promoted by the United States also had the effect of widening sensitive gaps between rich and poor, between city and countryside, and between regions in many Third World countries. With aggregate growth as the dominant yardstick, issues of distribution and of alleviating poverty and inequality received scant attention. Yet as long as growth persisted without excessive unemployment or inflation, few were disposed to doubt the American postwar achievement. This achievement was in part related to the apparent ability of advanced industrial economies to use Keynesian mechanisms to smooth boom–bust cycles and welfare state policies to combine prosperity with a decent life for the least advantaged members of their societies. Once again American leadership seemed vindicated by its success in reducing poverty at home while sustaining strong economic growth.

The American story began to take a different turn as the postwar world came to an end. When OPEC abruptly raised oil prices in the 1970s, it hastened the end of *easy* economic growth, showing the extent to which low-energy costs had contributed to earlier economic success. Deeper factors of instability were also at work. Profit margins diminished, and trade imbalances and foreign borrowing rose to frightening levels. When the dollar began to weaken in the 1960s, primarily as a result of vast external holdings, currency fluctuations introduced added uncertainty, even an element of anarchy, into the world economy. The ability of the United States to manage the international economic framework was dramatically reduced, and unilateral approaches of a protectionist character spread rapidly. Domestically, pressures mounted against welfare spending. A deep recession ensued, combining unemployment, inflation, and stagnant growth, which took different forms in different regions of the world.

Furthermore, the recovery of Germany and Japan continued to shift the world economic balance somewhat against the United States without any compensating shifts in the Washington-based system for managing the world economy. Uneven growth among the leading industrial countries now worked against the United States, as did economic performance measured by relative increases in productivity and product quality. The Japanese challenge became particularly dramatic in the 1970s, reinforcing an impression of American decline (in the wake of its defeat in Vietnam, Watergate, and the growing strategic power of the Soviet Union). There were other challenges as well. Modernisation efforts in some particularly dynamic Third World countries generated products that could compete successfully with American goods. Moreover, nationalist sentiments led to restraints on the operations of multinational corporations and on private capital from the North.

In an important sense, resurgent nationalism everywhere challenged US economic primacy. In its most militant instances, economic nationalism prompted interventionary responses by the United States, such as in Iran in 1953 and Chile in 1973, which attempted to rid these countries of leaders who threatened to confiscate important US economic holdings.

The relative decline of the US position in the world economy was indeed dramatic, as a comparison of the key indicators for 1950 and 1980 reveals. In 1950, the United States was responsible for about 34 per cent of the world GNP, 60 per cent of the world's industrial production, and 50 per cent of the world's monetary reserves. By 1980, these figures had declined to 23 per cent of the world GNP, 30 per cent of its industrial production, and 6 per cent of its monetary reserves.[10] At the same time, the end of easy growth led to fiercer international competition for markets and drastic reductions of international liquidity, both of which increased protectionist pressures, currency fluctuations, and precarious patterns of heavy transnational indebtedness.

The decline of relative US economic dominance has resulted in a series of conflicts that are basically unrelated to East–West rivalry. The Soviet Union is not a major participant in the world economy, either as a trader or as an investor, although Europe's greater stake in economic relations with the Soviet Union has become an increasing source of tension between the United States and its NATO allies. Advanced capitalist countries retain full, unchallenged control over the world economy. Even governments that are ideologically and diplomatically aligned with Moscow often build their principal trading relations with the West. The end of the postwar world thus has meant that American dominance has been replaced by West–West rivalry, not by collective leadership for the common good. Hunter Lewis and Donald Allison put it this way in their polemical, but well-researched book:

If there is a single great fact of our era, it is not the continuing rivalry between Russia and the West. Instead it is the emergence of the first truly international market place and the struggle between leading trading nations and blocs – the United States, Western Europe, Japan, Singapore-Taiwan-Hong Kong-Korea, Mexico-Brazil, and potentially, China – to control this new global economy.[11]

It may go too far to omit the Soviet Union from the list altogether. Because the East–West rivalry has recently intensified, the significance and even the perception of the West–West rivalry, and what to do about it, has been muted. American foreign policy has virtually denied the existence of this rivalry, except as a series of friendly disputes over technical matters.

It is not possible to maintain or restore postwar economic arrangements based on American dominance. The relative economic power of states and regions today is dramatically different, and although the United States still has the most powerful single economy in the world, its relative strength is declining. The claims of nations whose economic position has been improving over the years must eventually be reflected in genuine power-sharing arrangements or rival trading blocs and severe struggles will ensue. It is questionable whether international economic policy can be successful if it takes into consideration only the distribution of economic power. Participation in the process of shaping world economic policy is a definite ingredient of full sovereignty; therefore, in some sense, all states have a valid claim to take part. At the same time, the international economic framework should not be allowed to become unwieldly. There is some *unavoidable* tension between efficiency and equitable participation implicit in the management of the world economy.

Yet, primarily through the use of tight monetary policies and high interest rates, the United State has been able to re-establish, temporarily at least, its economic dominance, especially over the countries in the developing world. The South is on the defensive and seems to have lost the leverage, cohesion and confidence that it possessed in the 1970s; its concerns have been pointedly ignored by the Reagan administration, notably at Cancun in 1980 and again at UNCTAD VI. It seems unlikely that Third World demands for the United States to support a reflation of the world economy or a partial debt moratorium will be effective. Nor is it likely that the United States will support a reconstituted framework for trade and finance that might prevent further deterioration of the world economy in the years ahead.

By insisting on retaining the structure of its foregone dominance without responding to the pluralism and rivalry that now characterise international economic relations, the United States supports a world order that is increasingly inefficient *and* inequitable. One source of inefficiency is the division of enormous resources to the essentially non-productive domain of military production. To soften the immediate consequences of this diversion, conservatives have proposed cutting into 'the social dividend' of welfare payments. The liberal response is little better, for without a drastic 'demilitarisation' of the Federal budget its greater empathy for the poor is inflationary. Postwar national security assumptions, constrained as they are by the bipartisan consensus, effectively preclude economic adjustment.

Global negotiations, roughly along the lines of the Law of the Sea negotiations, are needed to address the main components of the international economy – the management of money, trade and investment. The Law of the Sea negotiations, although thwarted in the end by the ultra-mercantilist and nationalistic inclinations of the Reagan administration, demonstrated that it was possible to negotiate a widely accepted global regime in an area of immense complexity. Admittedly, the negotiating process was frustratingly slow, some of its results were controversial, and some of the participants felt variously cheated by the outcome. Yet, it is hard to imagine an alternative process given the need to take account of both the reality of a world of sovereign states and of the growing need for coherence in the interplay of international economic forces.

American foreign policy faces a serious challenge to foster the creation of appropriate formats for global negotiations. The annual economic summits of the leading industrial democracies is a step in the direction of collective economic management. Yet the value of these meetings is greatly diminished by the pretension of finding only common ground and by the refusal of the participants to face controversial issues. To become more useful, they must explore growing West–West economic tensions and the adequacy of the existing international economic framework. Only on such a basis can political support be built for global economic reform.

Greatly complicating the pursuit of such objectives is the reluctance of even rich states to commit themselves to a free trade world economy. One telling expression of America's economic decline is its recent surge of protectionist measures, often in disguised forms, and the tendency of these measures to spread to other nations. Also evident is an 'affirmative action' dimension of economic policy, whereby weak economies have for several decades relied on protection-like measures to develop an industrial capacity, to follow a path of import-substitution, or more recently, to promote export-led growth under the auspices of state capitalist governments influenced by neo-mercantilist ideas of economic policy. The economic strengths and weaknesses of various nations and sectors are immensely difficult to assess. The transition of the Japanese economy from weakness to strength arguably has not been accompanied by mechanisms to open its economy to foreign competition, whereas the relative decline of the American economy has been treated like 'weakness' rather than as an indication of a need for *domestic* economic revitalisation.

The normative side of world economic policy also requires major rethinking. Earlier preoccupations with development assistance have virtually vanished. In the 1980s neither altruism nor paternalism could provide the underpinnings for a restructuring of trade, money and investment relations to create more favourable opportunities for the more disadvantaged states in the world. Constructive reforms are possible along several lines. Serious consideration is now being given to the creation of an affiliate of the World Bank to finance, on a subsidised basis, energy-related development projects. Another promising proposal is for the creation of a Third World Bank, to be capitalised primarily with Arab money, that would encourage South–South trade and underwrite investments on terms less constraining and exploitative than those now imposed by commercial banks and international financial institutions. American foreign policy now has the opportunity to encourage the construction of a global framework that would take account of power shifts and national disadvantages, that would seek to create a system combining attributes of efficiency and equity, as well as procedures for collective management.

Such leadership would be credible only if accompanied by a restructuring of the US economy. This restructuring would need to be similarly guided by considerations of efficiency and equity. It would require stronger national planning to facilitate the conversion of some economic sectors to areas of competitive advantage, the modernisation of other sectors, and the stimulation of still others. It would also require large investments in public infrastructure to ease the burdens of transition and coordination with relevant international mechanisms for collective management of the world economy. To make such a process work would presuppose unprecedented levels of economic democracy, as well as collaboration between government, private management and organised and unorganised labour. This cooperation is not immediately in the offing, but without citizen and group pressures in this direction, it is difficult to be optimistic about national economic policy, and hence about the prospects for the world economy.

The solution to America's economic decline must be based on distinctive national capabilities. It cannot be found by slavishly aping Japan's model. The restoration of public confidence in America's economic performance could weaken the impulse of US leaders to exaggerate external security threats. It might also allow leaders and citizens alike to appreciate more fully the limits on military power, as well as the massive waste of devoting resources to 'useless' weapons that only bring us closer to the brink of catastrophic war. This appreciation of the growing disutility of military force would be further strengthened by the double renunciation of nuclearism and interventionism.

Reviving Diplomatic Leadership

More impressive even than its military and economic prowess at the end of World War II was the unchallenged diplomatic stature of the United States. The postwar vision the United States held out to the rest of the world – a vision based on Western solidarity, an open international economy, and the United Nations – was hailed as a wise and prudent path to the future, everywhere but in Moscow. The United States itself was perceived as invincible in war, and yet as idealistic and dedicated to peace and decency, not only for itself but for humanity as a whole. The conviction that what was good for the United States was beneficial for the world not only was held by American leaders, but was supported by public opinion at home and abroad. There seemed to be no serious conflict between pursuing national interests and serving the global interest.

Of course, this mantle of leadership was never as secure as it may have seemed. The United States had, after all, scarcely considered what it meant to launch the nuclear age by attacking populated cities. The interests and ambitions of the United States were generally aligned with the status quo, to such an extent that it even rehabilitated some fascist elements in Western Europe to help avoid alleged dangers of communist takeovers. The anti-communist cast of American foreign policy gradually alienated a broad spectrum of Third World opinion by its rigid insistence on treating revolutionary nationalism as Soviet subversion ('indirect aggression', in John Foster Dulles' fire-eating language). Furthermore, America's world design included the dispatch of multinational corporate and banking power all over the world, which in turn was reinforced by the interventionary option, and ultimately by the nuclear option.

None the less, at the formal level of policy and leadership, the wishes of the US government prevailed. In the immediate postwar period, US foreign policy and the positions endorsed by the United Nations were virtually indistinguishable. The Soviet Union was able to defend its positions on international issues within the United Nations only by using its Security Council veto, and it learned a lesson it never forgot in 1950 when it boycotted the Security

Council in the early months of the Korean War, and later found the organisation committed to resisting 'aggression' from the North.

America's diplomatic strength at a time of waning US economic and military power was perhaps most vividly evident in the issue of Chinese representation in the United Nations. For years the United States struggled to deny the political significance of the communist victory in China. As a result, China's seat in the Security Council remained in the hands of Taiwan until 1971. Not until the 1960s did the annual vote on Chinese representation begin to shift. Had governments voted freely, without US arm-twisting, the Peoples Republic would have been given its seat years earlier.

In other words, America's natural role as leader of the postwar world eroded as the United States took increasingly unpopular positions on issues of symbolic importance. In the Third World, the United States came to be seen as a successor to the colonial powers and as a custodian of established interests. As such, it collided with the intense currents of Third World nationalism. This collision has been most evident in recent years in relation to the two main instances of thwarted nationalism – that of black southern Africans and that of Palestinians. In the 1970s, with the partial exception of the *early* Carter years, the United States found itself isolated on these issues and resorted increasingly to its veto to frustrate the will of the United Nations' majority. Even Western Europe and Japan were unwilling to go along with the United States on such issues. In a sense, the United States became as isolated on the international stage as the Soviet Union. Perhaps more so. Increasingly, both superpowers – their menacing arms race and their imperial tendencies – were perceived as dangerous to the peace and well-being of the world.

Combined with West–West tensions of a largely economic character, these diplomatic developments contributed to the appearance of a country in decline. Such a perception should not be overdrawn. As developments in the Middle East since 1973 have shown, the United States, despite its links to Israel, has been the only outside actor able to exercise diplomatic leadership in the region. Although the United States has not achieved its stated objective of Arab–Israeli peace, it has repeatedly played a critical role in the region and has enjoyed the related satisfaction of minimising Soviet influence. Moreover, the normalisation of US–China relations has caused a major shift in the global balance, again at Soviet expense, and has enabled the United States to exert added influence throughout Asia by 'playing the China card'. Finally, the rightward shift in the domestic politics of the main industrial democracies has elevated the national security agenda and alliance politics. This development has enabled the United States to reassert its leadership over the Western Alliance.

United States postwar leadership was a direct consequence of its general pre-eminence in the world. This dominance has been greatly diluted economically and diplomatically. As a result, the struggle to maintain American leadership has increasingly rested upon coercion and military prowess. Its diplomatic imagination has been exhausted by rearguard actions and its activity in global settings has become overwhelmingly 'defensive' rather than constructive. This perception, by Americans and others, has been strongly reinforced by a diplomacy that relies heavily on nuclear weapons and an interventionary option. To restore American diplomatic leadership requires a new interpretation of the global setting and of its specific challenges. Such leadership can no longer rest on a virtually unilateral capability to establish the frame and tone of international relations, but must rely upon creating more participatory procedures and pragmatic and idealistic goals for the community of nations.

To begin, the United States should make a genuine effort to minimise the role of nuclear weapons in international relations and begin to respect the autonomy of nationalist movements in the Third World. Following the example of West European governments, it should adopt a posture of non-opposition to the self-determination struggles of Third World peoples, including those of Palestinians and southern Africans. In the broadest sense, American foreign policy in recent years has been beleaguered on these issues and correctly understood in the United Nations, and elsewhere, as a position of support for remnants of the superseded colonial order of the Third World.

These reassuring steps should be accompanied by indications that the long-range direction of American foreign policy will be changed. Contingency planning for war should be matched by contingency planning for peace, the detailing of how various international settings could be used to increase the potential for reducing tensions, avoiding violence, and for establishing procedures and arrangements that would consign 'the war system' to the rubbish heap of discarded societal patterns, alongside slavery, infanticide and colonialism. Evidence of such a diplomacy of peace would assure a new leadership for the United States in the decades ahead.

In this regard, diplomatic leadership based on a demilitarised foreign policy should centre upon 'a return' to the United Nations. American leaders should not expect to control the direction of United Nations activity, but rather to participate in a series of collective processes seeking safer, fairer global arrangements. Such participation would be far more consistent with US interests than it now seems if it were accompanied by a renunciation of the nuclear and interventionary options. Ultimately, such a re-orientation would involve serious attention to the problems of the world's population, its environment, and its resources. US support for a world policy consensus on these issues would be to the benefit of all states and would protect the overall quality of the world. In the end, US foreign policy, if it is to be constructive and suitable for a pluralistic world in the nuclear age, must be based on non-violent modes of agreement and adjustment.

This new form of leadership, premised on the continuing importance and vitality of the American political process, need not be naive about persisting power/conflict realities. The prescriptive analysis offered here does presuppose the value of a demilitarised foreign policy, and the need for serious interest in disarmament, but it does not call for pacifism or for non-resistance to aggression. Obviously, the redirection of US foreign policy must involve an exploration of the potential for cooperative adjustment in a complex, fragile and dangerous world. This does not mean that the United States should abruptly reduce those military capabilities needed to deter and, if necessary, to defend against aggression, but that it should reorient its military capabilities and missions toward strictly defensive roles. The insistence that an alternative foreign policy implies power-innocent idealism is false; it has been used by reactionary social forces to confine our political imagination to a postwar frame of reference, including its Hobbesian imagery of international relations as the war of all against all.

A redirection of American foreign policy along these lines can be achieved without any comparable shifts in Soviet foreign policy, although it could be undertaken with more domestic support and greater enthusiasm if reinforced by corresponding Soviet adjustments. To anticipate Soviet adjustments is not completely unrealistic. The Soviet Union, too, has experienced a period of 'relative decline'. It has lost credibility as a supporter of decolonisation and has been increasingly less able to provide a positive model of socialist development. Furthermore, the latest rounds of the nuclear arms race have clearly imposed strains on Soviet resources and created anxieties for Soviet leaders. Soviet over-extension and failure in the Third World may make Kremlin planners more hesitant to undertake interventionary missions. Certainly, the West loses nothing by understanding the opportunities that now exist for a redirection of Soviet foreign policy, provided a kind of innocence does not emerge that relies upon them.

THE CASE FOR POSITIVE INTERNATIONALISM

It is true that individual liberals and moderates in both parties share many of the impulses that underlie the proposals made here. But it is also true that their mainstream advocacy is feeble, and gives way easily under pressure. The forces of the old bipartisan consensus have easily circumvented what meek opposition exists. This was made clear by the President's successful insistence that the public outrage over the Soviet downing of a Korean commercial airliner increased the justification for the administration's overall foreign policy agenda. On the basis of sloppy extrapolations, it now seems that opposition to the MX, to funding for US intervention in Central America, and to the general acceleration of the arms race will fade with that ill-fated airliner into the Sea of Japan. As long as no coherent conception of the US role in the world is put forward, the old assumptions and belligerent responses will hold sway under pressure.

It is in this sense that bipartisanship is a curse upon the republic at this stage. Earlier styles of foreign policy were premised on a dominance that no longer exists but which the United States continues to pursue by relying to an ever greater extent on the military instruments of diplomacy. The longer this tendency persists, the more entrenched and powerful become the militarist attitudes that undergird US foreign policy, and the harder they become to displace. The tendency to prefer the old ways is, to borrow and extend Robert McNamara's suggestive phrase, increasingly one of 'inviting war'.

The alternatives proposed here rest on a recognition that nuclear weapons and interventionary diplomacy must be renounced as instruments of foreign policy. They are incompatible with the most basic American values and with the protection of US interests in the world. The potential of the US economy remains awesome. This potential could be used to restore competitiveness to trading relations adapted to plural realities, and to create a cleaner, safer, fairer and more attractive and imaginative America.

Underneath such a proposed orientation is a call for political leadership with a different vision, one not still preoccupied by the postwar imperatives of dominance. This new leadership will at first be dependent on 'informal' patterns of popular support, and its 'credibility' will be assuredly undermined by the apologists for the old order. The substance of this new vision will affirm the challenge of building a diplomatic and economic framework that takes full account of plural power and that embodies great scepticism about any active reliance on military means to promote overseas goals. What is required in the deepest sense is a patient, yet unequivocal, strategy for peace, and in the case of the United States, a foreign policy that is rebuilt around an outlook that might be called Positive Internationalism.

The obstacles that currently preclude the effective embrace of Positive Internationalism are powerful. Overcoming these obstacles is the greatest challenge to the creative energies of political democracy ever posed since the US Constitution was adopted. It is also our greatest opportunity as a nation to make a contribution to the world and its future, while working to serve and save ourselves.

NOTES

1. Desmond Ball, 'U.S. Strategic Forces: How Would They Be Used?', *International Security*, Vol. 7, No. 3 (Winter 1982–83), pp. 31–60.
2 *Living with Nuclear Weapons*, The Harvard Nuclear Study Group (Cambridge, MA: Harvard University Press, 1983).
3. Ibid., p. 140.
4. Ibid.
5. 'Whole-Earth Security: A Geopolitics of Peace', Worldwatch Paper No. 55 (Washington, DC: Worldwatch Institute, July 1983).
6. 'Our Central American Myopia', *Newsweek*, 1 August 1983, p. 76.
7. Quoted in *Time*, 12 September 1983, p. 21.
8. 'Force Won't Work in Nicaragua', *New York Times*, 24 July 1983, p. E21.
9. *Time*, 22 August 1983, p. 12.
10. Nobuhiko Ushiba, Graham Allison and Thierry de Montbrial, *Sharing International Responsibilities Among the Trilateral Countries* (New York: The Trilateral Commission, 1983), p. 8.
11. Hunter Lewis and Donald Allison, *The Real World War* (New York: Coward McCann & Geoghegan, 1982), p. 8.

3 Nuclear Weapons and the End of Democracy*

Prospects for democratic governance are positively connected with the dynamics of hegemonic statecraft. For instance, it is notable, as Eqbal Ahmad has pointed out, that fascism flourished in the inter-war period precisely in those states among the capitalist industrial powers (Germany, Italy, Japan) that had been substantially excluded from the imperial game of colonising non-Western peoples and expropriating their raw materials.[1] It is also notable that hegemonic leaders of the day 'provoked' a lethal rivalry for colonial spoils that eventuated in general war.

In our own era there is an apparent link between post-colonial hegemonic tactics and anti-democratic interventionary diplomacy, part of an overall plan to make the world as safe as possible for multinational corporations and banks. Capital flows depend upon stable political environments that offer rewards by way of profits, and stable political environments can only be achieved, given mass discontent and mobilisation rampant in the Third World, by institutionalising repression. The widespread militarisation of the internal political order of the Third World

* This chapter was prepared as a contribution to a memorial volume on behalf of Gino Germani under the editorship of Luis Germani. An earlier version was discussed at the 1981 Workshop on Psychohistory held at Wellfleet, Massachusetts, and devoted to the theme of nuclear weapons and nuclear war. I am grateful to workshop participants for many helpful comments, as well as for the constructive suggestions made by my Princeton colleagues, Michael Doyle and Robert C. Tucker.

expresses the extent to which the functional requirements for order virtually require a permanent declaration of war by governing elites against restive citizenries. This hegemonic dynamic is reinforced in Third World countries by economic pressures to curtail inflation and labour demands, solicit further extensions of international credit, contain social demands for anti-poverty public services – that is, by the whole relatively recent International Monetary Fund (IMF) dimension of anti-democratic influence.

Such a geopolitical/geo-economic array of anti-democratic pressures is generally understood, at least in progressive circles. Gino Germani was an unusually perceptive interpreter of modern threats to democracy; he was particularly aware of the anti-democratic consequences of an emergent interdependence on all levels of international life. More than almost any contemporary political theorist, Germani sensed that democracy could no longer be reconciled with the fragmentary organisation of the planet into territorially separate and rival sovereign states, regardless of the political will or ideological predisposition of national leaders. Such an insight has revolutionary implications, suggesting, for instance, the absolute necessity of evolving a global perspective as a precondition for sustaining genuinely democratic modes of governance. Incidentally, a globalist outlook, as Germani also understood, need not be centralist in aspiration, but might most plausibly work toward superseding statist dominance by decentralist withdrawals of legitimacy and the formation of a world system out of relations among what Christian Bay calls 'natural political communities'.[2]

In this chapter, my concern is with the *structural relevance* of nuclear weaponry and strategy to the future of democracy. The central contention is that the existence of nuclear weapons, even without any occurrence of nuclear war, interferes with democratic governance in fundamental ways. In other words, we don't have to wait for Armageddon to begin paying the price, as measured by the quality of democracy, for a system of international security constructed around the central imagery of nuclear deterrence. To presume this relevance of nuclear armaments and doctrines to democracy is itself somewhat unusual. For instance, one searches in vain the pages of the Trilateral Commission's notorious study, *The Crisis of Democracy*, for any reference to the erosion of democratic governance as a consequence of 'the nuclear revolution'; the Trilateralists' idea of 'crisis' is based on the alleged erosion of authority and stability through the undisciplined tactics of social movements demanding reform that surfaced in the late 1960s, a phenomenon described elsewhere in positive terms as the beginnings of a participatory model of democratic revitalisation.[3] In the background, of course, is a concern about the preconditions for capitalist efficiency under contemporary conditions, including a fear that the work ethic, achievement syndrome and greed impulse are being drained away by cultural developments, including a substantially alienated intelligentsia in so-called mature capitalist countries.[4]

The nuclear weapons question is inserted on the orthodox agenda of liberal democracy in a dramatically perverse way by David Gompert, overseer of an influential study, *Nuclear Weapons and World Politics*, a product of the 1980s Project of the Council on Foreign Relations. Gompert writes:

In the long run, the existence of nuclear weapons could fundamentally alter government–citizen relations. If, over time, the need of governments to field expansive deterrent forces is not appreciated by citizens who no longer sense a real nuclear threat, popular support for the maintenance of forces could fade – *and governments might feel themselves compelled to provide for deterrence without the consent of the governed.*[5]

Evident in this remarkable passage of unsurpassed reification, is a presumed priority being accorded 'the government' on nuclear military policy over and against the possible opposition of 'the citizenry'. Democracy is turned on its head, not out of any alleged emergency that prevents either consultation or the participation of representative institutions, but because the perceptions of 'the rulers' are favoured over the adverse will of 'the people' in an area of disagreement. Such a realistic vision of what has already become standard operating procedure throughout the nuclear age raises to the level of explicit ideology the dire impact of nuclear weaponry upon democratic governance.

Daniel Ellsberg, a former government official with responsibility in the nuclear policy area, confirms the extent to which American presidents were prepared to use nuclear weapons in non-defensive roles and far beyond what the American people were ever allowed to understand. He writes:

When I did most of my working plans in '59, '60, and '61, . . . I assumed that I was reading basically retaliatory plans . . . The generals knew better. They knew that these plans were not at all for retaliation because, on the contrary, the Russians had no ability to strike first. So all these plans were really initiative plans, first-strike plans.

And, then, more concretely:

What I discovered, going back to Truman who made such threats in 1950, is that every team of every president has seen the serious recommendation by the Joint Chiefs of Staff of plans involving the initiation of nuclear warfare under certain circumstances. More significantly, at least four Presidents have secretly authorised advanced preparations for such first-use, or have actually threatened adversaries with U.S. first-use in an ongoing crisis.[6]

Ellsberg has documented these assertions thereby suggesting that political leaders in the United States have failed throughout the nuclear age to consult with, or disclose to, the public the occasions on which the use of nuclear weapons was seriously contemplated. In this sense, the government's refusal to accept notions of public accountability in the nuclear domain has been consistent and bipartisan.

In one of the few attempts at a systematic discussion of the relevance of nuclear weapons to the constitutional processes of the United States, Michael Mandlebaum considers their impact largely as a matter of adding an 'enormous responsibility' to the presidency and of producing an unavoidable increase in governmental 'power'.[7] Mandlebaum even hazards the view that 'Perhaps the reason for delegating nuclear authority to the President is similar to the role that anthropologists have assigned to divine kingship: a means of coping with forces that seem beyond human powers of understanding and control.'[8] Of course, the view of 'delegation' here is very strained, as the Congress, let alone the public at large, are ill-informed about the nature of presidential authority with regard to nuclear weapons. In a formal sense it is true that this grant of authority seems consistent with the underlying constitutional conception of the President as commander-in-chief of the armed forces.[9] Yet more substantively, the actuality of nuclear weaponry is such, with its requirement of constant readiness, as to defy the constitutional expectation that the President must have the unchallenged authority to make battlefield decisions in wartime, an authority conceived of as pertaining only to that special circumstance of emergency and national unity that is presumed to exist during a properly declared war. As is obvious, and will be discussed later, nuclear weapons, by their very existence, forever obliterate the occasion of 'peace', thereby, in my judgement, depriving a democratic polity of one of its most essential preconditions. Even those optimistic about the capacity of the modern state to uphold democratic values generally concede that governing procedures for accountability by leaders and participation of citizens are substantially abridged in the context of 'war'. Thus, a permanent state of war, not by the nature of political will or the character of international antagonisms, but as a structural reflection of the nature of modern weaponry, casts a dark shadow across the very possibility of a democratic polity. Citizens of secondary nuclear and non-nuclear democracies, at least to the extent that their governments take part in the geopolitics of alignment via alliance relations, have 'delegated' this awesome authority over the deployment and use of nucler weaponry to leaders of another state! Here, again, such a delegation may conform to the formal logic of constitutionalism, but it shreds the fabric of democratic substance seemingly beyond repair.

More substantively, this new grant of powers to a particular leader does entrust an awesome actual capability to a fallible, flawed human being or, at most, to a small, often hidden, inner group of advisers. Traditionally, divine right prerogatives even if pathologically abused could only produce limited damage, although of a severe sort for a given time and place. Increasingly, the leadership of the main nuclear powers possesses a capacity for destruction commensurate with what traditional religions attributed to the divine, a capacity to cause in the fullest sense a global or human apocalypse. Authority and power to inflict such results by a single process of decision suggests the extent to which the citizenry is inevitably and permanently excluded from determinations that decisively shape societal destiny.

But it is not only the upholders of constitutional legitimacy that overlook the relevance of the nuclear weapons dimension. Sheldon Wolin, in an eloquent introductory editorial to his new journal of progressive opinion, pointedly titled *Democracy*, nowhere indicates that nuclear weapons may foreclose democratising prospects in unsuspected, unacknowledged, and crucial respects. His emphasis is on 'the steady transformation of America into an anti-democratic society' as a consequence of the increasingly authoritarian character 'of the country's primary institutions'. Similarly, Alan Wolfe in his excellent book, *The Limits of Legitimacy*, devoted to an assessment of anti-democratic pressures on the liberal state, neglects even to mention the relevance of nuclear weaponry.[10] Both Wolin and Wolfe are fully aware, of course, that nuclear weapons are crucial political 'facts' that are reshaping the modern state, but they interpret political reality on the basis of traditions of political thought oblivious to the reality of nuclear weapons.[11]

Perhaps, the failure to emphasise nuclear issues partly reflects an attitude that their relevance is so manifest as to be taken for granted or so 'structured' into our world context as to be beyond the domain of practical politics, however radical their intention. In either event, I believe the failure to address the issue of nuclear relevance is an important omission for any serious reflections on the current democratic prospect.

André Glucksmann writes: 'Everything subtle, profound, definitive and rigorous that has been said about nuclear weapons – which means not much – was said already a century before.'[12] By this provocative assertion,

Glucksmann is arguing that antecedent acquiescence in 'totalist thought' had completely vested in the state ample authority and modalities to subordinate ethics to considerations of state power – 'The nascent order of reciprocal terror was a feature of Western culture long before the invention of nuclear weapons.'[13] And, of course, such an observation is pertinent. The moral ease, for instance, with which American decision-makers adopted atomic tactics in World War II was definitely 'facilitated' by belligerent policies already routinised, especially terror bombing of civilian centres of population.[14] This striving for nuclear rectitude was, in a sense, reinforced by the Nuremberg Judgment that imposed criminal punishments for the 'immoral' political behaviour of the defeated leaders of Germany and Japan, but neglected 'the wrongs' of the victorious powers.

Taking at face value Glucksmann's contention that the secular triumph of totalist ideology had already destroyed the moral foundations of state power long before Hiroshima, I find myself unable to go along with the postulate of continuity as a way of avoiding the need for specific analysis and commentary on the distinctive relevance of nuclearism. In this regard, I agree with the important recent assessments of nuclear relevance by E. P. Thompson and Robert Jay Lifton, as well as the earlier wide-ranging analysis of Karl Jaspers.[15] Thompson, in an indictment of Left/Marxist thought for its failure to highlight the nuclear issue, analyses the contemporary political situation beneath the overarching, trans-ideological category of 'exterminism', that is, as underscored in his own title, 'the last stage of civilisation'. As is now widely known, Thompson's special concern is centred on the particular victimisation of Europe as a potential ' "theatre" of apocalypse' in a struggle waged by the superpowers who, in effect, seek to maintain their homelands as 'sanctuaries', that is, as 'off-limits' in the event of a nuclear exchange.[16] Thompson notes in passing that 'a prior condition for the extermination of European peoples is the extermination of open democratic process.' Underneath this assertion is the conviction that citizens would never knowingly give their assent to such a suicidal arrangement, and that therefore their rulers (not any longer mere leaders) must impair their access to knowledge and their rights to act on what they know. Repression at home, preferably by anodyne means designed to induce apathy, becomes a necessity of governance if security is to be premised, directly or indirectly, on the logic of exterminism. Again nuclearism and democracy collide in a specific, concrete manner.

Robert Lifton, whose writings probe the psychological and cultural significance of nuclear weaponry, reaches conclusions startlingly similar to those of Thompson. As he puts his emphasis, the new capacity for totalist destruction 'changes everything (fundamentally alters our ultimate and immediate relationships in ways . . .) and seems to change nothing (it is apparently ignored by much of the human race, which goes about business as usual).'[17] Note that for Lifton, the element of continuity is maintained not by the antecedent terrorism of state power, as alleged by Glucksmann, but by the failure of most people, including leaders, to grasp the radical novelty of nuclear weaponry. This novelty centres upon the sheer magnitude of potential destruction, giving secular reality to what had previously been a largely symbolic reality associated with the apocalyptic premonitions of religious tradition.

As Lifton goes on to suggest, the special aura of urgency in the United States around atomic espionage issues during the 1950s, culminating in the incredible ritual of capital punishment enacted in response to 'the crimes' of Ethel and Julius Rosenberg, was associated with guarding the unprecedented power and with anxiety about the potential vulnerability created by nuclear weaponry.[18] The full absurdity of the security pretext for internal repression became evident only two decades later when bomb designs were written up as undergraduate student exercises, and do-it-yourself bomb-producing technology became the subject matter of monthly magazine articles. What is not absurd, however, is the governmental need to frighten its own citizenry into subservience by insisting that no one challenge the awesome authority of the government to engage fully and secretly in the apocalyptic end-game of exterminism. We note the recent reflex outburst by Ronald Reagan's first

National Security Advisor, Richard Allen, in reaction to the European grassroots movement against nuclear weaponry. In a rare post-1945 breakdown of Atlanticist decorum, Allen publicly castigated the emergent European mood, saying that 'outright pacifist sentiments are surfacing abroad. One recent incident of concern is the split in the British Labour Party. Right now the second largest party in Great Britain has adopted as part of its official platform the renunciation of nuclear weapons. We are even hearing, in other countries, the contemptible "better red than dead" slogan of a generation ago.'[19] Allen's words lend substance to Lifton's fear of "the particularly dangerous radical right embrace of *American* nuclear weapons' that 'might well lead one to seek nuclear Armageddon as a way of achieving total purification'.[20] The animus of the revival of anti-Soviet, anti-communist hatred, the resumption of the Cold War and arms race, marks the current period as a pecularly dangerous phase within the wider context of nuclearism.[21] As such, we can expect an intensification of anti-democratic institutional initiatives. Such an expectation has been confirmed in the early months of the Reagan presidency by such steps as an upgrading of the CIA, a renewed stress on the linkage between national security and broad governmental prerogaives of official secrecy and surveillance procedures, an attack on the Freedom of Information Act, and an impending proposal to reinstate capital punishment in relation to the federal crime of espionage.

A concrete instance of this attitude of sufferance toward the citizenry occurred on 19 September 1980 when a monkey-wrench dropped in a Titan II silo located near Damascus, Arkansas producing a large explosion.[22] Local residents were naturally anxious to discover whether large amounts of radiation had been released. Astonishingly, the Pentagon took the incredibly arrogant position that it would neither confirm nor deny the reports that a nuclear explosion had occurred, or that there was a fallout danger. And more astonishingly, the public generally acquiesced in this display of official arrogance. Incidents of this sort, inherently revealing, are also indicative of a process whereby the citizenry is thoroughly demoralised with respect to citizen rights and duties, being subjected to an experience of learned helplessness.

One scarcely noticed dimension of nuclearism is the dubious legality of nuclear weapons.[23] In fact, the entire edifice of the law of war rests upon the central prohibition of indiscriminate killing of innocent civilians and includes separate prohibitions for weapons that cause victims 'unnecessary suffering' or disproportionate damage.[24] It hardly requires a learned disquisition to comprehend the radical inconsistency between the minimum reading of the law of war and the insistence on national discretion to threaten and use nuclear weaponry. Such an inconsistency is peculiarly significant for democratic polities as their deepest pledge is to govern within a framework of law (a government of laws, not men). Furthermore, all 'mature democracies' insist that every political entity claiming sovereign rights accept the obligations of the international legal order, virtually as evidence of its intention to participate as a state in international life. The hue and cry directed at the Iranian governing authorities for their failure to uphold the immunity of American diplomats and embassy premises during the 1979–81 Teheran hostage crisis was based on the apparent rejection by the Khomeini leadership of this behavioural standard.

The claims of international law in the war/peace area are particularly strong in relation to the United States' conception of political legitimacy. It was, after all, the United States that had taken the lead throughout the century to circumscribe sovereign discretion in relation to force and had, after World War II, insisted on criminal liability for political leaders who commit war crimes.

Some apologists for nuclearism contend lamely that under international law the sovereign is permitted to do everything that has not been expressly prohibited. There is some basis for such a contention in relation to certain subject matter, but it hardly seems applicable to nuclear weaponry. In this setting, law follows closely the minimum imperatives of morality; international law has, since the seventeenth century, been an uneasy blend of governmental consent for contrived rules and procedures and the natural law postulate. In our time, conventional moral outrage is concentrated upon 'terrorism', the victimisation of the innocent for the sake of ulterior political motives. It hardly takes a master moralist to reach the conclusion that nuclear weaponry and strategy represents terrorist logic on the grandest scale imaginable, yet the popular discussion of terrorism usually exempts nuclear weapons despite the currency of such phrases as 'the balance of terror'. The point here is that law and morality converge to condemn nuclearism, an acknowledgement increasingly being made by religious and cultural leaders of independence and stature.[25]

To suggest that nuclear weapons are illegal and immoral, and that leaders who threaten or contemplate their use are guilty of crimes of state, is to raise core questions about the legitimacy of *any* governance structure. Reliance on nuclear weapons is not just one of many governmental functions, it is in many ways the decisive undertaking of national political leadership, the one upon which, almost everyone agrees, all else hinges. If that undertaking is perceived by a substantial fragment of the citizenry as a criminal enterprise, then it will be impossible for political leaders to achieve legitimate authority. Deception, secrecy and coercion will become increasingly indispensable instruments of governance, not to handle anti-social deviants, but to prevent citizens of the highest moral authority from challenging the absolutism of the state. Criminal prosecutions of those who dare expose this state secret of illegitimacy disclose the inevitable dilemma of 'democratic' governments that embrace nuclearism.[26] Either the government ignores such protests and acts of resistance despite the loss of legitimacy, or it prosecutes its clearest moral voices despite the loss of legitimacy. There is no way for a democratic political leadership to retain its legitimacy in the eyes of its citizenry for very long if a sustained campaign around the legal and moral status of nuclear weapons is mounted. Some overarching questions emerge. Can democratic forms retain even provisional vitality when their substance is so deeply perverted? Or do these forms become atrophied rituals that disguise the passing of democracy from the scene? Can the nuclear question be kept cordoned off from the overall, routine administration of state power? Responses to these questions vary from country to country and depend on the consciousness of the citizenry and the perceptions of national leaders, as well as upon the tension level of international relations. In general the higher the tension level, the greater the anti-democratising impact of the legitimacy dilemma arising from the existence of nuclear weaponry.

The focus on the United States is not meant to exempt the Soviet Union from scrutiny, but since the Soviet system seems procedurally anti-democratic in its essence it falls outside the strict scope of this inquiry. To the extent that the Soviet political leadership relies on nuclear weaponry, a crucial dimension of authoritarian governance is added. By now, whatever may be said about its earlier ambivalence, the Soviet Union seems to be fully committed to a reliance on nuclear weapons as a means of upholding its interests.[27] Because secrecy is so extensive and public participation so curtailed in the Soviet political system, there seems to be little opportunity for citizen opposition to nuclearism, while at the same time, reliance on nuclear weapons places formidable, rarely acknowledged constraints on the possibilities of democratising reform taking hold within Soviet society.[28]

Of course, I am not arguing that nuclear weapons nullify all democratising impulses at the state level. It is certainly possible to alter government citizenry relations in a democratising direction despite a reliance, directly or indirectly, upon nuclear weapons. It is rather a matter of structural constraint that bears on the most essential issue of state power in a manner that is anti-democratic in an extreme sense (here, democracy refers not only to the consent of the governed, but also to the idea of a government of laws, not men, which given shared human vulnerability has to include policies at the state level bearing on war/peace, resource use and environmental protection).[29]

The broad implications of this analysis are twofold: the restoration of democratising potential at the state level depends on the downgrading and eventual elimination of nuclear weapons as an element of international political life; secondly, normative opposition to nuclear weapons or doctrines inevitably draws into question the legitimacy of state power and is, therefore, more threatening to governmental process than a mere debate about the propriety of nuclear weapons as instruments of statecraft. The Machiavellian question is foremost: can a system of sovereign states ever manage to get rid of a decisive weapon by which an unscrupulous leader might impose his will? The course of international history strongly supports a negative reply. In effect, democracy, as a political framework, seems to be a permanent casualty of the nuclear age, although democratic forms, as an increasingly empty shell, can persist, disguising for some time the actuality of their inner collapse. The trend towards authoritarian governance, although prompted mainly by other factors, may also be, in part, a consequence of the anti-democratic influences of totalist attitudes and capabilities operative even in non-nuclear states (often reinforced by way of alliance or acceptance of 'a nuclear umbrella').

Of course, there is an apparent paradox present. The erosion of democracy by way of nuclearism is, at the same time as the European movement suggests, a stimulus to democracy. It may yet be possible for citizens to organise in such a way as to exert some measure of democratic control over nuclear weaponry short of achieving its total elimination. Advocacy of a no first–use declaration and posture could provide a realistic goal for democratic movements seeking to restore balance in the relationship between government and citizenry and sanity to the quest for international security.[30]

The future of democracy then is at one with two intertwined explorations: the possibility of a post-Machiavellian international political order[31] and of a post-nuclear world.[32] In central respects, safeguarding and restoring the democratic prospect for mature capitalist polities depends on a comprehensive world order solution. The beginning of such a solution may involve delegitimising the state in the area of national security. For this reason the religious, medical and legal campaign against nuclearism seems of vital relevance to the very possibility of a democratic revival.

NOTES

1. Oral presentation, 'Abolition of War Conference', Institute for World Order, New York City, 6 June 1979.
2. Bay, 'Toward a World of Natural Communities', *Alternatives* VI: 525–560 (1981); see also Chapter III of Falk, *A Study of Future Worlds* (New York, 1975) for a presentation of a range of world order systems alternative to the present statist system.
3. For depiction of 'participatory democracy', see C. B. Macpherson, *The Life and Times of Liberal Democracy* (Oxford, 1977), pp. 93–115.
4. Michael J. Crozier, Samuel P. Huntington and Joji Watanuki, *The Crisis of Democracy: Report on the Governability of Democracies to the Trilateral Commission* (New York, 1975); Daniel Bell, *The Cultural Contradictions of Capitalism* (New York, 1976).
5. David C. Gompert and others, *Nuclear Weapons and World Politics* (New York, 1977), pp. 4–5 (emphasis added).
6. 'Nuclear Armament: An Interview', pamphlet of the The Conservation Press, pp. 1, 3, undated.
7. For discussion see Michael Mandlebaum, *The Nuclear Revolution* (Cambridge, 1981), pp. 177–183.
8. Ibid., p. 183.
9. Ibid., p. 182.
10. Alan Wolfe, *The Limits of Legitimacy* (New York, 1977).
11. It seems significant to note that Wolfe fails to enlarge the agenda even in the course of his otherwise devastating critique of the Trilateral Commission report, cited note 4. Wolfe, pp. 325–30.
12. André Glucksmann, *The Master Thinkers* (New York, 1980), p. 151.
13. Ibid., p. 150. Simone Weil and Stanley Diamond push the argument back further, maintaining that the fundamentally coercive nature of the state has been the ground for all subsequent modes of official violence. For a brief discussion of their views, see Falk, *Human Rights and State Sovereignty* (New York, 1981), pp. 128–31.
14. See a careful interpretation of the decision to use atomic bombs in Robert Jay Lifton, *The Broken Connection* (New York, 1979), pp. 369–81, including consideration of the 'moral' interposition by Henry Stimson, then Secretary of War, of reasons why Kyoto, because of its cultural stature, should be 'spared', that is, taken off the list of approved targets.
15. See Karl Jaspers, *The Future of Mankind* (Chicago, 1961).
16. Edward Thompson, 'Notes on Exterminism, the Last Stage of Civilisation', *New Left Review*, No. 121 (May–June 1980), pp. 3–31, at pp. 10–14.
17. Lifton, *op. cit.*, p. 335.
18. Ibid, pp. 354–6.
19. Text of 'Remarks by Richard V. Allen Before the Conservative

Political Action Conference 1981', Washington, D C, 21 March 1981, p. 10.

20. Lifton, *op. cit.*, p. 359.

21. This danger is heightened by adoption of first-strike strategic thinking, by new weapons innovations, and by conflicts and instabilities that threaten hegemonic patterns of Western influence over resource-producing countries in the Persian Gulf and southern African regions.

22. See, report, of 'U.S. Nuclear Weapons Accidents', *The Defence Monitor*, X, No. 5, (1981), p. 11.

23. Typical of this discussion is the assumption that international law currently imposes no restraints on the discretion of governments to use nuclear weapons. See, for example, Michael Mandlebaum, 'International Stability and Nuclear Order: The First Nuclear Regime', in Gompert, *op. cit.*, pp. 23–4, where such discretion is connected with the absence of express treaty restrictions and the general unenforceability of international law. For a refutation see Richard Falk, Lee Meyrowitz and Jack Sanderson, 'Nuclear Weapons and International Law' (unpublished paper, February 1981).

24. For a comprehensive treatment of this and related issues, see Falk, Meyrowitz and Sanderson, *op. cit.*

25. See, for example, James W. Douglass, *Lightning East to West* (Portland, Oregon, 1980); see also Delhi Declaration on the Prohibition of Nuclear Weapons (1978).

26. A notable instance of such civilian resistance has involved Catholic activists associated with Rev. Daniel P. Berrigan and his brother, Philip Berrigan. Their most recent undertaking involved entering a General Electric plant in King of Prussia, Pennsylvania, and damaging two nosecones intended for Mark 12A missiles. The eight individuals involved, known as the Plowshares 8, were prosecuted, convicted and sentenced in a trial conducted in a highly emotional atmosphere in which the defendants were determined to centre the case on their claim that nuclear weapons were illegal and immoral, and the judge was equally determined to rule such considerations out of order. For a brief evaluation see Falk, 'Shield for Civil Disobedience – International Law – a Counterforce Weapon Against Nuclear War', *Pacific News Service*, August 1981.

27. See Mandlebaum, *op. cit.*, pp. 202–3, for comments on the Soviet approach to nuclear weapons.

28. Jean-François Revel, for instance, reports that efforts by European anti-nuclear protesters to march from Copenhagen to Moscow, as well as Copenhagen to Paris, were refused, while at the same time the anti-nuclear protest was given Brezhnev's explicit blessing. Revel, 'The Strange Nuclear Diplomacy of Willy Brandt', *Wall Street Journal*, 19 August 1981, p. 29.

29. For my world order analysis of these issues, see Falk, *A Study of Future Worlds*, *op. cit.*

30. I owe the impetus for this paragraph to Robert C. Tucker, long a

forceful advocate of no first-use thinking. For Tucker's views on this prospect, along with the position of other commentators on international affairs, see Robert C. Tucker, Klaus Knorr, Richard A. Falk and Hedley Bull, 'Proposal for No First Use of Nuclear Weapons: Pros and Cons', Policy Memorandum No. 28, Center of International Studies, Princeton University, 1963; and Falk, Robert C. Tucker, and Oran R. Young, 'On Minimizing the Use of Nuclear Weapons', Research Monograph No. 23, Center of International Studies, Princeton University, 1 March, 1966.

31. Cf. Ferenc Feher, 'Toward A Post-Machiavellian Politics', *Telos*, No. 42 (Winter 1979–80), pp. 56–64; see also Stanley Hoffman, *Duties Beyond Borders* (Syracuse, New York, 1981).

32. The main focus of a book written jointly by Robert Jay Lifton and myself, bearing the title *Indefensible Weapons: The Political and Psychological Case Against Nuclearism* (New York, 1982).

4 Nuclear Weapons and the Renewal of Democracy

I

No public issue is more difficult than avoiding war; no public task more noble than building a secure peace. Public officials in a democracy must both lead and listen; they are ultimately dependent upon a popular consensus to sustain policy . . . (The Pastoral Letter of the US Bishops on War and Peace, *Origins*, 19 May 1983, Vol. 13, No. 1, pp. 1–32, at pp. 29–30.)

Typically, improving the prospect of peace in the world is associated with reforming the structure of international society (strengthening the United Nations, or more ambitiously, establishing a world government), altering the ideology of governing process in important states by supplanting extremism and crusading conceptions, or changing the way in which international security is understood and upheld (exploring non-military resistance, non-violence). Arms control and sometimes even disarmament are treated as largely autonomous projects that can be pursued within the framework of international relations. Obstacles are associated with geopolitical rivalries, distrust, bargaining complexities and, to some extent, the constraints on political leaders brought to bear by pressure groups associated with the military-industrial complex.

In my view, such interpretations of the most promising directions of global reform lack a political dimension unless they also examine the relevance of the relationship between state and society with respect to the formation and execution of policy in the war/peace area. By taking the particular situation in the United States into consideration, I wish to show that the erosion of the procedure and expectations of representative democracy greatly impair the capacity of the electorate to translate their mandate to reduce nuclear war risks into official policy; further, that this impairment is not generally understood, leading the bulk of the peace movement to seek 'solutions' that cannot hope to achieve more than nominal results given the character of bureaucratic control over national security policy and I wish to show concretely, for instance, that the effort to rely on Congress and a more enlightened elected leadership in the White House to end the arms race is naive in the extreme, or what amounts to the same thing, 'utopian'. The freeze movement as a *message* of concern is a brilliant political tactic, but conceived of as a *mechanism* to achieve results, it is a gift of an innocent citizenry to a recalcitrant and essentially antagonistic bureaucracy.

Gradually there has taken shape a societal consensus in the advanced industrial world that opposes reliance by any government, including our own, on nuclear weapons for purposes other than as an ultimate deterrent against nuclear blackmail or surprise attack. This opposition is of signal relevance to the possibility of avoiding nuclear war, and yet no major political candidate for the American presidency has been willing to endorse it. The explanation should not be, surprising.[1]

As matters now stand, a bipartisan approach to nuclear national security defies the directives of this societal consensus. As such, the entire rationale of governmental authority based on 'the consent of the governed' with respect to the most important question of human well-being is sharply eroded, if not undermined. Further, these official policies as to nuclear weapons use also grow questionable, if not illegitimate, to the extent they are increasingly perceived and analysed as fundamentally inconsistent with relevant notions of law and morality.[2] In effect, the official or governmental posture towards nuclear weapons raises serious questions about the legitimacy of state power that disclose a sharpening tension between the requirements of conscience and the normal duties of citizens to obey civic authority. As the Declaration of Independence affirmed, and surrounding political theory on societal rights to over-throw tyranny confirmed, when a government fails to uphold its basic social contract with society, then for the citizenry, in the *Declaration's* words, 'it is their right, it is their duty, to throw off such government and to provide new guards for their future security.'[3]

Under present circumstances, without revitalising the forms of representational government, there is little hope that any other approach to the reform of public policy can successfully challenge, except in a minor way, the current role of nuclear weaponry and related militarist dispositions in national security policy. The meaning of 'revitalisation' needs to be clarified in this policy context. It embraces a strategy of political action that falls short of making a revolutionary demand for the replacement altogether of our governing process, and yet acknowledges the current crisis of political futility that confronts a peace-minded citizenry intent on ending the nuclear arms race and minimising the role of nuclear weapons in the conduct of foreign policy.

This focus on nuclearism does not imply an indifference to the relevance of the broader concerns about either the decline of democracy or militarism.[4] For one thing, nuclear preoccupations cannot be usefully treated in isolation. There is every reason to fear that a side losing a war waged exclusively with conventional weapons, but possessing nuclear weapons, would be tempted to threaten, and likely to use, such weaponry, especially if enemy encroachments on national territory and political independence were otherwise feared. The United States culminated its drive for victory in World War II by dropping atomic bombs on Japanese cities without even confronting threats to its core interests. Israel, faced with very real pressure early in the 1973 war, reportedly was ready to introduce nuclear weapons rather than go down to defeat. Furthermore, non-nuclear war is also becoming ever more destructive and expensive, being fought with what Michael Klare calls 'near nuclear weapons. It seems politically dubious to allow the concern with nuclearism to make the world 'safe' for unrestricted conventional warfare, or somehow to meet the charge of 'pacifism' often hurled at the anti-nuclear movement by reassuring defenders of the national security status quo that existing interests could be protected by enhanced capabilities to carry on conventional warfare. Finally, in the United States since the Vietnam War there exists grassroots resistance to military intervention in the Third World, indicating that the societal consensus that has been mounted against nuclearism also could and should be extended to oppose interventionism for tactical political reasons of building the strongest possible anti-militarist coalition, if for no other.[5]

Analogously, the decline of democracy is of great independent concern aside from its dramatic expression in the war/peace setting. The quality of what is being secured depends to a significant degree on having a governing process responsive to an active citizenry, while being mindful of minority rights.

The peaceful character of democratic and majoritarian sentiments cannot, of course, be taken for granted. There is generally a reservoir of anger and pent-up resentment against foreign states in the populace that can be easily mobilised in an international crisis by politicians or clever pressure groups; as well, domestic frustrations can often be channelled into militarist overseas adventures and war fever. The calls to 'nuke the Ayatollah' during the 1979–80 Iranian hostage crisis were a chilling expression of a widely supported demand by the public for American military action, however senseless in relation to effects and even if the lives of the Americans being held would thereby be put in greater jeopardy. President Ford's handling of the Mayaquez incident or Prime Minister Thatcher's ardent embrace of the Falklands War suggest that militarist responses can be very popular at home, despite losses of life sustained by fellow citizens. Public opinion polls indicate that a majority of Americans wanted President Reagan to take even tougher anti-Soviet action than he did in retaliation for the September 1983 shooting down of a Korean commercial plane overflying Soviet strategic territory; even greater was the public enthusiasm among the American people for the massive unprovoked intervention by the US in Grenada later the same year.

There is a tradition of informed thought about diplomacy that regards the emotive tendencies of democracy and public opinion as impediments to the rational maintenance of order in international society. Walter Lippmann was foremost among those who argued that the need of governments in a democracy to mobilise popular support for foreign policy inclines the behaviour of these states towards undesirable extremes that lengthens and intensifies wars, as well as introducing a kind of moralistic dimension to conflicts among nations that interferes with the prudent, professional management of diplomacy. This notion of professionalism hearkens back, nostalgically, to the nineteenth century, and before, when statecraft was generally an aristocratic undertaking insulated from democratic pressures and procedures. In this earlier setting affinities of class, even of family, made it feasible to negotiate differences among states quite cynically if 'adjustments' were needed to achieve peace or avoid war. As manoeuvrings on the diplomatic stage were gradually exposed to public scrutiny by the press and as democracy's expectations rose, so the argument runs, diplomats and politicians were forced to justify their claims in terms that could enlist the moral enthusiasm and political support of their citizenry. As a result, this process of democratisation introduced irrational elements of national honour or adversary evil and made it more difficult to restrain or avoid conflict through rational methods.[6]

These factors act as qualifications on the generally held view that a constitutional order presupposes effective forms of citizen participation, especially in relation to war/peace decisions and national security policy. Indeed, the framers of the US Constitution were quite preoccupied with the task of devising a scheme of separation of powers that would assure far wider participation in decisions to go to war than had been associated with the royal prerogatives of dynastic rule. And generally, Western political thought has proceeded on the Kantian assessment that since the burdens of war fall disproportionately on the populace, rather than the leadership, democratic control of foreign policy is positively related to the preservation of international peace, including a reluctance to take on those financial burdens associated with preparations for war.[7]

We also need to question whether the underlying constitutional arrangement adopted by the United States in 1789 can any longer provide a democratising framework for war/ peace issue. After all, the Constitution was designed to operate in a sparsely populated agrarian society far removed by oceans from potential enemies and minimally governed from its federal centre in Washington. The new republic in its early days was deeply committed to a foreign policy of non-entanglement outside the western hemisphere. Ideas of representative governance, brilliantly synthesised by Madison in *Federalist* No. 10, antedated sophisticated pressure group politics, the formation of a huge governmental bureaucracy with an extraordinary resource base, the struggle for leadership being waged between two large national parties operating within limits established by pressure groups, large financial contributors, and the bureaucracy, not to mention prior to the existence of a large permanent military establishment linked to powerful overseas corporate and banking interests. In other words, even aside from national security, a strong case could be made in the 1980s for rewriting the social contract that binds state and society. So conceived, national security is only an acute instance of why earlier constitutional conceptions, despite much stretching, are no longer working to uphold the postulates of political democracy. And why, within this relatively restricted domain of national security, reliance on nuclear weapons accentuates this loss of democracy.

These general considerations take on a more menacing character if interpreted from the specific situation of the United States late in the twentieth century. The government is largely insulated from diffuse popular pressures that might inhibit war-making. At the same time, the temptation of politicians to strengthen their domestic hand with a military victory remains strong and dangerous. Furthermore, the governmental machinery has itself become militarised in a manner that makes it especially *autonomous* in the national security field of action.[8] As a result, challenging a militarist orientation will have to come, if at all, from informal political forces generated by societal ferment, including such acute dissatisfaction with official policies and procedures as to prompt direct action and civil disobedience.

Governmental autonomy as a central attribute of state/society relations substantially insulates national security policy from shifts in public sentiments. The procedures of representative democracy (political parties, campaign, elections and the operation of the legislative process) are constrained, and yet a dominant segment of the public does not yet comprehend the relevance of democratisation to their policy concerns in these underlying structural terms.

My intention in this chapter is to deal with a single aspect of this broad problem set – that of reflecting changed attitudes towards the role of nuclear weapons in United States foreign policy. I shall assume, what seems reasonable on the basis of public opinion polls and expressions of moral conviction by religious leaders and institutions, that there exists an unacceptable gap between official policies and the societal consensus on these matters. To pose the issue of constitutional order, however, it is not necessary to accept my empirical hypothesis. It is enough to inquire whether if such a gap existed, it could be closed given the way in which the state tends to deflect and ignore societal challenges.

In reformist terms the issues can be phrased as follows: how can representative democracy be revitalised to enable the societal consensus favouring a more restrictive role for nuclear weapons to be effectively imprinted on governmental policy and behaviour? Or failing this revitalisation, are there alternative ways to alter official policy, at least with respect to this crucial subject matter?

THE SPECIAL RELIANCE OF NUCLEAR WEAPONRY

The loss of democratic control over foreign policy in the American case is a cumulative process and has a variety of explanations. The expanded role of the United States after World War II meant a far larger share of government resources for foreign policy during peacetime. As a result, governmental vested interests associated with an activist foreign policy increased, as did efforts to mobilise popular support. This circumstance was tied to an interpretation of the world situation, especially turbulence in the Third World, that emphasised military intervention in foreign civil strife. Sustained intervention was inconsisent with a leading political myth of the United States that affirmed self-determination of nations as a basic right, and thereby led leaders to explain foreign policy in misleading terms to minimise popular opposition.

Of course, the alleged discontinuity of American foreign policy associated with recent times – say, from 1945 onwards – can be easily exaggerated. In the western hemisphere and across the continental expanse, the United States from the outset of its existence kept satisfying its geopolitical appetite for control and expansion. Yet, there was a new greatly increased set of possibilities in the postwar world. The former core powers of international society were largely spent forces, whereas the Soviet Union, although devastated by the war, seemed poised to challenge the primacy of the West. The United States acted not only as a global leader in the postwar world (i.e. from 1945 onwards) but also to reconstruct the economic and political orders of the main defeated countries and to fill the alleged vacuum being created by the collapse of the colonial system of imposed order in Asia and Africa. This globalist role led to an expanded and expanding permanent place for military influence in the governing process. As well, the strain on US resources, initially disguised by great economic strength, put an emphasis on cost-cutting by way, especially, of reliance on mobility and high-technology weaponry: capital instead of manpower. This priority was raised still further as a result of the long ordeals of land warfare, first in Korea (1950–52), and later in Vietnam (1963–73).

These policies, although subsumed under the Cold War and explained to the public as essential steps to take in order to make 'containment' work, became unpopular, especially as the dollar weakened and American lives were lost in the late 1960s. The latter stages of the Vietnam War exposed the shallowness of the foreign policy link between government and the people in the United States. As a consequence, 'a credibility gap' emerged, secrecy and the manipulation of information were used as devices to keep citizens from knowing what their government was doing or contemplating, and dissent beyond modest limits was harshly stigmatised.

Nuclear weaponry has a relevance to this decline of democracy throughout this period, although the relative weights of different, overlapping influences on the decline of democracy are impossible to assess accurately. The acquisition of nuclear weapons by a potential enemy, especially when combined with modern means of delivery, produces a permanent pre-war situation of anxiety and readiness. There is no longer a realistic possibility of demobilisation so long as readiness to defend against a nuclear surprise attack is a – perhaps *the* – prime requirement of national security. Furthermore, war plans and decision procedures involving nuclear weapons are completely cut off from democratic notions of agreed upon guidelines or modes of accountability, much less citizen or even Congressional participation. The President has assumed, as far as we know, absolute control over nuclear weapons policy, the most significant decisional framework that exists at the present time for the United States government. Whether the President has actual authority in relation to threats and uses of nuclear weapons remains, of course, untested and unknown.

The citizenry is kept completely in the dark, even being deliberately misled by official pronouncements. In general, it has been deemed more important by our leaders to have a potential adversary believe that nuclear weapons will be unpredictably introduced into conflict than it is to inform the domestic polity about the real guidelines governing the use of nuclear weapons. In effect, intimidating Moscow takes precedence over informing and reassuring the American people. For instance, Robert McNamara writes that when he was Secretary of Defence he had recommended to Presidents Kennedy and Johnson that nuclear weapons never be used first by the United States, no matter what.[9] At the time, the public doctrine definitely appeared to contemplate first use, especially in a European setting.[10] At other stages, the public is misleadingly reassured as when actual threats to use nuclear weapons are conveyed in secret.[11]

To legitimise this usurpation of the basic constitutional arrangement, including serious dilution of doctrines about separation of powers and checks and balances, especially pertaining to war/peace issues, justifications by officials stress 'national security', the need for secrecy, and the overall circumstance of persisting emergency. The death sentences imposed on the Rosenbergs during peacetime for allegedly conveying atomic secrets to the Soviet Union were indicative of this official attempt to convince the public that it was necessary for the government to exercise special protective and custodial authority. The inner war-like resolve of the governing elite to counter alleged Soviet designs to achieve world domination is vividly confirmed by the fervour of 'secret' national security documents recently declassified. NSC 68, a fundamental official consensus statement in 1950 of the National Security Council, is especially indicative of an ideological atmosphere that obviously subordinates state/society proprieties to the waging of a global struggle for survival against the Soviet Union.[12]

Over the years, also, an elaborate nuclear national security network has evolved, with important mutually reinforcing links joining Congress, weapons labs, think tanks, defence industries, elite universities, media specialists and foreign policy associations. This network vigorously supports reliance on nuclear weapons in the context of extended deterrence and is geared up to support the necessity for the continual innovation of improved nuclear weapons systems. There are, to be sure, inter-service rivalries about the best means to implement this nuclearist consensus, including differing attitudes of support and opposition toward various forms of arms control, and some degrees of disagreement on an individual or organisational basis as to the character of the Soviet threat and how best to respond. The nuclearist consensus, in other words, places limits on the range of debate, rather than embodies a rigid dogma that resolves every issue.

This formidable structure constrains competitive politics by establishing informal, but highly effective, boundaries on serious public discourse, electoral politics, and the institutions of representative government. Political candidates cannot hope to gain access to office, nor leaders to govern, without the tacit acquiescence of this nuclear national security establishment. If individuals or positions are seen as threatening to the nuclearist consensus, then official and quasi-official assaults on 'credibility' mysteriously occur with devastating effect. Without credibility of this kind an American politician is virtually finished. Henry Wallace, Eugene McCarthy, Fred Harris, Harold Hughes, Jerry Brown and George McGovern are a few examples of how rather diverse political figures lost their credibility and thereby rapidly move to the margins of the American political scene.[13]

Here is a summary of the main argument. Nuclear weapons are held by the armed forces for potential use at the sole discretion of the President, or some official delegated to act on his behalf. In effect, no representative institution or procedure is given a role to share the responsibility for establishing advance guidelines or initiating a use of nuclear weapons. Even if such a role were established, by way of consultation or membership on a crisis committee, its exercise would likely be rather nominal given the probable weight of military and intelligence 'advice'. Perhaps, this situation is partially unavoidable, at least at the outer limit of responding to a surprise attack. Unless a country like the United States were prepared to accept its nuclear vulnerability without creating a capability to retaliate immediately or even pre-emptively, then it must have in being a method to assure rapid decision and response. In fact, this plausibility of immediate or pre-emptive response has been taken as essential for the proper functioning of deterrence, and without deterrence, it is argued, war becomes more, not less, likely by tempting the adversary to strike first. This dimension of living with nuclear weapons could be mitigated, if the nuclearist consensus were so inclined. If nuclear weapons were strictly reserved in their role to retaliation against a prior nuclear attack, and this was unambiguous as to rivals, then a considerable effort could be placed in achieving a survivable second-strike capability that allowed a sufficient pause between attack and response to enable a procedure for collective decision that could possibly include meaningful participation by Congressional leaders and, conceivably, even involve some form of consultation and assessment of public sentiment. Of course, any post-attack decision process is bound to be laden with the absurdism of *any* contemplation of nuclear weapons use.

The present centralisation of this secret power of decision over the use of nuclear weapons stabilises an anti-democratic 'core' in the governing process, obscures the absurdity, and confines the most momentous of all possible subject matters to unknown and unknowable response mechanisms. It also tends to nullify both electoral politics and official institutions that rest their claims to act upon powers of representation. What also seems evident is that without fundamental shifts in either the organisation of international society or in restricting somehow the availability of technological capabilities for war-making, there is no acceptable way to overcome altogether these anti-democratic features of nuclear weapons policy.

Beyond this general circumstance of necessity, nuclear weapons have been relied upon as an instrument of American diplomacy in a variety of Cold War settings. On some twenty occasions threats to use nuclear weapons have been seriously made, or uses contemplated, by US leaders.[14] US strategic doctrine and war plans continue to rely on nuclear weapons to achieve 'extended deterrence', that is, to inhibit Soviet or other adversary non-nuclear provocations by the prospect of a nuclear response. It is well known, for instance, that the United States reserves the option of a nuclear response to non-nuclear attack or hostilities in Europe or Korea. These roles for nuclear weapons, quite inconsistent with prevailing views on law and morality, have never been clearly explained to the citizenry or endorsed by institutions of representative democracy.[15]

WHAT CAN BE DONE? SOME IMMEDIATE PRIORITIES

Having spent seven years as Secretary of Defense dealing with the problems unleashed by the initial nuclear chain reaction 40 years ago, I do not believe we can avoid serious and unacceptable risk of nuclear war until we recognize – and until we base all our military plans, defense budgets, weapons deployments, and arms negotiations on the recognition – that *nuclear weapons are totally useless – except only to deter one's opponent from using them*. Robert S. McNamara, 'The Military Role of Nuclear Weapons', *Foreign Affairs* 62: 59–80, at 79 (1983) (emphasis in original).)

This section explores the programmatic content of democratising demands with respect to nuclear weapons policy. The argument rests on the convergence of normative and pragmatic considerations – that societal well-being can be enhanced by certain steps if the institutions of representative democracy were able to operate to reflect an emergent societal consensus. Taking these steps would also promote the restoration of political legitimacy by reducing the gap between nuclear national security policy and applicable notions of international law and morality. Such reforms are consistent with non-idealist (or realist) assumptions about international politics.[16]

The mainstream deterrence theorists keep reminding us that we must learn to live with nuclear weapons, and not pretend that we can generate the political will to recreate the world according to some pacific design. There is a surface plausibility to this position. It is virtually impossible to contemplate nuclear disarmament without some guarantee against risks of cheating by others.[17] Such a guarantee seems unattainable. States, and, for that matter, the underlying political community of citizens that constitute separate states, seem unready to accept the potential vulnerability to nuclear threats or attacks by others that is implicit in total nuclear disarmament, whether achieved unilaterally or by agreement. In this central respect, there is no early prospect of establishing a universal political community that would effectively do away with national security consciousness, structures and capabilities.

Given this fixed resolve as to horizons of possibility, reformist energies are naturally focused upon *particular* steps that minimise risks arising from current arrangements and that reduce to the lowest possible level the prospect of the threat or use of nuclear weapons.

The peace movement for coalition-building and principled reasons has mainly concentrated on particular steps thought to have a minimising potential: opposition to the deployment of weapons systems with first-strike potential or that diminish crisis stability (e.g. Pershing II in West Germany; cruise missiles in NATO countries; Trident II submarines; MX missile system); opposition to strategic postures, deployment patterns and war plans that rely upon initiating uses of nuclear weapons (e.g. unconditional no first-use pledges or pledges restricted to specific theatres of operation, say Europe); proposals to exempt certain geographical regions or domains from nuclear weapons deployment (e.g. nuclear weapons-free zones in Central Europe, the Indian Ocean, Latin America, Africa, Pacific Islands; denuclearisation of Antarctica, the moon, ocean floor, and outer space); support for unilateral and negotiated steps to end the nuclear arms races (e.g. a mutually verifiable freeze on production and development activities); proposals for ceilings and reductions on different categories of nuclear weapons to improve the stability of the existing arsenal and to diminish current so-called 'overkill' capabilities (e.g. SALT process).

The emphasis of these particular steps is upon risk reduction and upon the central appreciation that nuclear weapons are, in McNamara's words, 'useless weapons' when it comes to foreign policy and statecraft.[18] Much of the danger in the world is that this simple *grundnorm* has never been accepted by policy-makers, strategists and leaders, especially in the United States.[19]

Correlative to this direct approach to denuclearisation is the more indirect possibilities of toning down geopolitical rivalry. This toning down could take two principal forms: renouncing interventionary diplomacy and seeking to re-establish détente in East–West relations.[20] Part of the nuclear temptation is bound up with American post-1945 geopolitical overcommitment – a range of involvements that cannot be satisfied at acceptable costs without relying to some extent on the nuclear option.[21] These involvements rest, in part, on the dubious foundation that the United States must stand ready to oppose national revolutions in a wide range of Third World countries. Tensions in East–West relations also heighten suspicions and encourage hostile interpretations whenever 'an incident' occurs. Past wars have originated in local incidents giving rise to pressures that culminate in full-scale confrontation. In other words, ending the Cold War as definitively as possible and renouncing Third World interventionism would remove occasions and pretexts for military action and reduce dangers of escalation that are now implicit whenever East–West interests collide.

The cumulative effect of these steps would be of great significance in advancing the cause of denuclearisation. Arguably under certain patterns of circumstances there could be one adverse effect – heightened prospects of nuclear proliferation, especially by governments no longer able to rest their security under an American nuclear umbrella (most significantly, West Germany, Japan, South Korea). It is by no means assured that such results would occur. Indeed, with careful diplomacy by *both* superpowers there is every reason to believe such results could be avoided. In any event, the United States cannot hold its own future 'hostage' to a position of great danger and immorality when it comes to nuclear weapons policy. My purpose here is not to make a specific substantive case around an overall strategy of partial denuclearisation, but only to suggest that there exists a wide range of particular steps that deserve debate and support far beyond what is now possible under current conditions of constrained democracy.

Of course, a particular initiative such as the freeze or opposition to a given weapons system is plausible even within the current framework, but its effects will be blunted or neutralised by having to pass through the filter of the national security bureaucracy which exercises a virtual veto power over the political process. What has normally happened, partly in response to popular pressures for arms control, is that a kind of bargain is struck – for example, opposition to the limited test ban was neutralised by the assurance of unlimited underground testing and an enhanced commitment to 'qualititative improvements' in weapons, such as MIRVing. Even McNamara's plea for a NATO no first-use posture is coupled with an unexamined endorsement of the need for increased overall defence expenditures to achieve a comparable deterrent with conventional weaponry; in effect, increased militarisation is the minimum price that the national security bureaucracy would be expected to exact for decreased nuclearism.[22] Such 'bargaining' is endemic in politics, but it creates here a dangerous illusion that democracy is alive and well in the national security sphere. The illusion takes the form of supposing that with sufficient public and Congressional support it is possible to move *cumulatively* against the arms race and militarisation. Exposing this illusion helps us understand the very limited sphere for freedom of action retained by the forces of political democracy.

REDEMOCRATISATION AND THE REDEFINITION OF THE REAL: THE ABOLITIONIST QUEST

I had always resisted the suggestion that war, as a phenomenon of inter-national life, could be totally ruled out . . . I am now bound to say that while the possible elimination of nuclear weaponry is of no less vital import in my eyes than it ever was, this would not be enough, in itself, to give Western civilisation even an adequate chance of survival. War itself, as a means of settling differences at least between the great indus-trial powers, will have to be in some way ruled out; and with it there will have to be dismantled . . . the greater part of the vast military establishments now maintained with a view to the possibility that war might take place. (George F. Kenna, *The Nuclear Delusion*, rev. edn, 1983, p. xxviii.)

There is an effort within the nuclearist consensus to limit 'responsible' debate to argumentation about how best to live with nuclear weapons and to invalidate abolitionist perspectives, whether directed towards nuclear weaponry, or more generally toward war.[23] As implicit in the Catholic bishops *Pastoral* and a variety of other religious and moral formulations, it is not possible to reconcile reliance on nuclear weaponry, or for that matter modern warfare, with minimal standards of human decency, nor with the pursuit of self-interested collective behaviour. At best, a provisional irreconcilability is acceptable, but only if combined with a search for total disarmament and the creation of positive peace or a durable world order system. Granted that the security of national societies against foreign enemies will remain a vital concern for the indefinite future, it seems still possible to work towards the realisation of arrangements over the years and decades ahead that could eventually make modern warfare as marginal to conflicts among groups as slavery has become to the organisation of work within society. Such abolitionist goals do not suppose any kind of perfectionist potential in either the collective or individual dimensions of human existence. Conflict, even violence, would likely remain widespread and multifaceted, as would scarcity and gross disparities between rich and poor.

The displacement of war in its modern aspect requires a different sort of evolutionary process that is closely associated with the revitalisation of democracy. The only feasible way to abolish war is for societal forces to reclaim and relocate the security function in 'the private sector' as part of their repudiation of war as the preserve of statecraft. As long as security is primarily entrusted to the state it will presuppose high technology and centralised management of internal and external power relations. This will necessarily include war as a natural limiting option. The idea of enlarging the public arena to encompass the planet does seem utopian unless a prior inward build-down of the national security bureaucracies occurs at the state level. If such a build-down takes place to an impressive degree, then one can imagine a greater willingness to endow collective security mechanisms, as contemplated by the UN Charter, with sufficient capabilities and autonomy to be a significant peacekeeping presence in world affairs. The essential step, however, is to fashion a citizenry effectively trained and mobilised for civilian resistance so as to make conquest and occupation an unattractive option for a potential aggressor.[24] That is, governments would no longer be expected to undertake the defence of territory and independence through centralised control over a military establishment.

Obviously, the process, of demilitarising the security function – and separating it from centralised state power – could probably only occur by confidence-building stages. Its pace would be deeply influenced by public sentiment, which in turn would be strongly affected by the presence or absence of reinforcing steps taken by adversary states. The essence of the process, in a sense, is a capability to assert a new set of democratic prerogatives on behalf of the people or the citizenry. Such a dramatic result would almost certainly require a substantial, sustained grassroots movement leading to the formation of strong demands for drastic constitutional reform.

At some stage, a Declaration of People's Security would need to be issued by the anti-statists to formulate their new vision of state/society relations, leading to the articulation of a relevant set of principles and rationales, possibly distributed at first by committees of correspondence and gathered together in a collection of 'People's Security Papers'. Whether such a call for constitutional renewal would be viewed as a subversive and illegal movement is unclear, but it would certainly create deep chasms and encounter every type of opposition from the various instruments of persuasion and coercion available to the modern state.

In essence, to realise the vision of an end to war does not depend centrally upon contriving international mechanisms to facilitate disarmament. It calls for re-establishing state/society relations in a manner to confer a much greater role upon the citizenry to work out new forms of defence and security appropriate to the special features of the nuclear age.

To the extent this analysis is correct, it does mean that moving the security framework beyond 'stability' depends on democratision of *all* major states. The existing trans-national peace movement, if it intends to address underlying issues, cannot realistically hope to achieve results merely by working towards enlightened state–state relations. Enlightened intra-state and transnational relations are indispensable, and thus the growth of peace movement activity independent of state control in the Soviet Union, Eastern Europe and elsewhere cannot be circumvented as a precondition for radical denuclearisation and the pursuit of abolitionist ends in international relations generally. The war system reflects a certain character of state–society relations with respect to national security policy that centrally embodies war-making and inevitably confers autonomous authority upon the political leadership of the modern state, with greater and greater adverse consequences, including the cultural consequences of 'waiting' for nuclear war. Such a structure, regardless of its ideological habitat, is incompatible with achieving security without war or threat of mass destruction.

NOTES ON PROSPECTS

Naturally, a detached assessment of the evidence yields little encouragement at the present time. The state remains firmly in control everywhere of the security function and only very rarely are denuclearising proposals or tactics associated with readjusting state/society relations. For minimising strategies, as discussed above, there is generally no challenge directed at all of the existing array of responsibilities of the state for security, but only the suggestion that these responsibilities can be as effectively met while greatly reducing the role of nuclear weaponry. Going further, conceiving of a positive peace system, as the *Pastoral* does, if undertaken at all, is most commonly identified with generating support for a global governmental authority – an enhanced United Nations that has the characteristics of a limited world government – that will remove war-making from the level of the sovereign state:

The hope for such a structure is not unrealistic, because the point has been reached where public opinion sees clearly that, with the massive weaponry of the present, war is no longer viable.
There *is* a substitute for war. There is negotiation under the supervision of a global body realistically fashioned to do its job . . .[25]

This centralised peace system will apparently continue to

conceive of security as a matter of war-making, but hopefully with the balance of forces being held by the global
arrangement and exercised on behalf of the world
community as a whole. The approach taken here towards
denuclearisation and the abolition of war is decentralist
and anti-militarist in emphasis, and rests on the potential
capacity of the citizenry to be largely self-reliant when it
comes to upholding societal security.

There are some reasons to be hopeful if the time-frame
is stretched out over several decades. The state is losing its
legitimacy in the national security sector, especially in
relation to nuclear war. Societal forces are beginning to
realise that the state is itself locked into war-making and
both a victim and abettor of technological momentum. It
seems likely that as the critique of the state and the states
system proceeds, the reformist focus will shift to an understanding of the impermeability of the national security
bureaucracy to a societal consensus relating to nuclear
weapons and war. Already seeds of such an understanding
exist, as in the suggestion, going back to President Eisenhower's warning in his Farewell Address about the menace
of 'a military-industrial complex'. But such a warning was
largely rhetorical, not a political challenge. The national
security consensus has easily outlasted and outwitted
temporary failures of public confidence, and usually struck
back effectively by way of well-orchestrated scare tactics.[26]

At the same time, however, there is some renewed realisation that only a social movement with the staying power
of the bureaucracy of the state can mount a societal challenge. The entry of churches into this struggle is crucial, as
it gives citizens vital institutional backing, normative
reassurance and a tradition of continuity.

A variety of religious perspectives has also inspired individuals to undertake exemplary actions of a variety of
kinds – for instance, blocking a train carrying Trident
warheads or seeking symbolically to interfere with the
production of first-strike weapons. These actions express
urgency and deep personal conviction (putting one's body
in the path of danger and accepting the punishments of
law), but more fundamentally, they express a loss of faith

in national security as defined by the state and reinforced by the overall workings of representative democracy.[27] Groups engaged in non-violent resistance are emerging at a rapid pace, although still consisting of only small knots of committed individuals, often part of religiously-oriented experimental communities. Their political consciousness is devoted mainly to negating the claims of the state to subject our lives and the future of the planet to a destiny of nuclear apocalypse. There are only the glimmerings that beyond the denial lies an affirmation of people's security based on the extraordinary potential for the empowerment of citizens to work out a variety of arrangements for the security of society without dependence on weapons.

Three phases of civic consciousness can be distinguished. Each overlaps with the others, even within the experience of a single citizen, yet in an optimistic interpretation of the future these three can be envisaged as stages in a scenario for revitalising political democracy in the United States, especially as it pertains to war/peace issues:

I. Resignation
A basic sense of despair about ending the nuclear arms race, avoiding nuclear war, and eliminating the shadow of nuclear danger overhanging daily existence. Without an emphasis on redemocratisation, despair persists in the form of unavoidable disappointment even for those who, responding to the encroachment of nuclear weaponry, seek various kinds of reform by way of arms control and disarmament. The nuclear national security state has sufficiently immobilised the institutions and procedures of representative democracy to render them almost ineffectual when it comes to challenging the fundamental content and framework of official policy in the war/peace area.

II. Resistance
A basic sense that the struggle against nuclearism has to be waged outside, and almost in defiance of, the normal constitutional order. In such circumstances non-violent, symbolic acts of resistance operate to redefine the meaning of good citizenship. Participation in political campaigns,

party politics and elections become meaningful almost only to the extent that their failure to address basic grievances about nuclear national security is exposed. Resistance tends to be mainly negative in its political energy, although not in its human motivation which enables the resister to believe in the possibility, often created by and with a deeply held religious view of reality, of a possible national political community based on love, fearlessness and sharing rather than hate, fear and possessiveness.

III. Renewal
A basic shift in emphasis from negation to reconstruction. The citizen is liberated from any illusions about political democracy as handed down and has understood the impossibility for forging solutions within old problem-solving frameworks. At this stage, the diagnosis of what is wrong is overshadowed by a broad collective effort to reconstitute the nature of security in international relations. As explained, the struggle emphasises a new constitutional arrangement that transfers predominant responsibility for security downward from the state to the individual, local, and semi-local level. This transfer is premised upon conclusive disillusionment with militarised, centralised, high technology security systems. The plausibility of such a transfer rests upon the creativity of the citizenry in designing various types of 'people's security' and in renewing the overall relationship between state and society so that political democracy can flourish again.[28] Implicit in such a process is not only a localising, decentralising spirit, but also a more cosmopolitan attitude towards the future that acknowledges a global political community as natural and necessary, despite the persistence and benefits of political diversity. This diversity is a positive attribute of global political community, provided only that the main sub-communities find ways to democratise the relationship of state and society in the war/peace context.

NOTES

1. See Chapter 3.
2. On their problematic legal status, see C. Builder and M. Graubard, 'The International Law of Armed Conflict: Implications for the Concept of Assured Destruction', RAND Publication Series R-2804-FF, 1982; see also Special Issue on Disarmament, *McGill Law Journal*, Vol. 28 (July 1983), esp. articles by Vlasic, Falk, Weston, Paust.
3. For a stimulating recent exploration of the *Declaration's* outlook, see Garry Wills, *Inventing America* (New York, 1973).
4. See Rober Jay Lifton and Richard Falk, *Indefensible Weapons: The Political and Psychological Case Against Nuclearism* (New York, 1982).
5. Argument developed in Falk, 'American Foreign Policy at the Crossroads: Lifting the Curse of Bipartisanship', *World Policy Journal*, Vol. 1, No. 1 (1983).
6. For argument to this effect, see Gordon A. Craig and Alexander L. George, *Force and Statecraft* (Oxford, 1983), esp. pp. 60–72.
7. For important qualifications on this standard view of the Kantian perspective see Michael W. Doyle, 'Kant, Liberal Legacies, and Foreign Affairs', Part 1 and 2, *Philosophy and Public Affairs*, Vol. 12, Nos. 3 and 4, (1983), pp. 205–35, 323–53.
8. This formulation has been influenced by Eric Nordlinger, *On the Autonomy of the Democratic State* (Cambridge, Mass., 1981), esp. pp. 1–41.
9. Robert McNamara, 'The Military Role of Nuclear Weapons', *Foreign Affairs*, Vol. 62 (1982), pp. 59–80, at 79.
10. See Richard J. Barnet, 'Annals of Diplomacy', Part II, *The New Yorker*, 10 October 1983.
11. For a helpful overview of the evolution of *actual* nuclear strategy, see David Alan Rosenberg, 'The Origins of Overkill: Nuclear Weapons and American Strategy, 1945–1980', *International Security*, Vol. 7 (1983), pp. 3–71.
12. For useful collection of declassified internal documents revealing the character of national security consciousness in the early postwar period, see Thomas H. Entzold and John Lewis Gaddis (eds), *Containment: Documents on American Policy and Strategy, 1945–1980* (New York, 1978); for the text of NSC 68, see pp. 385–442.
13. Incidentally, over-zealousness on national security policy can also lead to a loss of 'credibility', as was the experienced with Joseph McCarthy, Barry Goldwater and George Wallace. The national security consensus should, therefore, not be confused with rightist politics, although it is much more 'penetrated' by the Right than the Left.
14. Desmond Ball, 'U.S. Strategic Forces: How Would They Be Used?', *International Security*, Vol. 7 (1983), pp. 31–60, at 41–2.

15. See sources cited notes 2 and 9; cf. also the Pastoral Letter of the US Bishops on War and Peace, *Origins*, 19 May 1983, Vol. 13, pp. 1–32.

16. For discussion of international prospects from this perspective, see Craig and George, esp. pp. 146–153.

17. See David Deudney's discussion of 'transparency revolution', for the relevance of technological breakthroughs in monitoring capabilities to the much greater viability of disarmament in a world of acute distrust between rival superpowers. See Deudney, 'Whole Earth Security: A Geopolitics of Peace', *Worldwatch Paper 55*, July 1983, pp. 1–93, esp. 20–32.

18. See, also, to the same effect, George F. Kennan, *The Nuclear Delusion*, rev. edn. (New York, 1983).

19. There have been ups and downs in the attitude towards nuclear weaponry, ranging from Dulles–Eisenhower 'massive retaliation' to McNamara–Kennedy–Johnson operational minimisation. For more extended discussion, see the sources cited in notes 11 and 14.

20. I have argued at length in behalf of this effect in my 'American Foreign Policy at the Crossroads'.

21. For a recent pro-nuclearist reformulation in relation to a global array of commitments, see Lawrence W. Beilenson and Samuel T. Cohen, 'A New Nuclear Strategy', *New York Times Magazine*, 24 January 1982, pp. 34, 38, 39.

22. McNamara.

23. See e.g. the writings of Wiesentelier, Mandlebaum and McGeorge Bundy to this general effect; contrast Kennan, pp. xviii–xix, where he argues that sustainable denuclearisation cannot be achieved without ending war as a human institution; cp. McNamara where partial denuclearisation is offset by increased non-nuclear militarisation.

24. See Report of the Alternative Defence Commission, *Defence Without the Bomb*, Taylor and Francis, 1983; see also Michael Albert and David Dellinger (eds), *Beyond Survival: New Directions for the Disarmament Movement* (Boston, 1983).

25. See The Pastoral Letter of the US Bishops on War and Peace, note 15, at pp. 29–30. For earlier conceptions of positive peace see Grenville Clark and Louis B. Sohn, *World Peace Through World Law* (3rd rev. edn, 1966), and Falk, *A Study of Future Worlds* (New York, 1975).

26. For a telling, perceptive account of this process, see Jerry W. Sanders, *Peddlers of Crisis* (Boston, 1983).

27. See Chapter 13.

28. For a comprehensive study of experimental possibilities along these lines, see Gene Sharp, *The Politics of Non-Violent Struggle* (Boston, 1973); and *Social Power and Political Freedom* (Boston, 1980), esp. pp. 195–378.

5 The Global Setting and Transition to Democracy: Preliminary Conjectures*

INTRODUCTION

Democracy, in a fundamental sense, is a matter of degree. It is an evolving process, beset by setbacks and apparently constrained by the complex forms of labour specialisation that exist at all levels of social organisation. Simone Weil's arresting observation establishes a baseline of sorts for an inquiry into democratic prospects: 'What is surprising is not that oppression should make its appearance only after higher forms of economy have been reached, but that it should always accompany them.'[1] Obviously, this is not the place to consider the aptness of this sweeping generalisation, except to assert its underlying relevance to this more modest inquiry into democratising tendencies in the contemporary global context.

The objective of this chapter is to underscore the importance of this direction of assessment and to erect a few signposts for further inquiry. It hardly needs stressing that little prior work has been done on the relevance of global developments to democratic prospects. The emphasis of the earlier work that exists has been on 'domestic factors', 'case studies', of particular countries that may incorporate foreign influences, and on 'world system' constructs that proceed

* An earlier version of this chapter was presented at a June 1981 conference on 'Transitions from Authoritarianism and Prospects for Democracy in Latin America and Latin Europe', sponsored by the Latin American Programme of the Woodrow Wilson International Center for Scholars, Smithsonian Institution, Washington, DC 20560.

117

from a characterisation of the whole ('world') to an inference about the political makeup of the part ('state'). Most efforts to specify 'linkage' have been outer-directed, getting at 'the domestic sources' of foreign policy. My emphasis is on inner-directed linkage – that is, on 'the global sources' of democratising potential at the state level.

There is also the troublesome question of the viability of the enterprise itself. The causal connections seem argumentative rather than demonstrable, much less demonstrated. To some extent the answer (or evasion?) is to await 'further research', especially in the form of empirical studies organised around a framework that allows comparability and validation. In the meantime, an initial inquiry such as this proceeds by way of intuition, with anecdote presented as example, and with the construction of certain plausible-sounding conjectures that may explain, or give insight into, patterns of political drift. In effect, then, the objective is to formulate some general hypotheses and to make a tentative case for exploring the relevance of the global setting to democratising potential at a given time.

This notion of 'democratising potential' also deserves a comment. It is selective in relation to the overall drift of national political development. Indeed, given the militarising of politics at all levels of social organisation, an assessment of global forces contributing to anti-democratic or authoritarian state tendencies could be undertaken with greater plausibility.[2] One of the reasons for making 'democratising potential' a focus of inquiry arises from normative or policy preference in that it raises the possibility of enhancing democratising potential by policy recommendation or even by direct action. The most immediate meaning for democratising potential has to do with increasing the accountability of governmental leadership to the people through 'free elections'. Such a core sense of democratising potential must be connected closely, however, with a wider set of standards, values and rights. It is helpful to conceive of democratising potential in plural forms, as associated with two clusters of normative criteria:

1. the extent of protection of human rights, including rights

of the person, satisfaction of basic human needs, and participatory rights;

2. the extent of realisation of collective rights, including national self-determination with respect to political independence, territorial integrity, and social, economic and political autonomy; arguably, but less firmly established in positive international law are rights associated with freedom from the threat of 'illegal warfare' and from environmental decay.[3]

It may be worth exploring a 'values' approach to democratic potential as an alternative to this emphasis on 'rights'. The advantage of the rights approach is that established governments and political leaders have generally acknowledged the validity of these normative claims, thereby providing a juridical foundation for insisting upon the realisation of democratic potential. Such a foundation has, for instance, been used by Soviet dissidents to place their political demands on a legal base that had previously been endorsed by the Soviet government. The advantage of the values approach is that it provides a coherent normative framework that encompasses global as well as statist considerations, a coherence responsive to the increasingly integrated reality of political behaviour. The work of the World Order Models Project is illustrative.[4]

Both of these conceptions of democratising potential are more comprehensive than other approaches. The mainstream emphasis is upon minimum rights to be free from state abuse and to engage in political activity by way of public discourse, parties and elections; democratising potential is also generally connected with civilian rule, recurring consent by the governed, a tolerably free labour movement, and reasonably reliable protection for minorities who suffer from traditions and structures of discrimination. In popular usage, the image of democratic potential is more of a dichotomy between authoritarian and democratic forms of political order; in other words, one or the other condition pertains to any particular polity. For the purposes of this chapter, however, the idea of degree of democratisation is essential, especially to capture the drift that is occurring (and might be encouraged) within an essentially authoritarian anti-democratic political framework.[5]

The relevance of the global setting, as a hypothetical matter, should not be difficult to establish even if it is hard to measure. Patterns of governance seem to cluster in time and space in response to a play of social forces larger than the mix of factors in a given country. There are, for example, transnational waves of 'liberation' or 'repression' that virtually engulf entire regions within a few years of each other. The spread of liberal democratic ideas in Europe after the French Revolution is illustrative, as were the various revolutionary uprisings of 1848. The outburst of revolutionary nationalist movements (1978–present) in Central America represents a more contemporary democratic wave. On the other hand, the patterns of developments in the Southern Zone from 1964 to 1975 are suggestive of an anti-democratic regional wave.

These democratic developments cannot simply be explained by a similarity of circumstances in a series of separate countries. Indeed, such an explanation proves too much, as it undermines the stronger claim of national distinctiveness, namely, that specific national conditions and configurations largely shape the democratic prospect on a country-by-country basis. At the same time, we must be sceptical of international determinists who assert that a given condition of national politics inevitably follows from a given global or regional or sub-regional set of circumstances. The variations in democratic experience from country to country suggest that distinctive domestic factors are indeed influential.

There are two main approaches to the study of global linkage: a systemic approach and an actor approach.

Systemic orientation

The systemic approach attempts to specify the relevance of the world system, or its regional or sub-regional counterpart. It recognises that global structures of inequality and hegemony may be correlated to democratic potential in important respects. For example, the current obstacles confronted by Solidarity in Poland or the FMLN in El

Salvador involve to a significant degree the hegemonial roles of the superpowers. These obstacles are more numerous and formidable than just the ultimate threat of military intervention and occupation along the lines of the Soviet intervention in Czechoslovakia in 1968 or the US intervention in Guatemala in 1954. Such hegemonic patterns involve subtle but none the less real constraints to democratisation as well. Movements towards democratisation in certain regions will be opposed to varying degrees by fairly predictable patterns of indirect intervention, often involving support and encouragement for anti-democratic rulers or factions internal to the particular society. But the degree and form of external opposition to democratisation may be decisive. For instance, if the hegemonic actor is otherwise preoccupied (Soviet Union in Afghanistan), recently defeated in a comparable endeavour (United States shortly after Vietnam), lacking in effective capabilities to project specific military forces (United States in Iran, 1978), or widely opposed by internal and external political forces (current opposition to outside hegemonic uses of force in Poland and Central America), then the prospects for democratisation are enhanced as there is greater inhibition upon more blatant types of intervention. Hegemonic patterns may structure predispositions, but they do not by any means assure a given outcome. It should also be emphasised, however, that even if they are not finally controlling, hegemonic elements, as in Vietnam, make the eventual outcome much more 'costly' for all actors involved.

Democratising tendencies that erode hegemonial patterns, however, may not necessarily, on balance, be desirable even from a normative viewpoint.[6] For instance, if the efforts to inhibit hegemonial intervention raise superpower tensions and increase risks of general war, then possibly hegemonial patterns, even if they result in stabilising more authoritarian rule, should not be opposed beyond a certain point. Moreover, the pursuit of democratisation by radical means does not in each instance assure democratisation – already, for instance, comparisons are being drawn between the Shah's tyranny and that of Khomeini. In certain circumstances, of course, democratic prospects depend on radical means (e.g. South Africa).

Actor orientation

A second focus for inquiry examines the impact of outside actors on democratic potential. Of prime interest is the orientation of strategic actors towards democratisation. For instance, Jimmy Carter's early embrace of human rights diplomacy encouraged certain democratising tendencies, by promoting liberalisation of regime policies and by emboldening resistance movements in foreign societies. In this respect, there is a definite difference between the leadership and policies of the early Carter and early Reagan administrations relative to democratisation abroad. Leadership shifts in key actors are a definite factor to the extent that they concern themselves with 'stability' and 'democratising' policies.

The transnational roles of non-state actors such as religious bodies, labour unions and political parties are also relevant. For instance, the United States government's anti-democratising policies in Central America have been restrained to some extent by the efforts of the Catholic Church and Western European Social-Democratic political parties to promote democratisation, peaceful conflict resolution and non-intervention.

International financial institutions represent an especially critical and controversial kind of actor. The International Monetary Fund (IMF), for example, has significant leverage over the governing process of countries that are heavily indebted or that seek lines of credit. Anti-democratic effects have been attributed to the IMF's insistence on fiscal austerity and tight-money policies which interfere with social programmes for the poor, including even food subsidies. Not only do such pressures operate anti-democratically to the extent that they deprive people of their basic needs, but they indirectly encourage reliance on paramilitary approaches to internal security because austerity of this type stimulates militant discontent. Again, the wider policy context is not without ambiguities. Supporters of the IMF approach point to sound development policies as being eventually beneficial to all, or argue that without austerity outside capital sources would dry up, thereby causing even more severe austerity, more 'illegal' manifestations of opposition, and more anti-democratic forms of rule.

Then there are transnational non-governmental actors with an explicit democratising mission. Amnesty International is illustrative. By means of persuasion and adverse publicity, these human rights groups challenge specific political abuses in particular societies – for instance, torture as a practice, or the incarceration of specific political prisoners. The campaigns of Amnesty International have undoubtedly saved many lives and mitigated the sufferings of others, but it is generally difficult to assess their overall causal impact, partly because target governments rarely acknowledge bowing to pressures of this sort.

Finally, mention should be made of international political institutions at the regional and global level. Certainly, it is widely believed that the United Nations, assisted by the Soviet bloc countries, accelerated the process of decolonialisation in the non-Western world. The United Nations may also have helped to create a climate which promotes democratisation in southern Africa. Regional organisations also seem effective in select instances where sanctions of some sort are available or where symbols of international legitimacy are made dependent upon domestic political status. Some experts have contended that the EEC promoted the redemocratisation of Greece by its censure moves in the late 1960s and early 1970s, others that the human rights reports by the Inter-American Commission for Human Rights have discredited some authoritarian regimes and have exerted a moderating influence on others.

SOME GENERAL GUIDELINES

This survey of 'systemic' and 'actor' influences on democratisation raises more questions than it resolves. At a minimum, it does suggest grounds for concluding that the global setting, in interaction which domestic social and political forces, is relevant to democratisation. Yet it is equally evident that these crude indicators of linkage cannot help us much with our scholarly concerns about *the extent of relevance* under varying circumstances of time and place, nor with our prescriptive concerns relating to *policy recommendations* for realising democratic potential more fully. Too many factors are involved, secrecy and deception give us little access to the actuality of leadership perceptions, and different aspects of democratising potential react in contradictory directions to varying forms of outside pressure.

Does this suggest abandoning the quest for prescriptive understanding of democratising potential? Must we throw up our hands and get on with more modest, but 'do-able' analytic and normative tasks? I think not. Even grasping the general contours is a step forward. To turn away from these concerns would, among other things, reinforce prevalent cynical, militarist political orientations. It seems possible to set forth some general assertions that might help guide thought and action on the part of those who seek to promote democratic potential.

1. State actors, except in extreme instances, promote democratisation best by agreeing to respect the dynamics of self-determination and by refraining from intervention in the internal affairs of foreign societies. The principle of non-intervention is, in general, the best available protection in the present world-order system for democratisation.[7] Forcible 'humanitarian intervention' or intervention on behalf of democratisation, despite their pretensions, rarely seem capable of contributing, on balance, to democratic goals. Self-serving rationalisations by great powers often emphasise their commitment to democracy and freedom as their chief motive for intervening. Such rationalisations have lost their credibility as the effects of these interventions are generally now known to be adverse to democratisation. Consider the official US stress on preserving the appearances of democratic governance in Vietnam during the 1960s, or Washington's justification of its anti-Allende stance, or the Soviet's insistence that their interventions in Eastern Europe over the years have been designed to preserve socialist democracy. Note, also, that these claims of benign intervention also purport, usually unconvincingly, to be reacting to prior interventions by a rival state actor who allegedly has anti-democratic designs. The US government's 1981 White Paper on El Salvador uses an alleged Soviet/Cuban connection with anti-government forces as a basis for its support of the government. Similarly, the Soviet Union has tried to justify its invasion of Afghanistan in December 1979 as essential to neutralise prior external subversive efforts to build an anti-Marxist rebellion. Creating codes of conduct to restrain the superpower practice of hegemonial diplomacy might reinforce non-intervention and self-determination norms at the point where the structure of power in international life and patterns of geopolitical conflict make them weakest.

On the other hand, severe instances of domestic abuse involving the threat or practice of genocide present such serious normative challenges that the argument for intervention may, on balance, be persuasive – for instance, to remove leaders such as Amin in Uganda or Pol Pot in Cambodia. The non-intervention rationale also loses some of its force with respect to regional global actors entrusted with the promotion of normative goals. If, however, regional actors are little more than fig leaves for superpower hegemony, then their activity is subject to most of the same qualifications as unilateral state action. Similarly, to the extent that the political organs of the United Nations abandon constitutional procedures under the pressure of quixotic majorities, their normative role is compromised in relation to democratisation. In general, however, norms of non-intervention are positively linked to the achievement of democracy and independence, as the non-aligned movement has attempted to make clear since its inception in 1955 at Bandung.

2. Demilitarisation initiatives on all levels are conducive to the promotion of democratic potential. Other factors being equal, the militarisation of international politics works against democratisation. In this regard, the scale of North–South arms sales and the type of military training involved is especially important. To the extent that transnational links strengthen the military sector relative to others, they may tip the balance of domestic forces away from democratic governance. Such an imbalance is likely to be of even greater significance if officer training programmes emphasise internal counter-insurgency purposes and encourage repression as a necessary element of the military's mission to provide for national security. Latin American elites were directed along these lines during the 1960s by the United States.[8]

The dynamic of militarisation is, of course, related to the style of oppositional politics. To the extent that oppositional forces deploy illegal violence, especially terror against civilians, anti-democratic responses and justifications emerge, often winning widespread popular backing. If these violent disruptions of domestic order are further perceived to emanate, even in part, from external adversaries, then the pretext for repression is further strengthened. The tactics of the ultra-Left in Latin American and the foreign policy of Cuba in the early Castro years are illustrative. Non-violent mass demonstrations and movements, even if illegal in strict terms, usually give less reinforcement to anti-democratic tendencies. In fact, repressive leaderships often seek to provoke or stimulate revolutionary violence in order to lend an aura of legitimacy to counter-revolutionary terror. It is widely believed, for instance, that elements of the Shah's government started the fire that killed hundreds of civilians in an Abadan cinema in the midst of the Iranian revolution, both to frighten the Iranian people about religious fanaticism and to vindicate militarist tactics; the Reichstag fire is an even more prominent example.

Even strategic interaction bears on democratic potential at a given time. Arms races between major states usually increase international tensions, contributing to a greater stress on 'national security' in domestic politics, including secrecy, surveillance and the encouragement of militarist tendencies in foreign allied states.

3. Publicity, censure and withdrawal of the symbols of legitimacy by impartial international actors in response to authori-

tarian abuses generally contribute to the mitigation of authoritarian practices and to progress toward democratisation. All governments, even repressive ones, accept the normative framework of democratisation and human rights. Indeed, the legitimacy of political rule is to some degree based on this framework. Hence, persuasive withdrawals of legitimacy are setbacks for almost any anti-democratic government and for its leaders. Short of this, even the prospect of losing legitimacy may inhibit governments or lead them to correct some abuses.

The swing of the Catholic Church in the last decade or so in relation to the political future of Central America has been of great significance.[9] For one thing, those struggling for democratisation have enlisted the support of church officials, priests and nuns. For another, such individuals have become targets of official violence, creating ugly incidents. Such a dynamic generates transnational shock waves, as occurred after Archbishop Oscar Arnulfo Romero's assassination in San Salvador in 1980, significantly eroding, in this instance, popular support in the United States for intervention on behalf of the existing regime. The Catholic Church has considerable influence on such issues of political legitimacy in the United States, especially in relation to developments in predominantly Catholic countries. In this regard, US public opinion is without reservation in lending support to Polish democratising prospects despite the increased international tensions that result from confronting the Soviet Union within its primary sphere of influence.

Even the Reagan administration has tried to couple its accelerated military assistance programmes to informal commitments by recipient governments to the rhetoric of human rights and democratisation. The Soviet Union habitually claims that its interventions are motivated by the need to rescue democratic socialism from anti-democratic threats, abetted from abroad – a reasoning not dissimilar from that used by Henry Kissinger in *The White House Years* to justify US efforts to destabilise Allende's Chile. Notorious dictators like Pinochet periodically promise elections, liberalisation, and the like.

Of course, the nexus between legitimacy and democracy

debases political discourse, generates meaningless propaganda on these issues, and emphasises the importance of relying as much as possible upon actors with reputations for prudence and impartiality. In the last decade the United Nations has lost much of its moral authority on these matters because its votes of 'censure' seem arbitrary and selective, motivated to a considerable degree by partisan political coalitions. Some regional actors have fared better. Private public-interest organisations perhaps have done the best job of all, but these too have their vulnerabilities which are often a consequence of their limited budgets and the 'partiality' and 'sensitivities' of their funding sources.

4. Delegitimising interventionary options within the domestic arena of hegemonic actors is of great importance. Despite the formal mantle of approval routinely conferred on democratic governance, the real attitude of political leadership toward democratisation in key state actors, especially the two superpowers, is what is relevant. The issues here are partly pragmatic, partly normative, and partly a spillover from other domestic political issues.

The general proposition can be simply illustrated by the chilling impact of Vietnam on interventionary diplomacy during the 1970s. The pragmatic case against intervention is based on the recognition that military approaches do not work in the face of determined nationalist opposition, and that the prospects for US influence may be enhanced, not diminished, by accommodating various movements of national revolution in the Third World. This pragmatic approach also acknowledges that foreign leaders are more likely to govern effectively if they enjoy popular support, manifested through free elections, than if dependent on military rule. Thus, for instance, it is argued that the promotion of human rights in a country like South Korea helps assure the stability of overall US–Korean relations better than does repressive rule.

The normative case involves delegitimating certain practices (export of repressive technology, covert operations) in official arenas – what the US Congress has attempted in Section 502B of the Foreign Assistance Act and by various moves to contain CIA covert action. The normative case came under heavy attack in the late 1970s as being 'unrealistic' and as wasting 'assets' needed for an effective foreign policy. Conservative critics claimed that the US government needed greater flexibility to help its 'friends' and hurt its 'enemies' – that is, it needed anti-democratic interventionary options.

Domestic spillover involves unintended shifts in foreign policy, resulting from elections decided largely on other grounds. Ronald Reagan's ascent to the presidency is illustrative. In no serious sense can it be said that Reagan was elected to revive interventionary approaches to the Third World, notwithstanding Norman Podhoretz's protestations to the contrary. And yet, neo-conservative support for an enlarged CIA mandate and for less restrictive inhibitions on trade in the technology of repression works against the promotion of democracy.[10]

In the background is the calculus of costs and benefits perceived to result from democratisation in a given country or region. The Soviet Union is favourable to democratisation in South Africa or Argentina, but not in Eastern Europe. The perception of democratisation is also relevant. The Nicaraguan Sandinistas took many steps to reassure Washington that their victory in 1978 did not have to result in 'confrontation'. The Polish Solidarity movement tried to convey a similar message to Moscow. Beyond the reassurance is the question of feasibility. If anti-demoncratisation interventions fail or are very costly in terms of blood, money and prestige, then the inhibitions are likely to be much stronger than if a small stash of money and a handful of agents seem able to turn a government around, or over, without any substantial foreign publicity.[11]

In this calculus of costs and benefits, the legitimacy of possible anti-democratising foreign policy moves is an underlying issue for both the United States and the Soviet Union. The issue of legitimacy relates to overall political mood, which is quite unstable, waxing and waning dramatically. Nevertheless, there is little doubt that diminishing the legitimacy of interventionary attitudes and practices in hegemonic actors is of considerable relevance to democratising processes and prospects in Third World countries.

5. *Promoting normative activism in global and transnational arenas with respect to the protection of human rights generally encourages democratisation.* At present, there exists a formal commitment to the desirability of democratic governance, including the protection of human rights. All governments, regardless of other differences, have joined at a formal level in building this consensus. As a result, it is possible to maintain that modern international law reinforces the moral and political case for democratisation.

This consensus puts anti-democratic political leadership on the defensive. Authoritarian practices and policies are justified, to the extent acknowledged, as a temporary expedient to deal with exceptional circumstances. Internal opposition groups and external actors can invoke this normative consensus to encourage democratisation. This consensus also leads external actors, even those without much of a normative commitment, to indicate that their level of support for a foreign government depends on some degree of democratisation. Even if this expression of concern is *pro forma*, it is capable of creating a certain momentum for democratisation, at least up to a point.

Therefore, the strengthening of this normative consensus through additional international agreements seems useful, as does improved fact-finding mechanisms, reporting procedures, and the like, that call attention to progress and regress relative to democratisation. Such normative pressure seems consistent with non-intervention norms and respect for the sovereign rights of foreign states.

6. *Selective easing of short-term economic burdens through debt relief, extension of credit and foreign aid encourages democratisation.* Progress toward democratisation seems connected with greater economic flexibility on the part of national political leaders and international financial institutions. The Western willingness in early 1981 to reschedule Poland's debt payments was partly intended to moderate the pressure on the Polish leadership to crush the Solidarity

movement. To the extent that the IMF and private banks encourage debtor states to invest to increase foreign exchange earnings at the expense of a greater effort to meet minimum human needs, there is a political tendency to impose 'discipline' on the popular sector, especially on the organised labour movement. A massive foreign aid programme like that envisaged by the Leontief model, the RIO report, or in the Brandt Commission Report may help create a moderate political atmosphere via the rapid elimination of mass poverty.[12] Democratisation is more likely to flourish in an atmosphere of moderation than in the context of crisis.

7. *Critical scholarly and journalistic appraisals of the failures of anti-democratic regimes and the successes of democratic governance in relation to proclaimed goals may encourage democratisation.* Part of the anti-democratic pretext is a mixture of honest conviction and hypocritical pretension that repression is needed to save the country from its enemies, from socioeconomic chaos, or merely from the fractiousness of politicians. The military leaderships in Brazil or South Korea advanced claims that a certain amount of repression in the short term was the necessary price of rapid economic growth, and pointed to impressive economic achievements as confirming this. The Shah of Iran reportedly told critics that when the Iranians behave like Swedes, then Iran would be governed as is Sweden. In essence, such views contend that Third World countries do not have the cultural disposition for democratisation, at least not yet.

These contentions must be examined carefully. For instance, Jose Serra, in an important essay, effectively refutes the myths of economic efficiency claimed on behalf of the Brazilian alliance of technocrats and generals, and shows that much of the positive economic behaviour of the country after 1964 was attributable to favourable factors in the world economy and that the imposed discipline had failed to fulfil one of its main promises, namely, the control of inflation.[13] The partial redemocratisation of Brazil in the late 1970s can be attributed, in part, to a widespread acknowledgement that the economic benefits of anti-democratic rule have been wildly oversold. In contrast, the majority of the South Korean population seems acquiescent to dictatorship in the post–Park years partly because they continue to believe their nation's earlier economic spurt was a by-product of repressive rule.

In essence, then, critical thought and writing which both undermines the various rationales for anti-democratic practice and strengthens the impression that democratisation is fully consistent with the pursuit of economic and social goals is helpful. In this latter regard, publicising examples of governance that reconcile stability, economic progress and democratisation would be useful. There may be some difficulties here, especially involving the degree to which democratising can in general be shown to be also superior, or at least equal, to authoritarian governance *vis-à-vis* stability and economic achievement; at best, the record of achievement is mixed for both market and state-socialist polities.

It is also essential to examine critically 'showcase' democratisation, where the electoral process is used as a façade to suggest that a repressive government, despite all, enjoys the support of its people or that its government is moving towards democratisation. Lyndon Johnson's pressures on the Thieu government to organise free elections for South Vietnam illustrate a wider phenomenon. The elections were designed primarily to legitimise the US role on behalf of the Saigon government in the Vietnam War. It is helpful for critical forces to question such 'legitimising' activities and to expose them as shams and frauds to the extent warranted.

Finally, positive models of 'development' that relate resources to needs provide the basis for a transnational democratising learning experience. The work of the Bariloche Foundation on the sufficiency of regional capital resources for needs-oriented development in Latin America is illustrative.[14] In contrast, academic works that emphasise prospects for scarcity in the face of overwhelming population pressures lay the psychological and ideological foundation for anti-democratic governance, virtually as a matter of political necessity. Writings in the North that favour 'triage' insist upon 'lifeboat ethics' and discuss the political consequences of persistent scarcity exert an anti-democratic influence, even if this is not their intention.[15]

8. *The emergence of a new international economic order that equalises North–South relations and that strengthens the capabilities of all states to achieve self-determination would increase democratic prospects.* The international economic foundations for democracy at the state level are complex and controversial. Structurally, breaking down core–periphery relationships with respect to productive roles would be helpful. At the same time, so-called Newly Industralised Countries (NICs), such as South Korea and Taiwan, have not shown any correlated disposition to embrace democratic patterns of governance.

The persistence of demographic pressures that make it difficult for most Third World governments to satisfy the basic needs of their peoples seems related, in large part, to expectations of persistent poverty. Altering these expectations is mainly a matter of domestic social, economic and cultural reform; but it would be facilitated by a more equitable international economic order, one that allowed each government greater autonomy. Indebtedness, unregulated multinational corporations, and adverse terms of trade, all seem to work against the maintenance of moderate structures of government, the latter being a necessary, but not sufficient, condition for democratising progress.

9. *Transforming structures of world order in the direction of establishing the will and capability to protect global, as well as national, interests would generally work in favour of democratic prospects.* The state system, as it functions, reinforces coercive patterns of governance, including militarising tendencies. Demilitarising processes, especially those bearing on relations between strong and weak states and those lending external support to repressive regimes (by means of assistance, including transfers and sales of repressive technology), would enhance democratising prospects. No particular alternative structure of world order is

to be suggested here. There exists an array of possible global organisational frameworks within which democratic values could more easily flourish than is currently possible.[16] An appropriate leadership in dominant actors would be helpful – that is, a leadership that was sensitive to the overall risks of continuing down the militarisation path in the nuclear age and was receptive to positive alternative approaches to the attainment of security.[17]

A NOTE IN CONCLUSION

Exploring the global dimensions of 'democratising potential' is, as we suggest, elusive and complex. A given development can often be construed in a variety of ways. We do not know what will work, or to what extent. There are two broad types of policy activities: (i) reinforcing support for democratising potential, and (ii) organising opposition to anti-democratic political structures. There are also heavily ideological debates present–is Cuba more or less democratic under Castro than Batista? Is Iran more or less democratic under Khomeini than the Shah? Virtually all points on the political spectrum, even the most militarist, affirm their allegiance to democratising potential. This is a central source of confusion. Hence, it is necessary to cut through these polemical barriers and set forth some reliable criteria centring on the realisation of political self-determination. Another source of confusion arises because governments profess one set of goals, yet often pursue policies and practices that are motivated by contradictory goals. The hegemonic actor in international affairs loudly proclaims endorsement of non-interventionary standards, while quietly or covertly engaging in intervention.

The nine general assertions set forth above are framed in the light of these confusing actualities. Their purpose is to focus thought-for-action, as well as to delimit some of the ways in which the global dimension impacts upon democratising prospects and struggles.

NOTES

1. Simone Weil, 'Analysis of Oppression', in George A. Panichas (ed.), *The Simone Weil Reader* (New York: David McKay, 1977), p. 131.
2. This possibility of interpretation underlies my article 'A World Order Perspective on Authoritarian Tendencies', *Alternatives V*, 2, August 1979, pp. 127–193; also published as Working Paper No. 10, World Order Models Project, 1980.
3. For my overall orientation on these matters, see Falk, *Human Rights and State Sovereignty* (New York: Holmes and Meier, 1981).
4. See Saul H. Mendlovitz (ed.), *On the Creation of a Just World Order* (New York: Free Press, 1975); for a more general indication of a world order orientation, see Louis René Beres, *Peoples, States, and World Order* (Itusca, Ill.: F. E. Peacock, 1981).
5. The deep structures of antidemocratic statism are a main theme of Stanley Diamond, *In Search of the Primitive* (New Brunswick, N.J.: Transaction Books, 1974), esp. ch. 1; that is, democratisation as we explain it is decisively restricted by the modern state and the states system, yet there is a wide range of normatively significant variations in the way in which state and society are linked.
6. For interesting speculations along these counterintuitive lines, see Michael W. Doyle, 'Imperial Decline and World Order: The World Politics of a Mixed Blessing', *International Interactions* 8 (1981), pp. 123–50.
7. A strong argument along these lines is advanced by R. J. Vincent, 'Western Conceptions of a Universal Moral Order', in Ralph Pettman (ed.), *Moral Claims in World Affairs* (New York: St Martins, 1979), pp. 52–78.
8. Perhaps Alfred Stepan's work on Brazil has provided the most influential documentation. See Stepan, *The Military in Politics* (Princeton, N.J.: Princeton University Press, 1971).
9. For a good overall account of the shifting alignment of the Church in Central America, see Alan Riding, 'The Sword and Cross', *New York Review*, 28 May 1981, pp. 3–8; this story is also the central theme in Penny Lernoux, *Cry of the People* (New York: Doubleday, 1980).
10. Cynthia Arnson and Michael Klare, *Supplying Repression: U.S. Support for Authoritarian Regimes Abroad* (Washington, DC: Institute for Policy Studies, 1981).
11. The claim made in relation to the 1953 intervention in Iran. See Kermit Roosevelt, *Countercoup: The Struggle for the Control of Iran* (New York: McGraw Hill, 1979).
12. See Wassily Leontief *et al.*, *The Future of the World Economy* (New York: Oxford University Press, 1977); Jan Tinbergen *et al.*, *The Future of the World Economy* (New York: Oxford University Press, 1977); Jan Tinbergen *et al.*, *RIO: Reshaping the International Order* (New York: E. P. Dutton, 1978); and *North-South*: *A Programme*

for Survival, Report of the Independent Commission on International Development Issues Under the Chairmanship of Willy Brandt (Cambridge, MA: M.I.T. Press, 1980).

13. Jose Serra, 'Three Mistaken Theses Regarding the Connection between Industrialisation and Authoritarian Regimes', in David Collier (ed.), *The New Authoritarianism in Latin America* (Princeton, NJ: Princeton University Press, 1979), pp. 99–164.

14. Amilcar O. Herrera, et al., *Catastrophe or New Society? A Latin American World Model* (Ottawa, Canada: International Development Research Centre, 1976).

15. Such conceptualisations are to be found in Robert Heilbroner, *An Inquiry into the Human Prospect* (New York: Norton, 1974); and in Garrett Hardin, *Exploring New Ethics for Survival* (New York: Viking, 1972).

16. For such a depiction of world-order alternatives, see Falk, *A Study of Future Worlds* (New York: Free Press, 1975), pp. 150–276.

17. The emphasis on appropriate leadership is influenced by Robert C. Tucker's *On Political Leadership* (University of Missouri Press, 1981), especially chapter 4, 'Leadership and Man's Survival'.

6 Rethinking Neutrality in the Nuclear Age*

The large-scale deployment of nuclear weaponry exerts an enormous strain on traditional approaches to security in a world of sovereign states. One of these approaches is a foreign policy based upon unconditional neutrality in times of war and peace. One justification for neutrality is to increase the prospect for war avoidance.

In a sense that incentive persists, but is challenged in a special way by nuclearism. The challenge arises from the tendency of nuclear weapons to spread their lethal effects far beyond the territories of belligerent countries. One dramatic expression of this feature of any substantial use of nuclear weapons is the recent indications that a nuclear winter might well result, causing disastrous effects on climate and food production. The policy issue raised for governments that adhere to a stance of neutrality to avoid alliances and militarism is whether something more can be done to protect their future security in relation to the specific danger of nuclear war, including the anxiety associated with the risk of such a war in periods of geopolitical crisis.

Traditional criticisms of neutrality in wartime as amounting to a repudiation of collective security has been more recently joined to a geopolitical attack on neutralism from the perspective of the Cold War. Except in special cases (Austria, Switzerland) neutrality has been criticised by the US government as irrelevant or immoral. Such

* This chapter is adapted from the transcript of a lecture given at Trinity College, Dublin, on 18 April 1984.

attacks on neutrality were mainly focused on Third World countries until the advent of the European peace movement in the late 1970s.[1] It is argued that the only alternative to deterrence is nuclear disarmament, which conventional wisdom regards as unattainable. The bomb cannot be disinvented, rival states cannot be trusted, and the Soviet Union is not a reliable partner for disarmament because of the closed nature of its political order. Therefore the choice for rational policy-makers becomes not whether to live with nuclear weapons, but how.[2] In this respect, it is argued, reformist thinking should accept deterrence and gear its energies to make sure it works as effectively as possible.

Disappointment with the failure of collective security led Ireland to neutrality in the first place. Under the leadership of Mr de Valera, who at one time was briefly President of the League of Nations, Ireland originally strongly supported the notion that its foreign policy would be best served by contributing to a strong collective security system. Ireland did not adopt a neutralist foreign policy after it achieved political independence in 1923. It was the disillusionment of the de Valera government with the League of Nations failures in face of fascist aggression in the 1930s that led to a redefinition of Ireland's posture. In particular, it was the inability of the League to respond effectively to Ethiopia's pleas for assistance when it was attacked by Mussolini's Italy in 1935. It was in that context of failed collective security that neutrality became a second-best world order option for Irish foreign policy and it was this second-best option that was relied on by Ireland throughout World War II despite considerable pressure from both Churchill and Roosevelt to join in what was widely viewed as a just war against the evils of fascism and Nazism.[3]

The adoption of neutrality by Ireland expressed a very fundamental commitment to stay out of geopolitics as the basis of security. This posture of geopolitical aloofness is one of the options that remains available to those smaller states in the world that are in a position to exercise their sovereign rights. An understanding of the Irish adoption of neutrality has, of course, to be connected closely with its unresolved struggle for societal unity and its determination not to subordinate these nationalist goals to make common cause with the United Kingdom, whatever the provocation, until such time as partition is ended and full Irish territorial integrity achieved. Neutrality, then, is consistent with Irish priorities. If the national question had been resolved, even possibly a promise of favourable resolution might have been enough, then Irish leaders and public opinion might well have been induced to join World War II as a co-belligerent in the struggle against fascism. In addition to cultural and ideological affinities with the Allies, economic incentives and pressures from Irish-Americans favoured such a course.

So far as I know, Ireland is the only country to have made this shift from emphasis on collective security to a policy of neutrality in the determination of its foreign policy in the 1930s and 1940s. Several other countries decided to adopt neutrality as an alternative to participating in alliances. Sweden and Switzerland, for example, are culturally and ideologically part of the West European system and they are committed to capitalist political economy. Yet they adopted neutrality as a preferred war avoidance perspective without any particular experience of disillusionment with collective security. Rather they do not want to compromise their state sovereignty by participating in a wider alliance; they see non-participation in war as the best way to promote their particular national interests and they rely on a large armed capability to protect their neutrality. In other words, they seek to make themselves as unattractive as possible to potential belligerent powers that might covet their territory or other assets. In a technical sense, the option of neutrality imposes an obligation to enforce neutrality; if that obligation is not uphold, a refusal to respect neutral rights is legally ambiguous.

A third form of neutrality is that which is associated with Austria since 1955 or Belgium in the nineteenth century. In these instances the great powers imposed neutrality on a country because they feared that otherwise an unresolved international identity could be a cause of breakdown in general balance of power arrangements. This form of neutrality cannot be connected with any overall idealistic view of how to maintain order in the world, but represents an adjustment of the international state system to a particular set of local circumstances. Neutrality becomes a diplomatic instrument used to achieve stability.

THE PERSISTENCE OF PRE-NUCLEAR NEUTRALITY

Neutrality can be adapted to a variety of situations that reflect the particular history, geographic location and interests of a given country. Now if we consider the question of how neutrality policies have been operative in the world since the development of nuclear weapons, there are several things that seem worth noticing. The first is that the United Nations Charter system has proved relatively ineffective in avoiding warfare of a sub-nuclear variety, so that even the traditional notions of neutrality have been important in confirming the scope of that non-nuclear warfare during this period. Thus the effort to prohibit aggressive war has not done away with the importance of neutrality in its traditional war-limiting sense, so that the 1907 Hague Convention on land and naval neutrality and the 1928 Havana Convention on maritime neutrality still provide a body of specialised international law which is of real relevance to state practice, especially in the Third World and in relation to numerous interventionary situations which arise on the international scene from time to time. The concerns of this corpus of law relate to such matters as the duty not to provide troops for belligerent powers, the duty not to allow territory to be used as the base for hostile operations, the obligation not to provide transport for belligerent forces or supplies in time of war and the general obligation not to provide financial or other aid which can be translated into military capability, as well as the definition of maritime rights and duties as between belligerent powers and non-participants in a war situation. However, the overall law on neutrality has little relevance to the problems posed by the nuclear arms race.

The traditional position of international law on neutrality is based on the attempt to maintain a precarious balance between the will of belligerents and an acceptance of the existence of a sovereign right to opt out of war. Naturally the very nature of war–its tendency to a total abandonment of restraint–attaches a measure of irony to such attempts at its limitation. Belligerents will exploit or ignore neutrality if it inteferes seriously with military necessity. A viable neutrality can be established only if it is mutually convenient for both sets of belligerents, especially if, as in World War II, the belligerents are far more powerful than the neutrals. In the Gulf flare-up in 1983–84, especially Iraq's efforts to make neutrals suffer from the ongoing war, the apparent motivation is to draw the United States into the conflict to impose a solution.

Traditional neutrality rests on some practical consider- ations, as well as an abiding desire to reconcile state dignity with war-making. The practical element derives from the foundations of international law relating to core state inter- ests, that is that there exists a domain of reciprocal interests suitable for legal regulation between the combatants which is not generally perceived as legitimately central to the resol- ution of the military conflict. Examples would be the mutual interests in keeping each other's prisoners alive, sparing civilian society to the extent possible and leaving third coun- tries to their peaceful ways provided they show a posture of strict impartiality. The idealistic element in the law of war rests on a recognition that even though war is an uncon- ditional combat between states, the leaderships concerned do not deny the humanity of the enemy, so that a procla- mation of a willingness to adhere to law is a way of signifying to oneself and others an acceptance of a limit on the prerogatives to kill on behalf of the state.

It is problematic whether this law of war can retain much influence in face of modern technological developments or the fundamentalist religious aspect of some modern political conflicts (cf. the Iran–Iraq War, the Lebanese conflict, the Sikh movement in India). Of course the specialised law on neutrality survives as a mixture of positivist arrangements

of treaty rules and pragmatic expedients relating to the
interaction between belligerents and non-belligerents in
non-nuclear wars. However, it has little to offer by way of
sanctuary for states seeking to avoid the effects of the
nuclear arms race, or worse, the overall consequences of
a breakdown of deterrence. The overall characteristics of
nuclear weapons, as well as evolving doctrines governing
their intended uses shatter assumptions about reciprocal
limits on war-making that are at the core of the law of war
concept. Hence the problem for neutrality centres on the
degree to which nuclear weapons should be properly
regarded as violating international law, making reliance
upon them an illegal form of international security. Hence
it may be contended that in so far as the nuclear arms race
imperils both the members of international society and the
society itself, there is a direct challenge to the underlying
purpose of all law to enable human survival.[4] Following this
line of thinking suggests that the sovereign rights of non-
nuclear countries are being flagrantly violated by the *present*
structures of nuclearism.[5]

Questioning of the status of nuclear weapons in international law has greatly increased in recent years from
moral, political and legal viewpoints. The *Pastoral Letter* of
the US Catholic Bishops comes extremely close to deter-
mining that any use or threat of use of nuclear weapons is
unacceptable morally in the fundamental sense of being a
violation of the just war tradition which has governed Catholic thought and practice for centuries on matters of war
and peace. At the least, the *Pastoral Letter*, together with
the declarations of other religious groups in Europe, North
America and elsewhere, is beginning to give rise to a tension
between the definition of what is acceptable to modern
civil society and what is acceptable to the nuclear state.[6] In
political systems that rest on democratic principles this
tension may well become a source of serious instability to
the extent that it draws the legitimacy of the state itself into
question. This moral questioning is reinforced by cultural
groups such as Performing Artists Against Nuclear
Weapons, who have mobilised considerable cultural energy

against reliance on nuclear weapons, and by professional groups like Physicians for Social Responsibility, who have demonstrated to the American people that there is no medical possibility of recovering from even very limited forms of nuclear war. And finally there has emerged in recent years an active Lawyers Committee on Nuclear Policy that reflects, I believe, an emerging consensus among international law specialists that nuclear weapons are to varying degrees inconsistent with existing international law, fundamentally because of their indiscriminate and poisonous character.[7]

It seems to me that in this context it makes historic sense for neutral states to challenge as directly as possible the legal status of nuclear weaponry by linking much more explicitly the viability of their neutrality to a political programme aimed at the elimination of nuclear weapons from the military arsenals of the principal states in the world. The leaders of neutral states can point to the tendency of nuclear war to inflict harm on non-belligerents in a manner that ignores territorial boundaries. The extent of potential harm from existing arsenals of nuclear weapons has been shown to imperil permanently the maintenance of all forms of life on this planet. Even the use of relatively small proportions of existing stockpiles (100 of a total of 50,000) could provoke the phenomenon now known as 'nuclear winter'.[8] The large-scale use of nuclear weapons promises to destroy Alliance members and neutrals alike, and even the danger of such an occurrence undermines the security of neutral states. In such a context it may be contended that the sovereign right of non-participation in geopolitics and warfare is of little value even if it is respected in good faith by all belligerents.

Beyond this, nuclear national security entails a breakdown of the political assumptions relating to political democracy and representative government. The use of nuclear technology enables a fundamentalist or pathological leader, or even an errant submarine commander to exercise the power, without any foundation in constitutional arrangements or popular consent, to plunge much of the planet into a flaming cauldron that could extinguish life as we know it. Such a power cannot be humanly vested without creating the structures, procedures and habits of mind and practice associated with the most arbitrary patterns of domination associated in the past with tyranny. Traditions of civil society affirm an ultimate right of citizens to resist tyranny. It seems essential at this time to construct a new rationale for resistance to the structures of nuclearism. Meaningful political life for citizens is almost irrelevant, even in democratically organised societies, to the extent that nuclearism has become embodied directly (by possession) or indirectly (by alliance or territorial deployment) in the permanent structure of the state.[9]

How to exercise this right of resistance is a perplexing question which we must each ask and answer. I have been considering a response from only one standpoint, that of neutral countries using the restricted and somewhat compromised resources of international law to avoid complicity in nuclear war and to contribute to the process of denuclearisation both for their own country and for humanity. But it should be clear that the threat of such an outcome and its effects make it adopt a preventive stance. Neutrality has to be transformed from its reactive character to be sustained in relation to nuclear dangers. A policy of active neutrality is required. States cannot reasonably expect to establish the merits of the legal position in a postwar setting, nor can they reasonably be expected to wait. Removing the threat is the only plausible relief to consider, when it comes to overcoming the actual and potential menace of nuclearism.[10]

REINVENTING NEUTRALITY FOR THE NUCLEAR AGE

A movement by neutral states for banning of nuclear weapons in international law would offset and complement the effort by nuclear powers, and the pressures they have exerted through the Non-Proliferation Nuclear Treaty, to dissuade those countries that do not have nuclear weapons at present from acquiring them. The emphasis on non-proliferation puts the emphasis on the dangers of acquisition, whereas the emphasis of neutralist concern would be upon the dangers associated with possession, stockpiling and continuous acquisition, as well as with those associated with an active reliance on such weaponry. It is often overlooked that one aspect of the non-proliferation framework, embodied in Article 6 of the Non-Proliferation Treaty, was a commitment by the nuclear powers to pursue actively and in good faith the goals of nuclear disarmament. This pledge by nuclear powers, in conjunction with an effective commitment to non-acquisition of these weapons by others, would move world society towards their elimination.

Such considerations disclose this additional legal foundation in the Nuclear Non-Proliferation Treaty upon which all non-nuclear countries, including neutral states, can act to protect their sovereign rights not to participate in or be affected by illegal modes of warfare by exerting pressure for the repudiation of these weapons and of strategy related to their threats and use. The stance of non-participation in nuclearism thus becomes one of avoiding complicity in what is contended to be an essentially illegal security system, namely nuclear deterrence. Indeed even subordinate alliance members have begun to realise that their sovereign rights to initiate war has been delegated in a manner that imperils their survival more than a common enemy or threat; to be 'Finlandised' appears far less menacing than to be annihilated! Or put in another light, nuclearism is the worst possible form of Finlandisation.

Overall, I am arguing that traditional doctrines of neutrality have been eroded by the collective security/just war thinking of post-Versailles international law and by the emergence of a war technology that makes non-participation virtually meaningless, and certainly provides insufficient protection against the harm from this evidently illegal weaponry, entailing a permanent tragedy for all if deterrence fails. At the same time law is creative in the sense that it arises in response to emerging needs of the human community and evolves to reflect the practice of states arising from claims and counter-claims. The contemporary crisis of world order arises, in significant part, from the inability and unwillingness of the dominant states to play a creative role in overcoming the joint and several dangers of nuclearism. This analysis also suggests that the peoples of the world are not being adequately protected by their governments to the extent that the menace of nuclearism isn't removed, or at least diminished. Against this background, initiatives by neutralist governments would be widely received as positive contributions to world order and as constructive efforts to reclaim international legal process for human benefit.

A new form of neutrality is therefore required by the nuclear age that restates the case for impartiality and the right of non-participation, as well as establishing a duty of non-complicity in an essentially illegal international security system. This revival is premised on a series of interrelated developments: a reaction to the decline of the United Nations concept; the general ineffectiveness of collective security; the character of bloc relations; the failure to implement the central prohibition of international law against recourse to aggressive war (cf. the US–USSR response to the 1980 Iraqi invasion of Iran); and most of all, the dynamic of an arms race in the weaponry of mass destruction that necessarily undermines the sovereignty and self-determination of all states, and even compromises their internal constitutional order.

Can neutrality be revived and adapted to serve the extraodinary law-creative challenges arising from the present world situation? A movement of revival and adaptation can be based on the special claim of non-participants to have their future secured against the threat, as well as the actuality of nuclear war; for the prospect itself produces severe anxiety and to await passively for these harm-causing effects is completely unsatisfactory. Neutral powers can also act to fulfil the universal entitlement of all international actors to stop the commission of crimes of state. Thus if piracy is a crime in international law, punishable by all actors, so preparations to wage nuclear war should similarly endow states with the legal competence to act despite the non-territorial locus of their grievances.[11]

In pursuit of such a law-creative mission it seems helpful to obtain a General Assembly request to the International Court of Justice for an advisory opinion on the legal status of nuclear weapons and on the status of neutral rights to protect the sanctity of sovereign territory and the preservation of international society as a whole from threats to use weapons that manifestly lack the capacity to confine their harmful effects. Sovereignty in the most fundamental sense of self-preservation of these states must inevitably be violated, potentially in an irreversible manner. Furthermore, the rights of society, of peoples, and of earth stewardship are all at issue here.

Another activist initiative that could be useful in this setting, arising from the logic of the non-proliferation concept, would be an effort by either the neutral countries acting alone, or in conjunction with a grouping of less militarised states, to call an international conference for the prohibition of nuclear weapons, for the specific purpose of formalising a consensus as to illegality that has taken place in relation to poison gas, biological weapons, and even recently to so-called environmental warfare (that is, manipulating climate and such natural phenomenon as volcanoes and earthquakes as 'weapons').[12] This conference would seek to have nuclear doctrines, preparations, war plans and deployment considered contrary to international law and a crime against humanity, as well as to formulate an international treaty that would formalise the consensus and encourage as widespread adherence as possible. Of course, formalisation by itself is not enough. Recent indications of use of chemical weapons by Iraq in its war effort against Iran, and wider allegations of use, as well as an ongoing 'arms race' in chemical weaponry and suspicions of research and development efforts pertaining to biological weaponry reinforce the need to implement treaty obligations as well as to establish commitments more firmly.[13]

I believe that we have reached the point, in other words, where one cannot leave the practical pursuit of international security merely in the hands of the dominant states. Of course I recognise clearly, especially coming from the United States, that no international declaration as to the character of international law however widely endorsed is going to persuade superpowers to abandon their existing military strategies and their technological commitment to this kind of weapon. For the immediate future the importance of stressing the dependence of sovereign rights on the elimination of this weaponry is to contribute to a growing movement of citizens within the superpowers and elsewhere which is raising these same questions. Therefore the pressure that could be exerted by international law used effectively within international arenas like the World Court or the United Nations is to contribute to the growth of this popular movement within the leading societies of Western Europe, North America and Japan, and to some extent within Eastern Europe and the Soviet Union. Such a movement could be a moment of great awakening and education in the political life of modern state societies. For the first time the creative development of international law might play an historic role.

One cannot be optimistic in the short run about the effects of such an emphasis, but what does seem important as an initial step is the recognition that neutrality is something which has to be actively protected in a nuclear age in pre-war contexts and also that the strategic doctrines of the nuclear powers are a direct infringement of the sovereign rights of neutral countries. In other words, nuclear technology is so global in its nature that it undermines the legitimate choice by an independent state of neutrality as an option for itself. It seems to me that this effect of undermining the effective rights of a sovereign state to choose neutrality and the implicit refusal by nuclear powers to respect neutrality in working out strategic doctrines constitutes by itself an independent violation of international law which would, if suitably challenged, further strengthen the wider efforts throughout international society to prohibit this weaponry.

One may ask finally to what extent does this extension of international law find a basis in the way in which international law traditionally develops. It is all very well for me to say that neutrality nowadays should be conceived in this way, but is that assertion founded on anything more reliably grounded in the traditions and character of international political life? I would argue that all international law which does not develop through agreements is a consequence of governments and other international actors making claims to uphold their interests in a way that represents new responses to the challenges of international life. If one looks at the way in which the law of the sea has evolved (e.g. the gradual seawards extension of coastal jurisdiction and the emergence of vindicating legal doctrine), or the law of war (e.g. the move to include irregular forms of combat within its orbit), it may be seen as resulting from the interplay between old agreements and new life circumstances. Thus the very fact that a group of neutral states, or even one neutral state, asserted that its sovereign rights as a state in international society are being violated by the nuclear arms race would itself have an effect on the way in which international law was understood in this matter. Individual state practice itself can become a law-making force in world affairs in a setting where established legislative institutions that can discuss and resolve issues of this sort do not exist. It is not jurisprudentially unusual to advance this position, even if it is geopolitically difficult. What makes it so difficult is that to establish neutrality as viable in relation to this new threat it is necessary to alter the policies of the most powerful states, so that it is not feasible in any immediate sense to achieve this extension of neutrality. But one should bear in mind that this claim on behalf of neutral rights does complement a number of other social and political forces that are in any event a reaction to the nuclear arms race, so that it should be thought of as part of a much wider social process and by no means as an isolated expression of anti-nuclearist sentiment.

CONCLUSION

At this stage, neutrality, both as a minimum pragmatic and a normative position, is proving insufficient without the development of some kind of international community mechanism to create alternatives to interventionist diplomacy, deterrence, and so on. But is it reasonable to hope for so much? Are we not in the end condemned like Prometheus to endure this destiny of living with these terrible weapons? Such questions raise issues for other lectures. Suffice it to say here that there are conceptually feasible ways to treat nuclear weapons as 'illegitimate' (a first step), remove them from the scene by stages (a second step), banish their existence altogether from our political experience (the third step), and create a positive peace system (a fourth step). Certainly, it can safely be said that only by defeating nuclearism can the world be made safe once again for state sovereignty and hence for neutrality, and neutralism, as an option of foreign policy and international morality.

The unseen life here in our context is understood to be a world security system that does not rely on weapons of mass destruction and which may require a repudiation of war altogether. From a certain perspective this may seem idealistic, but I am afraid that the realists who are in control of superstate power these days are leading us towards catastrophe. In effect, these realists are illusionists of a destructive character. A life-preserving redefinition of realism becomes one of the most important political challenges of our time. As matters now stand, most of us, through the influence of the media and otherwise, find ourselves entrapped by the obsolete contours of the prevailing political imaginations. A policy of active and creative neutrality could help to establish one path that leads beyond the entrapping confines of nuclearism.

NOTES

1. For an expression of hostility toward 'neutralist' (and 'pacifist') tendencies in Europe, see Henry Kissinger, 'A Plan to Reshape NATO', *The Atlantic Community Quarterly* 22: 41–51 (Spring 1984). The underlying view is formulated as follows by Kissinger: 'We must not let our future pass by default to the neutralists, pacifists, and neo-isolationists who systematically seek to undermine all joint efforts' (p. 51).
2. The Irish Foreign Minister argued this position in debates about the

danger of nuclear war in the General Assembly of the United Nations. A recent influential study supporting this line of thinking was produced by a group of scholars at Harvard University and published under the title *Living with Nuclear Weapons* by A. Carnesale and others (New York: Bantam, 1985).

3. For accounts of Irish neutrality during World War II, see Patrick Keatings, *A Place Among Nations: Issues of Irish Foreign Policy* (Dublin: Policy Institute of Public Administration, 1978); Patrick Keatings, *A Singular Stance: Irish Neutrality in the 1980s* (Dublin: Institute of Public Administration, 1984), esp. pp. 10–32.

4. This link between law and the promotion of survival is a core contention of H. L. A. Hart's *The Concept of Law* (Oxford: Oxford University Press, 1961), esp. pp. 181–95.

5. 'Nuclearism' is a term relied upon by Robert Jay Lifton and Falk in our book *Indefensible Weapons: The Political and Psychological Case Against Nuclearism* (New York: Basic Books, 1982), to express the psychological and political consequences of reliance by governments upon nuclear weaponry to sustain national security.

6. For the text of the *Pastoral Letter*, see 'The Challenge of Peace: God's Promise and Our Response', *Origins*, 13: 1–32 (19 May 1983); for other documents see Robert Heyer (ed.), *Nuclear Disarmament: Key Statements of Popes, Bishops Councils and Churches* (New York: Paulist Press, 1982); *The Church and the Bomb: Nuclear Weapons and Christian Conscience* (London: Hodder and Stoughton, 1982).

7. Two symposia in law journals are indicative of this tendency. 'Special Issue on Disarmament', *McGill Law Journal* 28: 455–810 (No. 3, 1983) (see esp. Falk, 519–41; Weston, 542–90); 'Nuclear Weapons: A Fundamental Challenge', *Brooklyn Journal of International Law* IX: 199–335 (No. 2, Summer 1983); cf. also Sean MacBride, 'The Threat of Nuclear War: Illegality of Deployment of Nuclear Weapons', Action from Ireland, Third World Centre, Dublin (n.d.).

8. For a non-technical account of 'nuclear winter', see Carl Sagan, 'Nuclear War and Climatic Catastrophe: Some Policy Implications', *Foreign Affairs* 62: 257–92 (1983–84).

9. See Chapters 3 and 4.

10. There is a present encroachment on sovereign rights to the extent that the danger of nuclear war causes anxiety for the citizenry of non-nuclear countries and as a result of the exclusion from the formulation of war plans and deployment patterns that envisage nuclear weapons being used or causing harm to neutral states.

11. Planning and making preparations to engage in nuclear war is arguably an international crime that endangers the well-being of the entire planet, not just a prospective enemy. Put differently, the impact of such activity is upon all territorial states, thereby giving every state legal competence in a jurisdictional sense.

12. 1925 Geneva Protocol for the Prohibition of the Use in War of Asphyxiating, Poisonous or Other Gases, and Bacteriological Methods of Warfare; 1972 Biological Weapons Convention; 1977

United Nations Convention of the Prohibition of Military or any Other Hostile Use of Environmental Modification Techniques. For convenient texts see Josef Goldblat (ed.), *Arms Control Agreement*, (London: Taylor and Francis, 1982), pp. 124, 163–6, 194–7.

13. See Falk, 'Inhibiting Reliance on Biological Weaponry: The Role and Relevance of International Law', American Association for the Advancement of Science, paper presented at Annual Meeting, May 1984; 'Environmental Discription by Military Means and International Law', paper Geneva Conference, Swedish International Peace Research Institute, April 1984.

7 Beyond Deterrence: The Essential Political Challenge

Deterrence is such a slippery and diversely defined term that Freeman Dyson refuses to use it when analysing security issues (Dyson, p. 233). It is also a rather provincial terminology, being very American, or at least Western, in its role as a central element in strategic discourse about nuclear weapons. Nevertheless, deterrence remains a convenient focus for debate on security policy and the role of nuclear weapons in the West, as it stands guard over the main ideological tabernacle of militarism. Unless the monster of deterrence is slain, we shall be confined in reality, even in the imagination, to arguing about various forms of deterrence, that is, within a frame of reference that presupposes some continued reliance on nuclear weapons. Worse than this, by conceding the deterrence framework, yet addressing proposals for reduced reliance on nuclear weapons, the tendency is to forget 'politics' as the essence of any plausible demilitarising process, thereby assuring irrelevance (Cp. Schell, 1982 with Schell, 1984; the earlier more radical perspective exerted a far greater impact). Although 'deterrence' has a general meaning associated with the use of military power, in the form of credible threats of retaliation, its use in this chapter is confined to the use of nuclear weapons in such retaliatory roles (Art, p. 259).

A central uncertainty in doctrine, war plans and public consciousness is what sort of event would trigger nuclear retaliation. This uncertainty has been viewed as advantageous for the United States to the extent it keeps an adversary guessing, and thereby cautious about provoking a nuclear response. Some of the rigidity surrounding discussions of deterrence is a weakly acknowledged unwillingness to forgo a wide array of commitments (or to add sufficient, additional non-nuclear capabilities), ambiguously upheld under the rubic of 'extended deterrence'.

The case against deterrence rests on several independent grounds:

1. it may collapse, exposing either its bluff character or producing catastrophic devastation, including the possibility of a 'nuclear winter' as a secondary effect;
2. it produces a nuclear arms race that is expensive and productive of periodic outbreaks of acute public anxiety, especially during international crisis or at times when the public becomes convinced that nuclear war might occur;
3. it is not reconcilable with moral, political and cultural traditions governing recourse to war and violence, thereby straining relations between state and society, and tending towards the anti-democratic subordination of the latter to the former (Falk, 1982);
4. it induces public despair and apathy, as the continuous preparation for catastrophe, never more than minutes removed, necessarily produces a siege mentality, even if the persistence of the condition encourages escapism in various forms.

The conventional wisdom in the West, especially in the United States, suggests that no plausible alternative to deterrence exists. This view rests on the proposition that scientific knowledge is irreversible, and that once the weaponry exists, it is prudent to retain it to discourage others. Considered more carefully, this position assumes that nuclear pacificism invites blackmail, unilateral initiatives suggest weakness and invite 'aggression', and that nuclear disarmament rests on unattainable levels of trust and verifiability. Such a mainstream world view almost always rests on a Machiavellian image of human nature and international anarchy (Lifton and Falk, pp. 239–244). Since states are 'sovereign' and uninhibited, except by considerations of prudence, there is no lasting security except by way of deterrence/defence. Any questioning of these assumptions is discounted, if discussed at all, as 'utopian' or 'unrealistic'. These fundamental, timeless inhibitions are reinforced by the substantive identity attributed to the Soviet Union – a closed society, presided over by a militarised police state, sustained and legitimised by 'a grand design' of world dominance, if not conquest, and presented generally as inherently expansionist. They are also reinforced by certain historical 'lessons' that shaped the outlook of post-1945 leadership elites in the West–the encouragement of 'aggression' by appeasement ('the lesson of Munich'), the risk of surprise attack ('the lesson of Pearl Harbor'), and the costs of withdrawing from geopolitics ('the lessons of World Wars I and II'). The overall effect of these factors is to impose ideological blinders that constrain political imagination, and reinforce the impression that deterrence is unavoidable.

I believe the evidence suggests a more plastic, less definite identity for human nature, international relations and the Soviet Union. These basic aspects of international reality are continuously evolving under a variety of pressures and influences. The range of outcomes is wide, and essentially untested. Since the present narrow band of potential outcomes is self-destructive, it constitutes a decisive challenge to our capacities for cultural and political creativity to expand this range. Many times in the past constructive development for human society was blocked by intellectual and cultural inhibitions joined to power structures. Liberating the political imagination from a purely psycho-political definition of 'realistic' is essential if we are to explore the alternative lines of future development that remain consistent with the apparent outer limits of psycho-biological behaviour by the human species. To confine our image of human development and international political society to a warlike one is obviously circular as far as present policy debate is concerned, but worse, implies a very bleak future for the human race given its present nuclearist phase.

There are several theoretical ways out. One is to revive the plea ₁ for nuclear pacificism, unilateral initiative and nuclear disarmament on normative and prudential grounds, as preferable alternatives despite their specific risks. These paths are politically blocked at present by highly militarised states and by a consensus among elites as to what is feasible. The freeze as a moderate 'first step' does not address itself to the underlying obstacle of political blockage. Stabilising deterrence is another kind of calming response that may be better than some reckless strategic postures, weapons, initiatives and foreign policy tendencies, but fails to address the fundamental weaknesses of deterrence (Aspen Report).

A second image of a way out is to buy in 'defensive' technology to such an extent that no threats to use nuclear weapons in an offensive mode will ever have to be made, the so-called 'Star Wars' option contained in President Reagan's strategic defence initiative. There are reasons to doubt whether SDI is a way out at all. It induces a new arms race in expensive defence technology, as well as in means to foil the technology; it can be used and would be perceived along the way for 'first-strike' postures, thereby producing anxiety, tensions and faster arms ₁acing; its technical feasibility is in doubt, and it does not even purport to cover sub-atmospheric delivery systems associated with bombs or cruise missiles. It implies an abandonment of extended deterrence which relies on a willingness to initiate the use of nuclear weapons beyond retaliatory roles. For these reasons, SDI is wasteful of resources, utopian in the worst sense of proposing the unattainable, and its serious pursuit is quite likely to cause a decline in the current quality of deterrence (as measured by expectation levels about the likelihood of nuclear war).

At the same time, we can learn something from the official embrace of SDI, and the refusal even to consider nuclear pacificism, unilateral initiatives, or nuclear disarmament as serious options. SDI goes with the technocratic flow of the civilisation of modern state power, and of the cutting edges of capitalist dynamics, and takes for granted the

Machiavellian world view; as such, it promises to alleviate the normative crisis in Western civilisation posed by nuclearism without endangering the careers or special interests of those who benefit from and exert control over the modern state or its private sectors. It sustains the disequilibrium of state-society dominance, but abstractly offers to do so in a more reassuring form.

Nuclear pacificism, unilateral initiatives and nuclear disarmament have mainly opposite effects, although the technological capabilities summarised by Daniel Deudney as 'the transparency revolution' suggest some new 'realistic' possibilities for moving with the technological flow while demilitarising and denuclearising (Deudney). To the extent that this view of technological potential is correct, or even if it is only partially correct, it shifts the feasibility problem mainly to the nature and character of the militarised state and the dogmatic world view of its principal officialdom that associates security with levels and availability of military capability. Put more plainly, even without 'trusting the Russians', drastic forms of disarmament can now be made highly reliable; what is more, such reliability does not even depend on elaborate and objectionable inspection and verification schemes that have in the past proved to be a negotiating obstacle. To refrain from pursuing, or at minimum, exploring this path, then, is an expression of rigidity in the policy-planning process, reflecting such elements as cultural lag, special interests and ideological closure.

Beyond this, it would seem dangerous to foreclose liberating alternatives that rest upon an alternative geopolitical posture for both superpowers, a different calculus of human nature, and modes of conflict resolution among states less dependent on war and violence. In this chapter my main purpose will be to consider a more benevolent historical option for superpower relations in the 60-year period between 1945 and 2005. I seek to place that inquiry in a somewhat wider setting, however, by discussing briefly two dimensions of human and international political evolution that need to be considered to evaluate prospects for radical improvements in the quality of world order.

GEOPOLITICAL OPTIONS (1945–2005)

Both the velocity and character of the arms race, and the tenacity of deterrence as the lynchpin of security thinking in the nuclear age, reflect a particular course of geopolitics that emerged after World War II. It is often now forgotten that this course was not pre-set or necessary, although it can be argued persuasively that the configurations of power and of elite orientations deeply disposed the postwar world to unfold as it did, especially given the contradictory historical experiences and perceptions of Soviet and American leaders (Gaddis, pp. 1–31).

During World War II American leaders entertained several images of how to secure an advantageous peace in the postwar world. Unfortunately, these images were often not coherently developed, or were joined together in a contradictory fashion. As a result, it was not difficult for 'realist' tendencies to take over the policy-making process after a brief public endorsement of 'idealist' and semi-idealist alternatives.

American leaders during the war were eager to find a way of building a national, bipartisan consensus in favour of an active internationalist role for the United States. In part, the motivation was to redirect geopolitics into safer channels so that world war would not recur a third time. To achieve such a goal was thought to rest upon the following elements:

> the complete defeat of fascism (hence, the demand for 'unconditional surrender' and the postwar trials of leaders of the defeated Axis powers);
> the establishment of an international economic framework that protected free trade and assured confidence in monetary stability (hence, GATT and Bretton Woods);
> the creation of a mechanism for collective security that proposed to bring the weight of powerful states cooperat-

ively to bear upon any future aggressor (hence, the United Nations);

a promise of self-determination and equity for all nations (hence, the Atlantic Charter);

a commitment to work for disarmament and, after Hiroshima and Nagasaki, a commitment to internationalise control over atomic energy (hence, the Baruch Plan).

In practice, these goals were very unevenly secured or pursued. Fascism was defeated as planned, and effectively repudiated. An international economic order was established along the lines envisaged, and did facilitate a long period of expansion for all sectors of the world economy for more than 25 years. The United Nations was created and all powerful states became members, although the UN lacked the capabilities to carry out its main mission of preserving the peace; it lacked financial independence and peacekeeping capabilities, and its 'decisions' depended on agreement among the permament members of the Security Council. Such a structure cannot be expected to achieve the task assigned it, and therefore disillusionment was built into the architecture of its design. Or, perhaps, the United Nations was a meaningless concession to those elements of public opinion who rejected the old geopolitics of power-balancing, alliances and arms races. At best, it was a seedling that could only impinge upon geopolitics if major states gradually entrusted their destiny to such an internationalised framework of assessment.

The vague commitment by allied powers to self-determination and international equity on an international level was even less clearly considered. Self-determination was a commitment that could never be fully reconciled with either the Soviet insistence on a buffer zone of subordinated states in Eastern Europe, or the colonial powers' resolve to retain their empires. Wartime diplomacy both appeared to endorse these ideals and to promise, for the sake of Allied unity in the anti-fascist wars, a Soviet sphere of influence (Yalta). Out of this confusion grew the mutual recriminations over arrangements after 1945 in Eastern Europe, especially in

Poland. When Moscow imposed its political will it was widely interpreted in the West as evidence of Soviet bad faith and expansionist designs. The Kremlin apparently interpreted adverse Western reactions as a repudiation of the wartime arrangements and as confirmation that the capitalist countries were intent on reviving their hostile encirclement of the Soviet Union and of their struggle against communism. Note that little heed was paid to the comparable failure of the European colonial powers to respect self-determination in Africa and Asia. On the contrary.

The commitment to disarmament was never really tested. True, the Baruch Plan was presented at the United Nations, but quickly rejected by the Soviet Union, which countered with its own unacceptable proposals. These Soviet proposals, lacking any verification mechanisms, were regarded as mere propaganda, and immediately rejected by the United States. These efforts by both superpowers were half-hearted at best, and may never have enjoyed real political backing in either country. It is doubtful whether the United States would have relinquished its nuclear option when this was seen as a source of great leverage in the postwar world and as offsetting Soviet advantages in conventional manpower and ease of access to contested and tense areas in the world. (This reasoning is explicit in the famous policy overview contained in NSC-68, US National Security Council, pp. 385, 442.) In any event, these early efforts to denuclearise international politics were virtually discontinued in subsequent years, except in a spirit of propaganda.

Here is what we now know. Waiting in the wings during the ostensible idealistic trial period were realists armed with containment thinking and pressing the United States to take on the job of organising the defence of the 'free world' against the communist menace. This victory of pre-1945 geopolitics has several elements:

1. an insistence that the United States needs to be a constant participant in the effort to bring 'balance' to Europe (an end to isolationism);
2. an insistence that Soviet communism was 'aggressive' and should not be 'appeased' ('the lesson of Munich');

3. an insistence that Third World anti-colonial nationalism
   was a manifestation of Soviet expansionism and should
   therefore be opposed, or alternatively, that a vacuum
   would be created by the defeat of colonial overlords,
   that would be filled by Moscow if it was not filled by
   Washington;
4. an insistence on permanent mobilisation for war, with all
   the bureaucratic and ideological implications of such a
   stance;
5. an insistence on retaining 'the nuclear option', seeking
   to translate these capabilities into diplomatic results by
   secret threats;
6. an insistence on organising a set of American-led
   alliances to discourage Soviet aggression.

What was remarkable about this stance towards the world
was its failure to test or even explore alternatives. In the
background, was the cultural vitality of 'realist' ideology,
that is, a view that only military power at the state level
assures international stability. In this regard the United
Nations was always looked upon by the most influential
insiders as a propaganda forum, not a real political actor,
and disarmament was seen as ill-conceived in a world beset
by ideological rivalry in which the adversary could not be
trusted and placed great emphasis on secrecy.[1] These sceptical attitudes in the United States were strongly reinforced
by the realist geopolitics and by the anti-globalism of Soviet
diplomacy.

But why were not cooperative options considered and
tested more carefully on both sides? There was some
genuine misunderstanding about what would happen in
Europe after the war, but that might have been overcome,
or greatly mitigated, had not there been in place an elite
intent on militarisation. An important element was the need
to find a justification for taking on the colonial and counter-
revolutionary cause in the Third World in a manner that
would be accepted as legitimate by the American people.
Another was the pressure to construct an international
political environment that would be safe for multinational

corporations and banks, and hence, facilitate capitalist expansion and discourage the onset of a new depression.

In retrospect, the consequences of these 'adjustments' are very threatening:

1. intervention in the Third World has been costly, has not blunted nationalist energies, and has damaged US diplomatic prestige and leadership;
2. retaining the nuclear option has produced an expensive arms race that endangers human survival and undermines the legitimacy of the governing process, and produces high levels of public anxiety that surfaces from time to time;
3. challenging Soviet dominance in Eastern Europe has not facilitated self-determination, or even human rights, but has militarised the continent in a destructive, yet not symmetrical, arrangement of opposed blocs.[2]

In my view, each of these clusters of consequences is unfortunate, and suggests the importance of reconsidering the underlying geopolitical premises. In effect, I believe that ever since 1945 it would have been, on balance, beneficial to move US foreign policy in an opposite direction:

1. acknowledging Third World nationalism as largely autonomous, and as consistent with beneficial goals of self-determination; instead of adopting an interventionary diplomacy, efforts should have been devoted to strengthening a non-interventionary regime of norms and procedures and of resolving the severe tensions in the divided countries where stakes are high, contours of reasonable settlement ambiguous, and the temptation of the superpowers to intervene high; of course, many expressions of nationalist fervour produce destructive and undesirable results, but such outcomes are an incident of state-building in a turbulent era; intervention has a poor overall record of improving upon the play of domestic forces, although arguably in extreme cases where genocidal policies are being pursued, a persuasive case for intervention can be made (e.g. overthrowing or

ousting Pol Pot's regime in Cambodia, Idi Amin's regime in Uganda);

2. renouncing unconditionally the nuclear option as incompatible with cultural, moral and legal norms that underlie the political legitimacy of statecraft, and working tirelessly and credibly toward total nuclear disarmament;

3. accepting as a geopolitical *fait accomplis* Soviet hegemony in East Europe, despite its adverse consequences in terms of self-determination and human rights; such an acceptance by the West would not protect the Soviet Union against the fierce nationalism of these countries, but it would greatly reduce the plausibility of Western intervention and, hence, of the legitimating pretext for a Soviet military presence provided by this prospect.

There are several conclusions that emerge here. This geopolitical re-orientation might have prevented the worst features of post-1945 world order, although admittedly it has certain drawbacks of its own. Further, this re-orientation remains to this time virtually untested, largely unexplored and significantly promising. What is most remarkable is that secret, now declassified, documents in the fifteen years after 1945 show a failure by American policy-makers to entertain such possibility. The supposedly idealistic-normative side of American political culture has been effectively excluded from the commanding heights of governmental power. This exclusion moreover has occurred at an historical conjuncture when drastic adjustments in the conceptualisation of national or self-interest seemed desirable to many neutral, outside observers of broad historical trends. In fact, the cumulative strengthening of the national security sector of government has over the years widened the disparity between 'realist' assessments and more cosmopolitan imperatives of a cooperative framework of demilitarised relationships.

How to overcome this disparity is a great challenge. It is the real work of 'peace politics'. The central task is to demilitarise the state, opening up space for more constructive responses to the dangers of the current set of circumstances.

DEMILITARISING POLITICS

Underlying the world-order critique of the Machiavellian orientation is a mutually reinforcing mixture of normative and practical considerations. The destructive character of war as a conflict-resolving mechanism and the role of power and violence in maintaining a world system of great inequity are the root failures of the state system at this stage. In this respect, contemporary patterns of geopolitics can no longer even provide reasonable reassurance about human survival. This assessment can be vividly confirmed by considering two sets of actual circumstances – an unabated arms race that could produce a 'nuclear winter' if deterrence breaks down and a relentless famine of massive proportions in Africa that can make no claims (beyond charity) on surplus world food stocks (a contrast with the militarist threats directed at OPEC because of the cut-off of oil supplies).

With respect to behavioural patterns of states, the following adjustments to the menace of nuclear war have been made. In Europe arms are deployed in unprecedented quantities, with tensions periodically raised by regressions in East–West relations or by new provocative arms deployments. At the same time, great effort is devoted by both superpowers to maintaining a minimum structure of deterrence, thereby avoiding World War III. The situation is fragile and precarious, and it raises all the societal and inter-societal problems of preparing for and being prepared to engage in holocaustal warfare against innocent human 'neighbours'. At the same time, the Third World is made into 'a killing zone', in effect, a geopolitical 'free fire zone', where it seems 'safe' to carry conflict across thresholds of violence without causing global crisis that could produce World War III. The turmoil of decolonisation and its aftermath produced strong dispositions toward strife and warfare in any event. Yet it seems clear that the intensity and duration of the violence in the Third World is greatly aggravated by transfers of arms, by interventionary diplomacy, and by East–West geopolitical rivalry.

One crucial consequence of this process has been the pervasive and multifaceted militarisation of politics on a global scale. This militarisation has become 'normalised' in all societies, including those that retain the trappings of civilian leadership and sustain the formal character of political democracy. The essence of this militarisation, especially for the superpowers, is a continuous mobilisation for total war, the embrace of interventionary diplomacy, and the assumption of unconditional prerogatives to initiate and wage war, including terminal or apocalyptic war. As a consequence of this militarisation, a dangerous imbalance between state and society has developed, undermining the capacity of citizens to participate in any meaningful way in the definition of the public good, and sustaining a course of policy that seems acutely self-destructive. These developments impact also on the sovereign rights of all non-nuclear states, especially those outside strategic alliance networks. These states can be destroyed or severely damaged by a nuclear war, whether by nuclear winter, fallout or global disruption, without in any way participating in the policies or decisions that give rise to the catastrophe.

One manifestation of these developments is a deep-seated repudiation of the United Nations as a genuine source of peace. Instead, militarised members tend to view the various UN arenas as providing occasions to promote their particular agenda, often dominated by conflictual goals. For the United Nations to have evolved in a manner that could have come more seriously to embody the vision of a warless world presupposed a far less militarised set of outlooks among its members, especially the most important.

Normativity of Foreign Policy
Three lines of positive action seem important, and available, for those dedicated to a reversal of militarising trends. The first is to promote the normative dimension of policy-making. The present disposition toward norms, whether labelled 'realist' or Machiavellian, is neatly summarised by William Shawcross in a passage in *Sideshow* describing the

dissents of a number of Henry Kissinger's aides over plans by the Nixon administration in 1970 to extend the Vietnam War to Cambodia. Shawcross concludes: 'Lynn's [Larry] were the only arguments that seemed to impress Kissinger, because, Kissinger said later, he talked in terms of the military aspects of the invasion rather than emotion, law, morality or public opinion' (Shawcross, p. 142). Kissinger more than any other individual has expressed in words and deeds the full-blown implications of normless realism. He has exerted an extraordinary influence upon his Machiavellian brethren, even receiving a Nobel Peace Prize, suggesting that no part of the world political system has yet been liberated from the old way of handling power and politics.

In contrast to Kissinger's refusal to discuss 'emotion, law, morality or public opinion', the politics of demilitarisation would bring such perspectives to bear increasingly on training, recruitment, expectations about government performance and procedures of accountability applicable to public servants and leaders handling foreign policy. It is mainly a matter of nurturing a different type of political sensibility as 'fit for government service'. At present, those with normative concerns are either rejected or kept out of sight at low levels in the bureaucracy. I have seen over and over again that cynicism about values and legal restraints pays off, whereas some serious insistence on deference is regarded as alienated or foolish behaviour, virtually a revelation of disloyalty or immaturity.

To encourage this shift in outlook will require a major *societal* effort that includes a refashioning of 'realist' sentiment. International law and morality will have to be seen, as is increasingly the case, as serving *selfish* societal interests at this stage of international relations. We are better off, in other words, if our leaders are normatively constrained, even if others are not, or appear not to be. Of course, it is preferable to extend the reach of law and morality as far as possible in world affairs. To act 'lawlessly' or without moral compunction is self-destructive. Given the power of nationalism, the dangers of escalation and the tensions within domestic society, it is very difficult for powerful states to carry off a pattern of violative behaviour. Of course, as with any tendency, there are counter-tendencies and exceptions. The United States, it can be argued, pulled off successfully an illegal invasion of Grenada. Even this example is not without its normative ambiguity; the political situation had deteriorated after Bernard Coard's *coup* against Maurice Bishop's government, and the population of the island welcomed outside 'liberation', at least at the time of the invasion.

The complexity of politics and of public sentiment makes it difficult to generalise about normative influence, but the main purpose of such norms in the present world is to build into state behaviour the strongest possible bias against recourse to military solutions and political violence. This bias needs to be reinforced by respect for nationalism, societal self-determination and the sovereign rights of foreign countries. In this regard, the normative orientation toward reality is necessarily anti-imperialist in its conception of the ordering of relations among sovereign states of unequal endowments, or put differently, invokes a golden rule of mutuality to place boundaries on foreign policy.

In addition to strengthening the civic consciousness of leaders and advisors, a complementary development would increase the relevance of international law. At present, the only kind of self-imposed accountability for foreign policy performances in the war/peace area has to do with failure as measured by battlefield results and political outcomes. The United States, and it Allies in World War II, set forth a different, normative framework for accountability at the postwar trials of surviving German and Japanese leaders at Nuremberg and Tokyo (Falk, 1975, pp. 110–66). The essential idea was that leaders of states were accountable, and even criminally responsible, with regard to the fundamental content of international law bearing on issues of war and peace. In effect, this Nuremberg promise, made in the aftermath of world war, has been repeatedly broken in the postwar world. At most, it has survived as rhetoric and a call for a higher morality on the part of policy opponents. We have reached a stage during peacetime when it would be constructive for peace initiatives to insist upon its relevance, as a legal constraint.

This insistence will come about, if at all, only as a result of societal agitation. As we have stressed throughout, governmental circles are generally hostile to normative claims that challenge the unconditional character of sovereign rights. Only a peace movement that is engaged in a transnational struggle to demilitarise the state could conceivably serve as a vehicle of challenge. One minor indication of the importance of this normative dimension has been the emphasis recently being attached to international law and Nuremberg by peace activists. In numerous court trials for violating symbolically some law protecting property and public order, the defendants have tried to convince judge and jury that they were seeking to uphold a higher law and were carrying out the mandate laid down at Nuremberg.

An interesting 1985 case (*State of Vermont* v. *Jeanne Keller and others*) in Burlington, Vermont, suggests that the struggle to make an impact on legal process is not utterly futile. Twenty-six individuals of diverse backgrounds staged a sit-in at the Winooski, Vermont office of Republican Senator Stafford, and were charged with criminal trespass. Their motivation had been to oppose US intervention in Central America, urging the senator to hold a public forum on the issues and to refrain from voting monies to support the *contras*. Their elaborate defence centred upon an effort to persuade judge, jury and the public that the official policies towards Central America were indecent, illegal and contrary to the values embodied in American political culture. The judge in this instance was sufficiently persuaded that he charged the jury that if they felt that the defendants committed criminal trespass because they believed it necessary to curtail government policies that they reasonably believed to be in violation of international law, then they could be acquitted. They were acquitted after a short period of deliberation (*State of Vermont* v. *Jeanne Keller and others*). There is no way to assert with confidence that the international law argument was decisive, or even relevant, for the jury. Nevertheless, the judge's charge endorsed the view that American citizens have a direct interest in securing a foreign policy from their leaders that conforms to international law. The idea that the citizenry have a *direct* interest in constraining foreign policy within legal limits is a revolutionary idea, especially to the extent that it is coupled with the use of domestic courts and acceptance of the necessity defence in a criminal case. Such a tolerance for oppositional behaviour would definitely dramatise concerns about the militarised state and the general drift of the war system.

Institutionalisation

At some stage senseless patterns of conflict generate pressures for new types of order that improve the quality of security. The modern European state consolidated its power over a period of several centuries and rested its claims to legitimacy in large part on its capacity to provide a better quality of domestic order and to avoid the kind of pervasive strife at a local level that had often characterised feudal times (Miller, pp. 17–38).

Shakespeare expresses this strong societal impulse in the closing scene of *Romeo and Juliet*. After a cycle of bloody killings arising out of the senseless rivalry between the Montagues and Capulets, the Prince of Verona decrees an end to the bloody feud and a general framework of accommodation binding henceforth on both factions. The heads of the two great families accept with gratitude this imposed structure of peace, each promising to erect a statue in pure gold to honour the fallen favourite child of the other's family. Feuding had reached the end of the line in Verona with the death of the two lovers, Romeo and Juliet. The parties had exhausted their enmity to no positive purpose and were left with an enormous residue of grief. At such a conjuncture 'the new' can emerge. Weapons and prerogatives are gratefully discarded, belligerent pretexts that had earlier supported the most vindicative courses of action seem to evaporate.

If there were a global Prince of Verona one could imagine a similar intrusion upon the senseless rhythms of warfare and the drift towards nuclear catastrophe. Unfortunately, there is no global equivalent to Romeo and Juliet, that is, no surrogates who symbolise and embody the well-being of the wider communities of which they are members. In some respects, world figures and moral authorities such as the Secretary-General of the United Nations or the Pope have a wide moral authority that could conceivably mobilise public opinion at a moment of great world crisis, but as yet there is no serious tradition of global authority.

More plausibly, in the event of some kind of credible threat from space (a falling meteor, an approaching comet), world leaders would establish lasting procedures for cooperation and the exercise of authority by way of merged sovereignty. If cosmic aggressors could be identified, then political unification would seem easy to postulate as plausible within the old calculus of realities. Otherwise, the further institutionalisation of peace seems to depend on patiently awaiting the wreckage of global catastrophe, a kind of Godot which does not arrive, and if it does, might obliterate history by way of 'nuclear winter'. Whatever the original expectations, and they were always modest and marred by the cynical outlooks and anti-globalist suspicions of prevailing elites, the United Nations seems incapable of serious institutional growth, at least until the orientation of its principal members shifts in demilitarising directions that include a genuine conviction that supranational police and change capabilities are needed to compensate for the renunciation of state-centric militarism.

Here again, as with normativity, the domestic pressures of society upon the state and state system seems to be an essential precondition. As matters now stand, the definition of security by the state is predominantly military and paramilitary, complemented by other aspects of 'strength', including even morale and the moral enthusiasm of the public. Societal demands proceeding in this direction have surfaced in such diverse forms as the Green Party in Germany, the peace movement, and a variety of globalist religious formations. As yet, institutionalisation of peace, as a way of achieving governance on a global scale, has not been emphasised to nearly the extent than have demands to end the arms race, renounce first-strike weapons systems, and repudiate overseas militarism in the form of interventionary diplomacy. Such a relative absence of positive emphasis on institutional solutions partly reflects disillusionment with the United Nations, partly distrust of all large bureaucratic structures, partly a confused, and mostly inaccurate, conviction that advocacy of institutionalised imagery draws upon the discredited and utopian heritage of blueprints for world government.

Despite these genuine bases for concern, however, it seems essential to foster ways of institutionalising peace as an aspect of building confidence in a demilitarising, disarming process (Shuman, 1984). Norms without institutions are not likely to be widely respected or uniformly interpreted in a world setting as diverse and beset by antagonism and disparities as exists at present. At the same time, and here is the bridge, or linkage, between norms and institutions: the governmental structures, in place at the domestic level, could provide an important institutional element if top leaders and upper echelons of bureaucracies grow more cosmopolitan. International legal theory has long claimed a double function for national decision-makers, as officials of the state and agents of enforcement for international law (McDougal and Feliciano, pp. 39–40). This wider identity has been largely fictitious, given the strength of statist bias and pressures, and function at best in a rhetorical fashion; patterns of practice have tended to be nationalistic, self-serving and deferential to foreign policy priorities in the home country. The Vermont case is suggestive of another set of possibilities for courts. Property cases, and to a slight degree, human rights cases have also illustrated this cosmopolitan potentiality in the US setting (Falk, 1964).

Foreclosing the Political Imagination
One of the most discouraging features of statecraft in the postwar era has been the failure by leaders and elites to explore more cooperative paths of geopolitics. Ideological pressures have been relied upon to discredit demilitarising perspectives as 'unrealistic' or 'utopian'. Governmental settings seem intolerant of alternative thinking or thinkers if guided by cosmopolitan values or globalist politics. It is

not that these political structures and their policy-making elites are insensitive to rapid change or to the relevance of 'futurist' planning. On the contrary. The government, especially in matters pertaining to hardware and resources, is intensely preoccupied with planning for a rapidly changing future. Herman Kahn was the ideal 'futurist' from this viewpoint, reinforcing the realist orthodoxy, while spinning out optimistic fantasies about life in the next century, thereby affirming the capacities of existing leaders and structures to cope successfully with 'the challenge to change'. What reins in this kind of futurism and makes it 'valuable' is its acceptance of constraints on the political imagination.

Three sets of constraints seem especially prominent: (1) No investigation of how to charm enemies or rivals, thereby making them collaborators or partners; confrontation and encounter are taken as 'givens', although 'pieces' can be moved about on the big board (e.g. China). (2) No investigation of how to maintain national security without a primary reliance on the means and willingness to wage war, no serious study is devoted to how to dismantle the war system by stages, with the help of a transnational process of peace education, training in global citizenship (Barnet). (3) No consideration of the dangers of civilisational collapse under the pressure of continuous conflict and a loss of normative vision. (This perspective is a major theme in Toynbee.)

As we have noted in the discussion of geopolitics, the alternatives considered by US decision-makers who were in a most influential position after 1945 were quickly almost entirely dominated by Machiavellian scenarios of bipolar rivalry. There is considerable ambiguity on the level of explanation: perceptions of Soviet behaviour, building public support at home for an imperial foreign policy, inability to control the more cooperative frameworks such as the United Nations, failure of more 'altruistic' strategies (foreign aid, modernisation) to attain foreign policy goals (e.g. moderating Third World nationalism), ineffectiveness, expense and controversial quality of interventionary diplomacy, limited political utility of nuclear weapons, emergence of Western security allies as rivals in the world economy, perceptions and misperceptions.

The Cold War dominated the world political scene until a series of developments led to the brief interlude of détente in the 1970s. Frustrated by Vietnam, OPEC, the non-aligned movement and emerging Euro-Japanese economic challenges, American leaders sought briefly to shift geopolitical gears, diminishing the East–West axis of conflict and emphasising the economic dimensions of North–South relations, undertaking the so-called 'management of interdependence', epitomised during the decade by the outlook and writings of the Trilateral Commission and the Council on Foreign Relations 1980s Project. The militarisation of the state, however, interfered with this 'transition', as neither Moscow nor Washington were able to create the domestic political climate to sustain a more cooperative set of relationships. As a result, it was easy for militarists on both sides to revive the Cold War, by mindlessly blaming adverse developments in the world on Soviet ambitions and capabilities, an impression Moscow did little to avoid (Sanders).

At no point was the experimental adoption of a cooperative strategy separated from reigning Machiavellianism. Indeed, détente was engineered by two arch-Machiavellians – Kissinger and Richard Nixon. Their world view was consistently manipulative, informed by a gloomy and fatalist view of human destiny and human nature. Such a political sensibility presupposes conflict, is vulnerable to suspicions, and is quick to rely on military means to impose order. As far as we know, Kremlin counterparts in this period shared a pragmatic, anti-idealist and essentially opportunistic view of détente. Such a political imagination is both a product and cause of extensive and continuous dynamics of militarisation, a course reinforced by the militarised bureaucracies that remained entrenched throughout in both superpowers.

Here is the dilemma. As matters now stand, only arch-Machiavellians can gain the confidence of the militarised elements of state power to initiate cooperative ventures in international relations, but their predispositions lead to disappointment and policy reversals, producing reversions to high tensions and war dangers. Non-Machiavellians, however, are excluded from the upper reaches of state power and are in the closet to the extent they are present at all in the leading bureaucracies of power and wealth. Only a non-Machiavellian cosmopolitan orientation can envisage a cooperative community that rests upon adherence to norms, procedures of peaceful change, and the gradual institutionalisation of peace. To endow non-Machiavellian perspectives with credibility everywhere in the world is the genuine realist challenge of the moment.

EVOLVING HUMAN NATURE

An underlying conviction here is that 'human nature' is not fixed. It is enormously variable and is, in addition, subject to contextual pressures. Men and women can act with extreme aggression and cruelty, but also with intense love and generosity. The characteristic behaviour of large-scale organisations, public and private institutions, and collective frameworks (society, ideology, civilisation) is also an expression of historical circumstance, often encompassing contradictions. At present, the key institutions dominating our collective existence are closely associated with Machiavellian outlooks and practices. There are counter-traditions available to guard against deterministic inferences, even if these sources of resistance are seemingly weak or marginal at present. No one can, at the same time, question the reality of alternative potentialities.

Machiavellian outlooks and practices are an extension to public domains of patriarchical patterns. These patterns are beginning to be challenged in a variety of settings. It is too early to assess whether these challenges can catalyse a process of transformation, a new axiological age as Lewis Mumford has conceptualised, in which new values and cultural forms rapidly emerge (Mumford, pp. 59–81).

A recent film, *The Gods Must Be Crazy*, expresses a parallel realisation. It portrays the cultural superiority of the Bushmen, who live happily, cooperatively, if simply, in a kind of pre-civilisational bliss in the Kalahari desert (cf. also Diamond; Turner; Zinn). In contrast, modern societal forms, whether the urban madness of Johannesburg or the Third World turmoil of tension between petty dictatorship and capricious terrorist opposition, are presented in the film as self-denying and destructive. This film, using humour and insight, captures in vivid terms the obsolescent implications of the Machiavellian orientation under modern conditions, even without alluding to nuclearism.

We have little understanding about how the great religions spread, how Christianity moved rapidly in Roman times from persecution to dominance, from the catacombs to the very halls of imperial power. We cannot assess whether current gropings, evident in many settings, are expressions of a receptivity that is far wider than that now can be appreciated or is being acknowledged. We do know that the old Machiavellian ways are trapped, offering only an indefinite holding pattern, and seem incapable of promoting a positive future. There is evidence in the upsurge of ecological and conservation movements around the world, of non-violent forms of resistance, of the growing potency of informal politics, that new values and methods are being tested. Will this testing of societal resources for renewal yield something more substantial? Can the dominant structures be replaced without a terrible crash? Will the crash interfere with recovery prospects?

We cannot know. It is also difficult to locate ourselves in a cycle of civilisational change. We do know that generally transitions to new stages emerge abruptly (perhaps, catastrophically), and not by increment. 'The Hundreth Monkey' phenomenon is suggestive. On a Japanese island where monkey colonies lived, a young female monkey worked out that washing sweet potatoes made them taste better. She taught her female elders, who then spread the new knowledge. At some point, a threshold was crossed, the 100th monkey had learned to wash its food. At this point, all the monkeys on the island acquired the new behaviour.

It has been understood for a long time that the human species has contradictory traits of character. It has displayed great ingenuity in adapting to a variety of conditions on earth, and beyond. The impulse to survive, individually and as a species, seems basic and powerful. The conditions for ensuring biological survival are being tested and eroded in many ways by the scale and nature of modern technology. Longer-range survival does seem to depend on increasing the role of cooperative behaviour, increasing equality and sharing, and finding an identity that attaches importance to unity and solidarity of all peoples, moves towards the acceptance of non-violent conflict resolution, affirms the sacredness of life, seeks to protect 'innocence', and to perceive others as 'neighbours', not 'strangers', or 'enemies'. In one sense, a central purpose of education and socialisation becomes a fostering of 'global identity', not to displace other aspects of identity, but to connect these various elements of identity with the historical situation of modern times.

It is not necessary to embody these aspects of a counter-tradition in some coherent world view. It may be enough if these contrary claims and outlooks begin to shape fundamental responses, providing a new backdrop for the pursuit of security arrangements at various levels of social organisation, but including a sense of whole earth security, and possibly a trans-planetary feeling for the even wider 'presence' of galaxy and cosmos. As we become direct and vicarious space age travellers this expansion of consciousness is likely to ensue, but it is capable of exerting either colonising or liberating influences upon politics.

NOTES

1. The lesson of Munich learned by post-1945 leaders was that appeasement encourages potential enemies and makes general war more likely. On this basis, disarmament tends to be regarded with extreme suspicion as a policy option and various postures of military strength viewed with favour.
2. The US relationship to Western Europe is far less coercive than is the Soviet relationship to Eastern Europe.

REFERENCES

Art, R., 'To What Ends Military Power?', in Matthews, R., Rubinoff, A. and Stein, J. G. (eds.), *International Conflict and the Management of Conflict* (Scarborough, Ontario: Prentice-Hall of Canada, 1984), pp. 257–76.

'Aspen Report on Managing East–West Conflict', *New York Times*, 27 November 1984, A14 (partial text and commentary).

Barnet, R. J., *Who Wants Disarmament?* (Boston: Beacon, 1960).

Deudney, D., 'Space: The High Frontier in Perspective', Worldwatch Paper 50 (August 1982), pp. 1–72.

Diamond, S., *In Search of the Primitive* (New Brunswick, N.J.: Transaction, 1974).

Dyson, F., *Weapons and Hope* (New York: Harper & Row, 1984).

Falk, R., *The Role of Domestic Courts in the International Legal Order* (Syracuse, N.Y.: Syracuse University Press, 1964).

Falk, R., *A Global Approach to National Policy* (Cambridge, Mass.: Harvard University Press, 1975).

Falk, R., 'Nuclear Weapons and the End of Democracy'. *Praxis International*, Vol. 2, No. 1 (1982), pp. 1–11.

Falk, R., 'Toward a Legal Regime for Nuclear Weapons', 28 *McGill Law Journal* (1983), pp. 519–41.

Gaddis, J. L., *The United States and the Origins of the Cold War* (New York: Columbia University Press, 1972).

Lifton, R. J. and Falk, R., *Indefensible Weapons: The Political and Psychological Case Against Nuclearism* (New York: Basic Books, 1982).

McDougal, M. S. and Feliciano, F., *Law and Minimum World Public Order* (New Haven, CT: Yale University Press, 1961).

Miller, L., *Global Order: Values and Politics in International Politics*. (Boulder, Col.: Westview Press, 1985).

Mumford, L., *The Transformations of Man* (New York: Harper & Brothers, 1956).

Sanders, J., *Peddlers of Crisis* (Boston, Mass.: South End Press, 1983).

Schell, J., *The Fate of the Earth* (New York: Knopf, 1982).

Schell, J., *The Abolition* (New York: Knopf, 1984).

Shawcross, W., *Sideshow: Kissinger, Nixon and the Destruction of Cambodia* (New York: Simon & Schuster, 1978).

Shuman, M., 'International Institutional Building: The Missing Link for Peace' (unpublished manuscript, 1984).

State of Vermont v. *Jeanne Keller*, 1985.

Toynbee, A., *A Study of History*, 11 vols. (Oxford University Press, 1954).

Turner, F., *Beyond Geography: The Western Spirit Against the Wilderness* (New York: Viking, 1980).

US National Security Council, '*NSC-68*: A Report to the National Security Council), 14 April 1950, in Etzold, T. and Gaddis, J. L. (eds.), *Containment: Documents on American Policy and Strategy, 1945–1950* (New York: Columbia University Press, 1978).

Zinn, H., *A People's History of the United States* (New York: Harper & Row, 1980).

8 Can Decency Guide the Quest for Peace?*

THE MAIN PLANKS OF THE POSTWAR US CONSENSUAL FOREIGN POLICY

Since World War II, with two notable qualifications, it is accurate to regard US foreign policy as firmly anchored upon a national consensus embracing the leadership of both main political parties. This consensus possessed two notable elements: an agreement that the fate of Europe could no longer be principally entrusted to the Europeans, and a commitment to resist the expansion of Soviet power and influence to the extent feasible, while, if at all possible, avoiding yet another world war.

The shaping and sustaining of this consensus is a relatively familiar, although hotly disputed, matter. I think it can be safely said that the concern about Europe was based on the notion that it would adversely recast the global balance if Europe became dominated by any political tendency hostile to political democracy and industrial capitalism (fascism, communism) and that it was no longer practical to wait on the geopolitical sidelines until a challenge materialised in the form of war. In this respect, postwar American foreign policy was directed towards the prevention of World War III and the maintenance of the postwar configuration of geopolitical influence on the European continent. These

---

* This chapter was originally delivered as a paper at a conference at Vassar College held to commemorate the 100th anniversary of Eleanor Roosevelt's birth. It is published here in revised and modified form with the permission of the conference organisers who hold the copyright.

goals were promoted by a combination of the industrial and military reconstruction of Western Europe and the integration of defence policies through the formation of NATO. In the process, the consensus frayed somewhat from unresolved problems: how to prevent the extension of Soviet influence by the legal forms of political competition in those Western European countries that had strong communist parties; and whether to accept as legitimate the geopolitical divide between Eastern and Western Europe.

The containment doctrine was less geographical in its scope, although it certainly encompassed Europe. The essence of the containment idea was the identification of the Soviet Union as an overall threat to a stable world order built around Western principles of political democracy and free market economics. This danger was a multifaceted one that could not be reduced to any single threat. Again, it was unacceptable to meet the danger by appeasement or by waiting for war to erupt. It was essential to blunt the danger without going to full-fledged war. As a consequence, a state of perpetual readiness, together with a predisposition to defend geopolitical boundaries, became the heart and soul of American foreign policy, no matter which political party occupied the White House. The Korean War and the Vietnam War exemplified this notion of containment, as well as exposed its weakness as an agreed guideline. Underlying containment were three ideas—a threat to Western interests needed to be dealt with in a manner that avoided, if possible, a third world war; the Soviet Union and its ideological militancy posed such a threat; and only the United States could mobilise the will and capabilities to respond adequately.

The overarching tactical question was how to intimidate the Soviet Union without provoking general war. The United States chose to leave troops in Western Europe, to build up a string of air and naval bases surrounding Soviet territory, to brandish nuclear weapons, and to enter into a series of alliances and quasi-alliances with non-communist governments throughout the world. Events at three places had informed the learning experience of postwar leaders, and helped produce this foreign policy consensus: Munich, Pearl Harbor and Hiroshima.

Unsuccessful Challenge To The Consensus

On two occasions this consensus was briefly, and unsuccessfully, challenged. The first moment was the immediate postwar period when a portion of the American leadership believed that the wartime alliance with the Soviet Union could be sustained in the postwar world, or at least that the grim prospect of a catastrophic war in the future could be eliminated. The centrepiece of this view was the Baruch–Acheson–Lilienthal proposals for internationalising the control over atomic weaponry. The Soviet rejection of this plan, together with its reluctance to endow the United Nations with either capabilities or legitimacy, helped convince the more internationalist wing of American political leadership that there was no tenable way out of a renewal of geopolitics, and the consequent bipolar rivalry.

The second moment of challenge arose in the 1970s. The combination of America's defeat in Vietnam, OPEC's challenge to world economic arrangements, and the rise of Western Europe and Japan as formidable economic rivals shook the foundations of confidence in the consensus that lay at the core of the Cold War world-view. With great skill, Richard Nixon explored the possibility of re-orienting American foreign policy in the post-Vietnam years. He was well endowed to play this role as both his realist and anti-communist credentials were impeccable, and hence his vulnerability to attack from the Right was not great. Normalising relations with China, in part, acknowledged the diplomatic opportunities for the United States and the West arising from splits in the communist world; détente signalled a willingness to move from confrontation to cooperation in US–Soviet relations; and 'the Nixon doctrine' indicated the growing reluctance of the United States to participate through direct military action in efforts to destroy revolutionary movements in the Third World.

This set of diplomatic moves succeeded brilliantly, at first, but was discredited by the end of the 1970s. Improved relations with China did not depend on more moderate relations with the Soviet Union; quite the contrary. Further, the apparent accommodation with the Soviet Union did not pay high enough geopolitical dividends, especially for the United States. Adverse national revolutions in the Third World were associated with American decline, whether or not the Soviet Union benefited by, or contributed to, the results. Events in Iran provide the best illustration. Khomeini's blatant anti-Americanism, culminating in the 1979–80 seizure of the American embassy and hostage humiliation, created a confirming impression that Washington's abandonment of the Cold War stance was contributing to American decline in the world as a whole. Jimmy Carter's indecisive presidential style certainly added to this pattern of disrespect. And the Soviet Union did not help. It became more adventuresome, even provocative, in the Third World, especially in Africa, and persisted in building up its strategic forces at a rate that reinforced conservative anxieties that détente was a one-sided affair that was being exploited to promote a basic shift in global power in Moscow's favour.

As we know, Reagan's foreign policy has been a rather crude effort to restore the pre-Vietnam, more militarist consensus. Its most notable 'victory' was the invasion of tiny Grenada, an action that was popular at home and won support from even leading Democratic Party figures. Reaganism represents the least sensitive application of this postwar consensus, but it should still be understood primarily in terms of its continuity with earlier foreign policy. There is one important change in emphasis. Europe is less central to the new Cold War than it was to the earlier one. In some sense, the Pacific has replaced Europe as the centre of East-West struggle, but perhaps it is more accurate to suppose that the Pacific Basin has been added as a critical arena of equivalent significance to the Western position in the world.

Consensus refurbished
The resilience of this American consensus reflects several factors. On the one side, there is a resolve to maintain the US position in the world against all challengers, East and West. This resolve depends upon a tense international

environment and a willingness to intervene, as necessary, that is backed by public opinion. On the other side, there is the widely shared view that deterrence keeps the peace, while appeasement and withdrawal lead to decline, and then war. It is not entirely correct to attack the Reaganites as warmongers, although it seems persuasive to contend that their approach to peace needlessly increases the risk of war. Their endeavour, I am convinced, is directed towards keeping a favourable peace. Its plausibility depends on the image of the Soviet Union as strong and expansionist, a country that can be deterred from taking aggressive steps only by superior American forces and a credible American willingness to risk everything to hold on to its zones of primary influence in the world. There are some who argue these days that the real Reagan objective is to put so much financial pressure on Moscow that it is weakened by the burdens of keeping up with the United States, and so, on its knees, sues for geopolitical peace on terms favourable to the West – in effect, a scenario for winning the Cold War without fighting World War III.

What is relevant here is that postwar American foreign policy has been centrally preoccupied with the maintenance of peace (in the restricted sense of the avoidance of World War III). On the conservative side, this preoccupation has tended to emphasise military postures and capabilities to a greater extent, whereas, on the liberal side, this preoccupation has combined military approaches with a geopolitics of idealism. This idealism has been expressed in the form of a series of undertakings: foreign aid, arms control, the United Nations, human rights, the Peace Corps, Alliance for Progress. Conservatives are cynical about these initiatives, and regard them as either hypocritical window-dressing, or worse, as inconsistent with their conviction that world peace depends on Western military capabilities and resolve. On occasion, liberals emphasise the military component of the foreign policy consensus, as John F. Kennedy did when he attacked the Eisenhower administration for allowing the so-called 'missile gap' to develop, for its failure to develop counter-insurgency capabilities to meet actual Soviet challenges, and for its over-reliance on nuclear weapons. Ironically, the more liberal side of the foreign policy consensus, while less military oriented, also tends towards more interventionary postures, regarding political challenges as equivalent to military ones, and viewing the spread of American ideals as an appropriate goal of foreign policy. Yet, this liberal proclivity to intervene is often matched by the more ideologically assertive stance of conservatives, as is illustrated by the Reagan approach to Central America. In some respects, the attitude towards intervention reflects whether the party in office has associated itself with intervention or not.

It is useful to acknowledge that this broad, underlying consensus excluded positions on both extremes. On the right, it excluded both Fortress America isolationism, perhaps best articulated by the Ohio senator and presidential aspirant, Robert Taft, and suggestions for a preventive war, advocated behind the scenes by military leaders from time to time and by the right-wing fringe, on the theory that since war was unavoidable, it was best to choose the time and occasion of its occurrence. On the left, the consensus excluded the views that the wartime alliance with the Soviet Union should be maintained at all costs and that its collapse was primarily the fault of war-mongering by capitalist interests, a position associated with Henry Wallace's splinter presidential campaign of 1948. Also excluded were a variety of pacifist positions that repudiated war altogether as an instrument of national policy, as well as the stance of those who, like the world federalists, insisted that world government and complete disarmament was the only way out of international danger.

As of 1984, this postwar foreign policy consensus is stronger than ever. True, Reagan has been attacked by the Democratic opposition for his anti-internationalism and militarism, but not for his fundamental emphasis on containment and the build-up of US military capabilities.

As a means to sustain peace, this foreign policy consensus seems especially dangerous at this stage of international politics, as well as incompatible with the normative identity of America that has been important to liberals over the years. What is especially troublesome is the failure of the

American political process to generate alternative approaches to peace other than that espoused by the consensus.

A CRITIQUE OF LIBERAL INTERNATIONALISM

The liberal view of international politics is in conflict with a variety of more conservative and cynical positions. Liberals are far more optimistic about the possibilities for global reform than are conservatives. Conservatives tend to be fatalistic about international structures, and to the extent that they are optimistic, as in the case of Ronald Reagan, they believe in the potency of domestic structures and solutions, as well as in the dynamic effects of world trade and market mechanisms, for promoting investment and business operations. The ultra-right section of the Republican Party, including Ronald Reagan, had attacked even such a mildly internationalist venture as The Trilateral Commission, contending that it was a disguised plot to establish world government. Almost as threatening to conservatives as the spectre of communism is the alleged liberal embrace of internationalism, culminating in world government. The word 'alleged' is crucial here, as few liberals favour world government except in some vague futurist sense that they do not suppose will ever happen; and, ironically, notable conservatives such as Edward Teller and Herman Kahn have affirmed the desirability of world government, but only if it could be reliably established.

One focal point of liberal/conservative disagreement concerns the value and validity of international law and institutions, and, hence, the nature of their participation in them. Sharply divergent attitudes toward the United Nations exemplify this disagreement. It was softened in the early Cold War years, up through the Korean War, by the extent to which UN policy resembled US foreign policy. With the emergence of the anti-colonial movement as a social force in the world, the costs of internationalism seemed to grow greater if measured by reference to US policy objectives. Underneath, however, was a structural issue: the degrees to which national interests could and should be served by trimming sovereignty at the edges, and whether sovereignty trimming was a kind of international preparation for an eventual assault upon the war system.

Internationalists viewed prudent sovereignty trimming as beneficial to national interests. They held an evolutionary view of progress in international affairs that looked towards the gradual erosion and eventual displacement of sovereignty. The liberal tendency has been all along determinedly optimistic. It believed in the liberating role of reason, in progress, and in a steady growth of moral consciousness. Ultimately, then, its instrument for the promotion of change was education, contrasting its orientation with Marxist viewpoints that insisted upon contending social forces, especially class conflict, as the only source of change.

In a favourite liberal image, by substituting over time the rule of law for the rule of force, a structure of enduring peace would be established. But the liberal side of the position also sought to allow others to share the blessings of the American political, economic and cultural achievement. Liberalism is inherently interventionary, but with an idealistic, self-righteous, internally incoherent, somewhat self-deceiving, rationale. The recurrent American foreign policy debate, now emphasising Central America, reflects liberal viewpoints and confusions (e.g. a hostile policy toward the Sandinista government; negotiations and a variety of pressures to coerce improved protection of human rights; advocacy of a quarantine of Nicaragua if negotiations fail: and opposition to covert operations because they are 'counterproductive')[1] The more geopolitically-oriented conservatives see the world in terms of power, and regard progress as resting on relative military and economic capabilities, including the willingness to use power for national goals.

Liberals regard the fortunate as having both moral and pragmatic obligations to help the poor, to alleviate suffering and hardship to establish a path to a better life, and to contribute to anti-revolutionary goals of stability. Liberalism, at home and abroad, is often paternalistic, accepting the mandate to have government intervene actively to foster a fairer, more decent, set of societal arrangements. The conservative alternatives are more market-oriented, regarding societal achievements as best promoted by self-reliance, manifested through individual efforts and rewards. Conservatives are sceptical about bureaucratic approaches to welfare, arguing that the efforts rarely help those in need, invite corruption, and sap incentives. Conservatives favour minimal government when it comes to welfare programmes and social issues, but tend to support government control over labour activities and political dissent, and generally support maximal defence and intelligence capabilities.

Agreements Beneath Disagreements Between Liberals and Conservatives

The Cold War and the attitudes toward protecting Third World countries against political radicalism seem to be shared by liberals and conservatives over the years, although liberals tended to favour 'hearts and minds' negotiations and non-military forms of intervention, especially in reaction to frustrations and defeat in Vietnam.

These divergencies obscure a more fundamental shared outlook. Both liberals and conservatives defined the postwar world increasingly as requiring a mobilisation of resources to meet the global challenge of the Soviet Union and political radicalism ('Marxism-Leninism'). As such, both broad positions endorsed the Cold War, including the early phases of the Vietnam War. Liberals became disaffected and divided as the Vietnam War persisted (*normative* liberals defecting first: *pragmatic* liberals defecting only after the Tet offensive in February 1968, when the various costs of intervention rose). By way of comparison, *ideological* conservatives were disturbed from the outset by Nixon's détente diplomacy, while it was being celebrated by *opportunistic* conservatives.

With the failure of détente for the United States because of both principles and pragmatics, it was evident that a return to Cold War diplomacy and an accelerated arms race would occur in the 1980s regardless of which political party was in the White House. Foreign policy differences between the two major political parties have been reduced to matters of nuance, and do not reflect divergent world views.

We find ourselves in the mid-1980s with an exhausted liberalism. It has lost the political and psychological battle to a resurgent movement among conservatives. Few among the electorate seem convinced that these differences matter very much, at least when it comes to foreign policy.

One element in this liberal decline is the loss of its idealistic content. Liberalism no longer regards the United Nations as the foundation for a new world order capable of institutionalising peace. As such, liberals are thrown back, however reluctantly, on a policy of 'living with nuclear weapons' indefinitely and of remaining ready to intervene anywhere to uphold the global scale of US interests. The most they can reliably promise is to refrain from jokes about unleashing the apocalypse.

In the end, this kind of liberalism fails the basic American test of effectiveness. This failure was epitomised by John Kennedy's sponsorship of the Bay of Pigs operation designed to overthrow Castro in 1961, doing enough to offend legal and moral sensibilities, but not enough for the mission to have much prospect of success. Deputy Secretary of Defense Fred Charles Iklé has affirmed the Reagan goal as 'victory' in Central America, while the liberal opposition bemoans the means but shares the goal. As such, the liberal approach is incoherent and unappealing as an alternative.

The basic problem with international liberalism today is that its moderate stance seems inconsistent with geopolitical success, yet it no longer seeks any genuine transformation of geopolitics. Therefore, it accepts geopolitics, but half-heartedly. Of course, liberals continue to seek modest improvements through the adoption of such managerial arrangements as SALT agreements and the Law of the Sea Treaty. But let's not fool ourselves. These arrangements have not arrested militarising trends within and among states and they provide no prospect of an alternative to deterrence as a basis for security. As such, liberals have no antidote for those forms of cultural despair tied in some way to the nuclear dilemma or for our apparent entrapment within the framework of state sovereignty.

THE QUEST FOR PEACE RESTATED

If decency is insufficient, and perhaps even diversionary, how then should the quest for peace proceed? There are two responses that appear fruitful. I am excluding a third, namely, 'imperial peace', the idea of extending the domain of influence of a given power centre to embrace the world or its most important societies. No less a pacifist than Bertrand Russell has proposed, with evident seriousness, that the United States use its postwar monopoly of atomic weapons to coerce Soviet disarmament. And, possibly, the missionary forms of liberalism ascendant in the early phases of the Vietnam War could be viewed as an exploration of how far it would be possible to actualise an imperial dream in the form of Pax Americana.

The Geopolitical Road Not Taken
The first of these approaches assumes the persistence of international structures. It considers possibilities for peace arising from the political choices available to principal leaders. In particular, it asks whether postwar international relations might not have been very different if the two superpowers had placed a higher positive value on their wartime cooperation. In a sense, this perspective carries realism to its limit, and asks whether there might not have been a more practical way to carry on with geopolitics after the victory over European fascism and Japanese militarism.

From the American position as dominant actor (along all dimensions of power) in 1945, it seems plausible to have ceded Eastern Europe to the Soviet Union as a security belt or, more vulgarly, as a geopolitical sphere of influence. Included in this cession would have been the sort of reassurance accorded (yet recently somewhat withdrawn) 30 years later in the Helsinki accords that the division of Germany would be permanent and accepted as legitimate. If such arrangements were endorsed diplomatically, with reciprocal assurances to the United States about Western Europe, then the bases for postwar cooperation between Moscow and Washington would have been quite strong. An essential element in such an approach would have been an immediate and unconditional renunciation of atomic weaponry as a legitimate weapon of war and diplomacy. The necessity of this renunciation casts considerable doubt on the geopolitical wisdom of bombing Hiroshima and Nagasaki, suggesting that postwar planning in the later stages of the Pacific war should have discouraged recourse to such 'gratuitous' attacks, especially as there seemed to exist alternative means to end the Pacific phase of World War II rapidly and victoriously.

If this cooperation extended to a non-interventionary but sympathetic and supportive attitude toward anti-colonial nationalisms in the Third World, then Soviet–American relations might have remained reasonably stable, with adjustments and rivalries (in Asia) negotiated, or dealt with informally. This path of diplomacy would undoubtedly have induced severe tensions with the colonial powers, especially Great Britain and France. It would, also, have implied a Marshall Plan for the Soviet Union and Eastern Europe. As is known, the United States abruptly halted wartime aid to the Soviet Union as soon as the fighting stopped, even halting the delivery of supplies that were at sea *en route* to Soviet ports. To make this alternative genuinely plausible one would also have to suppose that Stalin was not completely determined to embark upon a period of hostility towards the United States in the postwar period, and that he might have made reassuring responses to American initiatives.

I am not suggesting that this Soviet-oriented postwar option would have worked, or that it was altogether desirable. I do argue that it might have at least created a basis for enduring peace and averted both a strategic arms race and an international milieu permanently shadowed by nuclear arms. Of course, there would have been costs and resistances. There would, first of all, have been fierce resistance at home from anti-communist and Atlanticist ideologues, both powerfully represented in American leadership circles during World War II. Secondly, there would have been vigorous opposition from important capitalist interests concerned with the rapid reconstruction of European markets, the protection of foreign investment, control over

Third World resources, and a generally favourable atmosphere for capitalist expansion. Thirdly, there would have been a West European backlash, a rupturing of Alliance relations over the failure of the US to support European efforts to retain their colonial possessions. Given the prestige of leaders such as Churchill and de Gaulle, it might have been impossible to line up public opinion behind a Soviet–American entente. Fourthly, interventionary and repressive results in Eastern Europe that would have been associated with Soviet dominance would especially inflame constituencies within the American electorate possessing ethnic affinities, and create a powerful domestic political pressure to reverse course. This pressure, when associated with these other adverse factors, might well have proved irresistible to any conceivable American leadership. Such a conclusion is further reinforced by the failure to foresee the adverse results of the Cold War (ideological) path chosen.

Nevertheless, the road not taken remains attractive to contemplate in retrospect. The main reasons for adopting a hostile approach to the Soviet Union have not been vindicated. Eastern Europe has fallen within the Soviet sphere, and perhaps more harshly than might otherwise have been the case; Western revisionist posturing that continues until today lends credibility to Moscow's claims of national security dangers. The US retention of the nuclear option has produced an expensive and dangerous arms race that seems impossible to stop. Holding on to the advantage enjoyed at the end of World War II did not yield positive results along the way, nor would great vulnerability have existed without it (despite NATO doctrine to the contrary). Finally, the Third World has gone in nationalist directions despite US efforts to block these tendencies and, arguably, US opposition radicalised several key nationalist movements.

The question I mean to emphasise is whether an American leader with geopolitical vision and great domestic political prestige might not have shaped a peace-oriented postwar world premised on the possibility of US–Soviet cooperation, accepting even some form of condominium as a lesser evil than the kind of Cold War that ensued. I realise that this would not have been an altogether satisfying arrangement, but it might well have avoided much of the massive bloodshed associated with the decolonisation process; it might also have lessened, if not avoided, the menaces we now associate with nuclearism. At the very least, our political imagination never seemed to contemplate this alternative geopolitical stance and, therefore, was insensitive to its attractions and to the costs of the stance adopted. Liberals, especially after FDR's removal from the scene, seemed virtually incapable of 'seeing' this option, and thereby forced its espousal off respectable political terrain in the United States (for example, Henry Wallace's pro-Soviet leftist politics), with the brief exceptions noted.

Obviously, there is no assurance that the Cold War (and the nuclear arms race) could have been avoided even if more openness to post-1945 US–Soviet collaboration had existed. It is almost impossible, for instance, to assess the degree of Soviet responsiveness, and whether Soviet leaders would understand the importance of reassuring US leaders and public opinion by some reciprocating gestures and by not seeming to take advantage. Soviet behaviour in the 1970s during détente is not encouraging in this regard. At the same time, however, Soviet leaders to this day still seem to be saying that a more cooperative approach to the postwar world might have worked had it been tried. In a broader sense, I am indicting the postwar generation of American leaders for fastening on to a premature consensus about the geopolitical situation. Their ideological closure has stilted the political imagination, and has reduced the diplomatic potential for promoting more peace-oriented styles of geopolitics. This failure persists unto the present moment, and it includes most liberal internationalists active in the political mainstream. George Kennan's 'retraction' of a geopolitical approach anchored to anti-Sovietism has barely registered upon those who are proposing foreign policies for the future.

A World Order Project for a Peaceful World
Part of my analysis of the failure of reformist hopes associated with the United Nations was the apolitical character of

the commitment. Somehow, liberal confidence was placed within a framework, mechanisms, and an enlightened public opinion. Little was done to offset the intense passions associated with sovereignty and nationalism. Even far-reaching plans, such as the Clark–Sohn proposals, were essentially proposing a world order bargain that cut against the grain of statism and self-reliance at the state level.

Liberal internationalists in the United States, and elsehwere, came to recognise the need for public support. They sought to build this support either by showing that statist goals could be more effectively realised via an internationalist framework or by abandoning visions of a new world order as utopian illusions, and advocating, instead, small, practical, evolutionary, steps. At the same time, they endsorsed the Cold War as the central basis of US foreign policy, and questioned none of its main tenets (arms race, nuclearism, interventionism). The result was disappointment on all fronts. As the UN changed, as a result of decolonisation and non-alignment, the international environment became hostile to US foreign policy goals and the small steps seemed to add up to very little, even if selectively useful.

For a world order project to succeed it must link up with a social movement that challenges entrenched attitudes and structures. Such a movement is unlikely to be able to develop within the formal patterns of political democracy. Put differently, the Democratic Party has proved incapable of espousing not only the values but also political demands necessary to advance an effective world order project. Its centre of gravity has been oriented around an acceptance of Cold War thinking, and the single partial exception of McGovern's 1972 candidacy had proved divisive. Besides, more liberal Democrats, eager for the presidency, fight for a greater hold on the centre by moving farther right, thereby establishing their Cold War and militarist credentials (for instance, Humphrey and Mondale).

The essence of a world order project for peace would include a social movement dedicated to transcending (or at least transforming) currently militarised states. Even in a country such as the United States, where the formal trappings of political democracy remain, the state manages the boundaries of political conflict in such a way as to frustrate world order challenges. Since liberal internationalism has never broken with the state (that is, it is not a world order challenger) it cannot possibly provide the ideological basis for this sort of transnational populist movement.

The contours of a world order movement can be discerned at this stage, although whether there is enough organisation and commitment to regard certain 'signs' as adding up to 'a movement' is doubtful. The elements of a world order movement can be enumerated, but cannot be discussed here in detail: a critique of existing arrangements and an alternative vision that is centred upon the moral significance of the human experience and seeks fundamental changes; a dedicated cadre of followers who are prepared to make sacrifices, even unto death, so as to realise the vision; leadership that inspires followers and draws upon hallowed societal values and traditions in the search for support; erosion of self-confidence by the elite that is operating the power system, and a consequent loss of its legitimacy; tactical initiatives that expose the moral contrast between the present evil order and a future benevolent alternative; a favourable conjuncture of circumstances that deprives existing arrangements of their practical justifications and creates greater receptivity to change.

The transnational peace movement, especially in Western Europe, possesses several of these elements, although it is admittedly in an inchoate form; it lacks a coherent, fundamental vision, and it may also lack a cadre of adherents that perseveres. The direct action wing of the American peace movement exhibits both a dedication to goals and a clear understanding of the inability of liberal politics (or traditional Left politics) to lead its followers and society to a sustainable peace and to a form of security not tainted by genocidal overtones (that is 'nuclearism').[2] Whether the seeds planted by nuclear resisters, usually organised by religious groups identifying with pre-Constantine Christianity in the form of direct action, will grow into something sturdy and expanding remains to be discovered. My claim is that these nuclear resisters are at least evolving a plausible basis for promoting a world order project.

CONCLUSION

No approach to peace has ever worked well in the practical realm of interstate politics under the pressures of conflict and change. The global setting impinges now in complicated, cross-cutting and menacing ways. It is doubtful that existing state structures are even vehicles for the sound promotion of selfish national interests these days. The course of foreign policy is more properly, even in countries where liberal institutions and procedures persist, guided by concerns about regime stability and the satisfaction of special interests in the economic sphere.

One important step towards peace at this time is to strip away the illusion that democracy can by itself protect the interests of human society. Of course, democratic procedures and rights are indispensable, but they are not sufficient, given the character of modern militarised states. Civil society is now challenged to transform the state by pressing the case for orientations towards power and security that take account of the importance of demilitarisation at all levels of governance, both to enable a genuinely democratic politics to function and to assure that resources are much more directed toward the satisfaction of human needs than is currently the case. The normative goal is to assure that political leaders at least serve the longer-run well-being of their own countries. To do this effectively requires the further step that the national interest is becoming inseparable from the protection of the global interest, or put differently, to be a good citizen requires a global perspective. Such an evolution is life-enhancing without in any way undermining the more specific attachments to culture and history. There is no tension between global identity and the affirmation of diversity within and among sovereign states.

NOTES

1. See e.g. Walter Mondale interview, *New York Times*, 18 September 1984, p. B6.
2. For extended discussion see Robert Jay Lifton and Richard Falk, *Indefensible Weapons: The Political and Psychological Case Against Nuclearism* (New York: Basic Books, 1983).

9 Normative Initiatives and Demilitarisation: A Third System Approach

NOTES ON PERSPECTIVE

The tension between a militarised global system and a goal of demilitarisation establishes the context for this inquiry. The global dynamic of militarisation continues to prevail, incurring serious economic, social, political and cultural costs, as well as generating a spiral of danger that could end in catastrophe for the peoples of the globe. Militarisation is, in part, a by-product of the fragmented organisational structure of the state system in which each polity defines its minimum security by reference to the military capabilities required to secure vital interests, especially the internal security of governing elites and classes and the integrity of its territory, but also the resources needed to keep a given economy and polity viable. Militarisation is also related to the hierarchical structures by which powerful states exert varying degrees of hegemony over weaker states.

By contrast, demilitarisation implies a comprehensive restructuring of world order and international security. Demilitarisation involves an assault on fragmentation and hierarchy, and hence entails, above all else, a shift away from violence to sustain organised political life on the planet. What has to happen to permit this redirection of energy to occur? At this stage, the dynamics of and preconditions for demilitarisation remain virtually unknown and largely unexplored. International political experience has been dominated by different forms and velocities of militarisation.

Although bureaucratic structures are not monolithic, governments generally are overwhelmingly hostile to, and suspicious of, demilitarisation as a principled process of transformation. Some governments may favour partial demilitarisation so as to improve their relative position within the framework of a militarised world. Indeed, all governments favour the relative demilitarisation of other governments except for those who are their allies or arms customers. Such *tactical demilitarisation*, the essence of arms control as a perspective on the war system, involves tinkering with the geopolitical setting, making it marginally safer, cheaper or more manageable. At best, arms control achieves temporary relief from the dangers and burdens of unregulated militarisation; it may also involve an effort by military elites to concentrate spending on particular types of weaponry or to discourage rivals from specific arms development. *But tactical demilitarisation, whatever its guise, offers no challenge by governments to the fundamental role of military power and violence or their linkage to the international structures of fragmentation and hierarchy.*

The focus here is upon *principled demilitarisation* that sets as its goal the abolition of war and defence establishments, and conceives of its task as the initiation of a political process that moves towards that goal. Preconditions for achieving the goals of demilitarisation are the substantial erosion of fragmentation and hierarchy in the present world order system. In their stead, demilitarisation proposes the goals of *coherence and equality*, structures by which planetary concerns are protected by institutions of a global identity and relations among actors based upon mutuality and respect.

Given this outlook, it becomes crucial to identify the location of *creative space* for innovation within the world political system. In effect, demilitarisation is a political process, that is, a struggle to carry out a radically revisionist programme of a specific sort. As such, it is bound to encounter resistance from the main institutional actors of the state system and its prominent supportive organisations (including multinational corporations, international financial institutions and private banks). In this respect, even international institutions with idealistic mandates, such as the United Nations, should be understood primarily as extensions of the state system, being dependent on voluntary financial contributions from leading governments. The UN lacks even a fully autonomous enclave of territorial space outside the jurisidiction of sovereign states, and possesses no independent enforcement capabilities. Militarisation is firmly entrenched, and because the technology of war evolves so rapidly with such disquieting potential, it is exceedingly difficult to gain any official support for principled demilitarisation. This reality is made even more formidable because of the confusion caused by assimilating some aspects of tactical demilitarisation into the overall militarisation process itself by way of arms control, peace rhetoric and nominal statist support for human rights. Semantic confusion is inevitable, as antagonist social forces accord lip-service to the same values and goals. As a consequence, world opinion has grown sceptical about professions of faith in peace and justice.

The path to demilitarisation is also blocked by the main traditions of opposition to militarism, which are themselves based on theoretical and practical reliance upon political violence. The widespread acceptance of armed struggle as an essential precondition to the pursuit of drastic reforms at the societal level illustrate the pervasiveness of militarisation. Of course, not all oppositional politics is militarist in character. Important non-violent, anti-militarist movements exist, and have achieved some notable successes. Gandhi's movement against British colonial occupation of India, Martin Luther King Jr's movement against racial discrimination in the United States, the popular movement that overthrew the Shah of Iran, and the Polish workers' movement (Solidarity) are a few prominent examples. Unfortunately, none of these instances has altogether sustained its demilitarising achievements, either embracing militarising methods once a certain threshold of power was crossed or disintegrating under the militarist pressures of entrenched forces.

As an initial step in a demilitarisation campaign, a determined effort is needed to cut through the mystifying language and refute the distorted claims of power-wielders. First, is the misleading contention that existing elites, even in the superpowers, would welcome a trustworthy path of demilitarisation. Secondly, is the derivative claim that demilitarisation is not feasible because of the specific qualities of the enemy, or because of the way the world is structured, or even because of the inherent characteristics of human nature. Thirdly, is the fatalistic belief that it is necessary, in the sense of being unavoidable, 'to live with' militarisation, even at the level of nuclear weaponry, and that all that can be done is to minimise risks and costs to the extent possible. Fourthly, is the view that constructive action should not attempt more than to contain the velocity and some wasteful or menancing features of the militarisation process. Fifthly, is the general claim that prudent militarisation as a permanent posture will succeed at least in preventing general nuclear warfare and will keep the peace among the advanced industrial countries. And sixthly, is the counter-claim that only oppositional militarism can displace and surmount the oppressive structures of entrenched militarism.

This ideological underpinning of militarisation enjoys the overwhelming support of all elites in the North, including the Northeast or Soviet sphere of influence. Militarisation also seems to be accepted, as well, although accompanied by varying degrees of distress, by the leadership of international institutions. A credible demilitarising challenge, then, will have to come from the popular sector, perhaps activating certain currently subdued voices within prevailing structures of political power. On the ideological level, the challenge of principled demilitarisation will have to be clear about its goals, its strategies, and its visions of the future. In essence, such an image of demilitarisation implies moving toward the realisation of a world order system in which collective violence is minimised, if not eliminated, in which economic well-being of all people is assured, social and political standards of justice realised, and ecological quality restored and protected. To attain these ends in a coherent form requires several decades of concerted effort, presupposes struggle, and implies the restructuring of power, wealth and authority at all levels of social organisation. The vision of restructuring at least implies a diminished role for states in the dominant sector of world society: a selective destructuring of state power, combined with the emergence of carefully constrained central guidance capabilities to express the underlying unity of planetary life and to protect effectively the general human interest in a sustainable environment and an undiminished stock of renewable resources. At the same time, by destructuring state power, the underlying diversity of planetary life would also be assured, thereby accomplishing an entirely novel blend of centralisation and decentralisation in the world order system.

Thus, our starting-point is the search for creative space in an atmosphere dominated by the dynamic of persisting, indeed intensifying, militarisation. In this atmosphere any fundamental challenge is ignored if possible, and repressed as necessary. To mount a challenge at this stage is primarily a matter of political education, piercing through the pacifying mystique of militarisation as an inevitable feature of the human condition. The setting is adverse, and yet there are some positive signs. For one thing, nuclear weapons have revealed the horror of war to a new extent and their spread to a variety of governments makes it seem increasingly unlikely to a growing number of moral and religious leaders that nuclear peace can be maintained indefinitely. Secondly, state leaders are increasingly faced with a series of non-military problems that they are unable to solve within the constraints of the present world order system, and their capability for effective and humane governance seems to be steadily declining. Thirdly, the diffusion of power by means of decolonialisation, by the spread of military and economic prowess, and by the growth of Third World solidarity has posed a threat to the established, Western controlled *hierarchical* arrangement of geopolitical relations in the world. Fourthly, the growth of interdependence – economically, ecologically and culturally – has exposed the inadequacy of this *fragmented* and *adversary* structure of secular power and authority in the world. As a consequence of these four developments, the legitimacy of militarisation is being eroded in the short run by the economic squeeze, in the longer run by its genocidal style of risk-taking. In effect, powerful social and historical forces are undermining militarisation at its apparent point of maximum momentum, but this subversive process is slow, uncertain in its effects and non-linear in its path (there are numerous regressions with the possibility always present of a decisive regression by way of World War III).

Therefore, the active, explicit challenge of demilitarisation requires a feeling for how, when and whether to intervene in the social/political dynamic surrounding the role of war, and more generally of political violence. Above all else, meeting this challenge requires clarity about noncreative or sterile space that reinforces the dynamic of militarisation while pretending to oppose it. To expect institutions in the dominant sectors to shift to demilitarisation by the serious espousal of genuine disarmament proposals is one familiar instance of meaningless gesture. Similarly, to suppose that arms control agreements will lead in the direction of disarmament is another venture in sterile space – although such agreements may be valuable as short-time managerial instruments, reinforcing tendencies toward prudent militarisation. Furthermore, to put faith in the victories of progressive movements of resistance is to overlook the extent to which virtually *all* politics is encompassed by the framework of militarisation, in thought as well as in action. To explore and identify creative space in the struggle against militarisation is the purpose of this chapter. The proposal of particular normative initiatives needs to take account of the political structure that exists in different regions and state polities. Under this framework of constraints, we seek those normative initiatives that both enhance *understanding* and promote *realisation* of world order values.

THREE SYSTEMS OF POLITICS

Basic to this line of analysis is the primacy of *the third system* for the work of *principled demilitarisation* given the present global political situation.

For purposes of clarification, the three systems of political action can be distinguished:

The First System. The system of power comprised by the governing structures of territorial states; in short, the state system, including its supporting infrastructure of corporations, banks, media; a system that is hierarchical, fragmented, and in which war and violence are accepted as discretionary options for power-wielders and in which armies, weapons, police and military doctrines play a crucial role within and among states.

The Second System. The system of power comprised by the United Nations, and to a lesser extent by regional international institutions; this extension of the First System enjoys a verbal mandate that remains nominal, a mere promise of substantial achievement; a system that is supposed to mitigate hierarchy and fragmentation; as well, it repudiates the discretionary option of states to make war or use force to advance their particular ends; states, as members, are the primary actors in Second System arenas.[1]

The Third System. The system of power represented by people acting individually or collectively through social movements, volutionary institutions, associations, including churches and trade unions; a system oriented around challenging the domestic manifestation of militarisation, and subject to regulation and repression by the First System on 'law and order' grounds; the Third System is the main bearer of new values, demands, visions, although its proposals may be co-opted or subverted to varying degrees by the First System, or even on occasion, by the Second.[2] Third System successes can often be jeopardised either by remilitarisation (e.g. Khomeini's Iran) or by vulnerability to uncontained militarist remnants (e.g. Allende's Chile). Such opposed dangers pose the dilemma of violence for Third System approaches to fundamental social change.

The idea of *normative initiative* is one of changing the terms of permissible action, by placing a boundary, or at least an inhibition, on what is discretionary. The international law of war represents a normative initiative of the

First System. The prohibition of force except for purposes of self-defence in the Charter of the United Nations is a normative initiative of the Second System. The campaign against torture conducted by Amnesty International is a normative initiative of the Third System.

In essence, the argument here is that as matters now stand the First System has been increasingly mobilised on behalf of the logic of militarisation; this process has spread around the world by way of arms transfers, sales and the development of indigenous war-making and repressive capabilities. The northern sector of the First System has also relied upon militarisation to maintain favourable aspects of *international hierarchy*, especially in relation to the southern sector. Finally, governing structures in all sectors have embraced militarisation to maintain *intranational hierarchy*, organised along class, ethnic, religious and regional lines.

These generalisations stand up despite the concessions made by the First System to demands for demilitarisation, especially in the aftermath of World Wars I and II: for instance, the creation of the Second System (League of Nations superseded by the United Nations), the advocacy and proposal of general and complete disarmament, and the renunciation of war as an instrument of foreign policy by way of an international treaty (Pact of Paris, 1928).

The Second System is a creation and largely a dependency of the First System. Yet, it has a normative logic and even a limited institutional momentum of its own. The Charter of the United Nations establishes a tension between statism (sovereign equality) and supranationalism (global community activity). The normative mission of the United Nations ('. . . to save succeeding generations from the scourge of war . . .') is tantamount to a call for demilitarisation. Yet, the Second System remains dependent upon the First System, although subject to varying orientations depending on shifting internal coalitions among member governments. The Security Council and the General Assembly are its most important organs. Membership consists of states represented by political appointees who act under instructions from their governments. The Security Council, alone empowered to make decisions binding on members, even partially incorporates the hierarchical feature (in the name of 'realism') of the First System in the form of permanent members enjoying a right of veto. Furthermore, the professional staff of the United Nations is financially dependent upon contributions made by member states, especially a few rich and powerful ones. And despite the promise of the Charter, no effort has been made to endow the United Nations with autonomous peacekeeping capabilities.[3]

The capacity of the Second System for demilitarising initiatives, then, is neutralised by its dependence on the First System; it is insufficiently autonomous to pose a structural threat to militarisation. Nevertheless, the Second System has made some helpful contributions to demilitarisation, especially through the General Assembly on North/South issues of hierarchy: support for decolonialisation and national self-determination, for the new international economic order, for human rights, for the prohibition of nuclear weapons, and for environmental protection are notable in this regard. The General Assembly has also endorsed normative initiatives helpful and relevant to the struggle for demilitarisation: the Universal Declaration of Human Rights, the Covenants of Human Rights, the Nuremberg Principles, and calls for a global effort in the area of disarmament.

These notable achievements have to be linked to social forces in the Third System, however, in order to transform behaviour. Movements for national liberation and OPEC have implemented Second System normative initiatives with structural consequences, whereas endorsements of the Nuremberg Principles and prohibition of nuclear weapons have not had any impact, as yet, because they have not been connected with a political process capable of altering behaviour. Their significance is mainly latent or potential, possibly symbolic, as tools or catalysts available for the appropriate social movement. We can illustrate this question of potency by reference to the anti-apartheid campaign waged so vehemently in the Second System. The normative initiative represented by the so-called anti-apartheid norm means little by itself, until coupled to resistance struggles or intervention threats. Then, however, by shifting the balance of legitimacy to the anti-apartheid side, it alters the status of First System rules of the game in a significant manner, validating normally 'illegal' anti-regime intervention and invalidating normally 'legal' pro-regime intervention, or at least shifting perceptions of crucial First System actors on matters of validity.

The Second System can be directed toward a demilitarising orientation by several developments:

> any evolution that accords its institutional elements greater autonomy, thereby making it more likely to lend weight to its natural mission which is to dismantle the war system, to put peace on a secure footing, to promote equality and dignity at the expense of hierarchy;
> a repudiation by critical First System actors of the militarising path, thereby using the Second System as a strategic political arena;
> a growth of Third System movement around the goals of demilitarisation that regards the Second System as a strategic political arena;
> a broadening by Third World countries of their attack upon the adverse effects of the First System hierarchy to include its military dimensions. The importance of the Second System for demilitarisation is therefore considerable, even if its role remains largely latent and symbolic, awaiting catalytic stimulus from without.

The Third System is segmented as a result of the degree of control exercised over political space by territorial governments that constitute the First System. There is no free space where people could promote demilitarisation without interference from the First System. Indeed, the First System sets the rules of the game for the Third System. These rules are confusing because they are not uniform. The diversity reflects the different strategies of governance and dominant political ideologies that control the definitions of the rights of people within any given sovereign state. In theory, each government purports to represent and protect the overall interest of its people, yet it continues overwhelmingly to resist pressures for fair and representative governance by falling back upon the logic of militarisation (that is, law and order, security through military strength and claims of emergency powers). Also, the First System overwhelmingly controls the dissemination of information and the educational process, assuring that the public is assaulted by militarising propaganda from cradle to grave. Again the segmented character of the First System results in different degrees and forms of control.

As does the Second System, the Third System suffers from a lack of *autonomy*, thereby greatly restricting its role in promoting demilitarisation. In overtly repressive polities, this pressure on the Third System is direct, as well as indirect as through propaganda. In more liberal polities, this pressure is mainly indirect, although the boundaries of dissent are policed: to date, First System actors have successfully relied upon various forms of mystification and pacification to obtain support for the policies of militarisation from a large majority of the population.

There are, however, certain tendencies that are threatening the credibility of First System domination over the Third System. The potency of popular discontent has been evident throughout this entire historical period. The outcome of the Algerian and Indochina Wars of Independence suggested the limits of transnational First System military superiority. Gandhi's movement against colonial rule in India, the popular movement against the Shah's tyranny in Iran, and Solidarity's movement against hardline bureaucratic rule in Poland revealed the power of non-violent mass movements when highly mobilised and well-disciplined.

On the level of legitimacy, the First System has weakened its claim to unrestricted authority by acknowledging the validity of certain normative restraints: international law; United Nations; specifically, human rights, including the Nuremberg Obligation. In the Soviet Union, for instance, dissenters have long invoked the human rights commitments formally made by the Soviet government as one basis of their attack upon certain features of domestic hierarchy; in 1980, Polish strikers insisted, among their other grievances, that the Polish government abide by conventions governing the rights of labour that had been formulated under the auspices of the International Labour Organisation.

Because of the carnage of past wars and the danger of future wars, the First System is on the defensive. It concedes at a verbal level the legitimacy of demilitarisation. This concession is reinforced by virtually universal moral and legal normative orders. This normative foundation provides a solid footing for Third System activities, including challenges directed at the First System.

One formidable constraint on the Third System is the tendency of the popular sector to restrict itself to territorial goals, that is, to reform only the national governing process in specified ways. To the extent that Third System goals are directed against various expressions of *hierarchy* within the national polity, it is important to emphasise the linkages that exist to global hierarchical structures. Beyond this, and more difficult to convince Third System activists about, is the importance of overcoming on a global scale specific types of *fragmentation*. Those that tie a state into the path of militarisation are of special relevance, exposing ordinary people to the hazards of nuclear and other types of war, as well as to the waste of previous resources through military expenditures and to a reliance upon military elites in the governing process, thereby tending to erode the protection of human rights at home. As well, economic, ecological and cultural interdependence create a Third System stake in the emergence of global capabilities to protect the public good of the whole. In particular, there appears to be a shared human commitment, as a matter of species identity, to the avoidance of irreversible catastrophe by way of mass war, environmental decay or depletion of natural resources. Furthermore, the popular sector has an interest in impartial limitation of territorial power through effective procedures for enforcing human rights, that is, on balance assuring *autonomy vis-à-vis international patterns of hierarchy* and providing *global community* protection *vis-à-vis intranational patterns* of *hierarchy*. A Third System movement for demilitarisation depends on the emergence of a planetary consciousness that is alive to the interlinked dimensions of militarisation and understands that autonomous liberation on a national scale is only partially attainable and not fully sustainable without reinforcing transformations of the state and statism. A transnational series of Third System initiatives alive to the global dimension of militarisation is the most hopeful prospect in the years ahead. Part of the process of encouraging such a development is within the realm of Third System normative dimensions where obvious interconnections exist between the domestic demand for reform and its dependence upon corresponding shifts in global policy.

Of particular importance are normative initiatives relevant to demilitarisation that can be undertaken in the Third System; that is, initiatives that challenge the root assumptions of militarisation by insisting upon certain norms of procedure and substance that rest upon some adequate moral/legal foundation. For this reason, the movement to prohibit the use of threat or even the possession of nuclear weapons is of significance beyond the effort to constrain governmental discretion. The movement for European Nuclear Disarmament (END) is a most spectacular example of Third System potency in this domain. Demonstrations by hundreds of thousands, backed by the support of many grassroots peace groups and by established religious organisations, are altering the political climate within which First System security policy is determined for Western Europe, and beyond, Romania, in particular, has been seeking to extend the demilitarising initiatives of END to embrace Warsaw Pact as well as NATO countries. The intention of such initiatives is to mobilise effective opposition to militarisation in all three systems by altering the normative climate. Such new climate would create new creative space within both the First and Second Systems enabling demilitarising moves to win wider backing.

Normative initiatives are not the only important activities of the Third System with respect to demilitarisation. The movement against nuclear power in the Third System Northwest is questioning domestic hierarchy in some critical respects. Its wider implications extend from a concern with safety of the nuclear fuel cycle, to the safety of any nuclear activity, including those related to military purposes. Comparable issues of safety in mining plant operation, waste disposal, and transporting and safeguarding of fissionable materials exist in the military nuclear sector, and perhaps are even compounded by secrecy and the absence of public scrutiny. By discrediting nuclear power, the Third System will go a long way towards agitating Third System concern about nuclear weapons, and even about traditional (militarised) conceptions of national security, although the reverse dynamic is also possible – namely, that to reinforce the prohibition on weapons, other nuclear activities will also fall under an increased barrage of criticism. The anti-nuclear power movement, important as it is for demilitarisation politics, nevertheless falls outside the main focus of this chapter, since it is not an initiative whose dominant motivation is to establish or enforce a norm.

As is obvious, there are positive and negative feedback relations among the three systems. At present, the main strategy is to alter the orientations of First System leaders by building pressure directly upward from the Third System, as well as by way of the Second System. As segments of the First System shift towards a comprehensive demilitarsation orientation, the political current of energy works its way back down via the Second System to other segments of the Third System, and then back up again to new segments of the First System. In this regard, it is necessary to view the three systems as interconnected and flowing parts of a unitary evolving global political order.

The political opportunities (and challenges) also cross system boundaries. It is easy to contemplate, for instance, the formation of a pro-demilitarisation coalition joining activist social forces in the Third System Northwest, with the leaders of segments of the First System South, and with elements of the Second System. A global demilitarisation movement, then, is likely to partake of all three systems to some extent.

NORMATIVE INITIATIVES IN THE THIRD SYSTEM AND DEMILITARISATION

There are several reasons why normative initiatives are an attractive focus for demilitarisation. For one thing, every government in the First System, no matter how repressive, acknowledges its accountability to moral/legal norms; hence, a universal basis for seeking adherence to these norms exists. This is especially important for Third System activity, as it is often constrained by boundaries of First System tolerance; that is, since the entire world (except for high seas and Antarctica) is divided into territorial states each Third System arena is governed to some degree by a First System actor.

Secondly, the ambiguity of authoritiative norms, including the distinction between what is forbidden and what ought to be forbidden, creates 'space' for prescriptive politics in most First System settings. This ambiguity extends to questions of what is binding by reference to international law upon a particular First System actor (e.g. are the Nuremberg Principles binding because declared and endorsed by the General Assembly and affirmed by an array of international law experts?). The point is that Third System activists committed to demilitarisation can act as if the Nuremberg Principles are binding, and thereby raise questions of accountability in many First and Second System settings.

Thirdly, a normative dimension for demilitarisation emphasises two possible grounds for an overall challenge: it vindicates the right of resistance against illegitimate political authority at the First System level and suggests the possibility that a comparable right of resistance should be postulated at the Second System level, that is, to the mode and manner by which global interests are protected.

The locus of normative concern in the Third System needs also to be explained. The First System is the principal source of authoritative norms because of its dominance of the international legal order, but it is unwilling and incapable of implementing those norms supportive of demilitarisation (e.g. prohibitions on aggressive war, nuclear weapons, abuses of human rights). The Second System keeps these norms alive in the public imagination because its credibility depends on some expression of minimal concern about the dangers confronting human society; yet it is paralysed politically as a result of its dependence on the First System.

Hence, it is only among elements of the Third System that there is a clear commitment to the enforcement of demilitarisation norms by securing First System adherence. Even in the Third System, misinformation, hostile propaganda, pacifications, intimidation and reactionary priorities confuse most people about their real stake in demilitarisation. Also, different First System settings condition Third System priorities and openings. Human rights concerns seem paramount for those First System settings where the domestic hierarchy is most oppressive. More global (Second System) concerns may be more permissible in these settings even if felt to be less vital, although any attempt to insist that one's own government take demilitarising initiatives because of a normative obligation to do so is likely to encounter stiff opposition.

The problems facing the Third System are different in the North and South. The centre of militarisation is in the North, as divided between the Northwest (USA-dominated) and the Northeast (USSR-dominated). The liberal orientation of the governing process in the Northwest allows explicit concentration on the demilitarising imperative of its own First System actors as a matter of first priority. Such a priority seems sensible both because the repressive features of the Northeast are generally resistant to external pressure and because First System actors in the Northwest pretend to be already committed to demilitarisation. This presence can be exposed for what it is, partly by normative initiatives in the Third System Northwest (e.g. a demand for disarmament, an insistence on the illegality of nuclear weapons, a claim that the sort of threats to use nuclear weapons contained in strategic doctrine are themselves instances of 'crimes against humanity'). This exposure can arouse public indignation, as well as demonstrate the need for imaginative normative initiatives that operate beyond the boundaries of conventional politics.

The ideological orientation of the governing process in the Northeast also has implications for the Third System. It creates a natural umbrella for demilitarising concerns, although First System apologists in the Northeast blame the Northwest, that is, the main capitalist sector of the First

System, for militarist tendencies in the world. Secrecy and control of information in the Northeast also makes it more difficult to mount useful Third System campaigns on demilitarising themes, except as proposals by relatively isolated intellectual dissenters (e.g. Sakharov) whose impact seems to be largely transnational. Issues of human rights (domestic non-economic hierarchy) enjoy a manifest demilitarising priority in the Third System Northeast–USSR and Eastern Europe. Such realities expose the absence of 'creative space', and reveal a failure by First System actors to protect the human interests of their own citizenries. For the non-Soviet portion of the Third System Northeast, special questions of international hierarchy (that is, Soviet domination) are added to issues of intranational hierarchy. Struggling against these repressive features will not necessarily contribute directly to the global demilitarisation process, except by opening up space in which the pursuit of normative concerns is accepted as legitimate activity for citizens.

In the South, the weight of militarisation is partly felt in the North South hierarchical structure, especially to the extent that the militarising tendency is associated both with international dependency and intranational repressiveness. The Iranian Revolution against the Pahlavi dynasty illustrated a Third System movement of extraordinary force animated by opposition to these two interlocking aspects of hierarchy. The main normative element in the Iranian revolutionary process was the stress on human rights, including gestures of solidarity, especially in the Third System Northwest. It remains unclear what will be the eventual character of the Islamic republic as a First System actor, but it seems probable both that its anti-dependency posture will have a short-term major demilitarising significance (cancellation of arms purchases, refusal to supply oil beyond Iranian captital requirements, support for liberation movements) for Iran, although not necessarily for the region, and that its governing process will generate a new agenda of severe human rights concerns.

In general, the Third System in the South is concerned with opposing the continued hierarchy dominated by the

North; the anti-neocolonial struggle goes on in the period of formal independence of the states in the South. To the extent that international hierarchy is linked with domestic hierarchy, as when outside actors from the North help keep a First System elite in power, then the struggle for human rights at home is also a struggle against the militarisation of the planet as a structure. Unlike the North where the First System actors are the main agents and beneficiaries of militarisation, in the South the First System actors are, at best, subordinate links in the system, having been to sharply varying degrees socialised into 'the military habit'. Indeed, acquisition of weapons, even nuclear weapons, in the South is ambiguous, as it can be partially viewed as a necessary step to achieve autonomy for a given state or region, and possibly to shock the North into some denuclearising initiatives of its own.[4] Partly for these reasons, normative initiatives emanating from the Third System of the South are directed mainly at First System actors in the North, thereby attributing responsibility for global militarisation (e.g. normative demands to renounce nuclear weaponry and strategy) mainly to those few states, especially the two superpowers.

SPECIFIC PROPOSALS

Which Third System normative initiatives have most promise when it comes to demilitarisation remains to be considered. A long list could be compiled. What follows is illustrative and tactical, suggesting the kind of proposals that seem most appropriate and the ones that have the most promise.

Global scale

The most significant Third System normative initiative at the global system level may be the projection of credible images of a comprehensive demilitarisation process. This effort needs to be centred in the Third System, consisting of various individuals and groups linked together by collaborative arrangements, perhaps with the informal backing of some progressive First System actors. It is normative to the extent that demilitarisation is a way of specifying what is preferable, that is, what would be normative for the politics of the future. The academic foundations for such an outlook are being developed under various rubrics: world order studies, future studies, peace studies, utopography, macro-history, dialectics of the future, 'soft' science fiction. Its essential feature is a conviction in the possibility and necessity of an encompassing transformation of the present orientation of First System elites so as to combat the increasingly pervasive militarisation of the planet. What is needed in the Third System is the dissemination of these images beyond the community of academic intellectuals in forms that are accessible to people in various circumstances of consciousness and literacy. Also necessary are a trans-national consensus-building process around the issue of what demilitarisation implies and reliance on various means to promote its goals in different areas, depending especially on First System constraints varying from country to country. Although image-forming is principally a Third System initiative, it would be helpful to have strategies for promoting demilitarisation advocated from within the First and Second Systems.

The second area of normative initiative on a global scale would involve generating pressure for all varieties of denu-clearisation, especially in the military domain. On no issue is the global and human interest more evident than in the delegitimation of nuclear weaponry. Normative consensus would contribute to this result by placing a stigma upon reliance on nuclear weapons and strategy. Illustrative of such directions of initiative are the issuance of two non-governmental declarations, each informed by the ethos of denuclearisation: the 1978 Delhi Declaration for a Just World[5] and the 1980 Lisbon Declaration on Denuclearis-ation for a Just World: the Failure of Non-Proliferation.[6] Both documents, drafted and endorsed by concerned citizens from around the world, express in unambiguous terms their conviction that any threat or use of nuclear weapons would be a crime against humanity. The Delhi Declaration even insists that the mere possession of nuclear weapons is a crime against humanity; the Lisbon Declaration also regards possession as criminal but not until a time definite has been formally established by the joint initiative of non-nuclear states. The Third System consensus on the menace of nuclear weaponry is an important element in a global movement for denuclearisation. A recent expression of the consensus can be found in the Rajgir Declaration in which Buddhist communities of Asia and individuals from many countries join to condemn nuclearism.[7] In the Northwest, the struggle against nuclear power, as unsafe and authoritarian in implication, combines certain elements of resistance to *intranational hierarchy* – anti-democratic structures – with opposition to the war system as the fundamental expression of *international hierarchy*.

A third area for normative initiative concerns direct opposition to militarisation tendencies. Here again the circumstances of a given national setting suggest the specific form of struggle. The domestic arenas of the two superpowers are obviously critical, both very different from one another. In the United States, movements against draft registration, opposition to specific weapons systems (MX, Trident), and opposition to specific arms transfers (e.g. to repressive regimes) and to increases in defence spending are important. In the Soviet Union, national security policy as such seems beyond citizen scrutiny, but calls for more consumer goods and denunciations by dissenters of interventionary use of Soviet military power work in a demilitarising direction. The basic demilitarising imperative in the Soviet Union, however, remains the struggle for human rights, which is in its essence a demand for domestic demilitarisation. If this struggle were to enjoy success, the demilitarising effects would exert influence on the Soviet approach to international security.

Throughout the world, also, it would be helpful to promote the efficacy of non-violent approaches to conflict. India, with its rich Gandhian legacy, is especially situated, although not by its own recent defence policy, to gain a global hearing for non-violent politics. Academic efforts to discover and highlight non-violent, pacifist and altruistic elements in the various great cultures of the world would help to convey the understanding, so needed at present, that non-violence has universal roots and many practical successes. To be serious about the abolition of war as a social institution implies putting something in the place of violence; necessarily then, images of non-violent polities of varying dimensions must be fed to the political imagination of peoples throughout the world seeking relief from a destiny of apocalyptic war.

Regional scale
Regional enactments of global scale initiatives are obviously appropriate and, on occasion, timely. The recent surge of Third System efforts in Western Europe has been prompted by specific insensitive First System security policy, especially proposed provocative weapons deployments that seem to increase the prospect of 'limited nuclear war' on a regional scale. Beyond this, regional and sub-regional efforts to decouple their security systems from the menace of war would be beneficial. In this regard, nuclear-free zones, non-alignment postures, intra-regional peacekeeping and disarmament moves, and general efforts to insulate Third World regions from superpower competition and ex-colonial intervention are beneficial moves in the appropriate direction.

Sovereign state scale
Normative initiatives directed at the governing process in sovereign states are of great importance at this stage of history. One important line of effort would be to restrict force structures and military doctrines to defensive conceptions of the use of military power. Admittedly, the defensive/offensive distinction is difficult to draw as so much depends on intention and context, yet the insistence that international force be used defensively, if at all, is vital at the experience with private violence within states suggests. The struggle for governmental accountability in the use of force as an instrument of foreign policy is a mode of exerting restraint, one sanctioned by Nuremberg. Keeping governments within a framework of law, subject to interpretation by an independent judiciary, is also obviously relevant.

Again demilitarising priorities will be diverse, even contradictory, from setting to setting. For instance, the demilitarising priority in South Africa may require front line states to augment their war-fighting capabilities in the short run, or a Third World beleaguered state such as post-1978 Nicaragua might do well to increase its defence budget as an inhibition against intervention.

As suggested, especially in anti-imperial contexts, certain apparent contradictions exist. Short-term belligerence may be required as a foundation for a more durable peace; at the extreme, additional proliferation of nuclear weapons capabilities may be a precondition for denuclearisation.

Individual scale
What one does with one's own life is a primary political statement. The shift from militarised to demilitarised allegiances will be expressed, in the first instance, by what people do with their lives. Refusal by scientists and engineers to design weapons, or at least weapons related to mass destruction or offensive use, is one dimension; refusal to engage in secret research on security issues; tax refusal; draft resistance; more radical forms of civil disobedience – pouring blood on the gates of the Pentagon, blocking the completion of a Trident submarine base – illustrate the range of undertakings. Activities by professionals in the United States (Physicians for Social Responsibility; Lawyers Committee on Nuclear Policy) around the normative viability of nuclear war and weaponry are indicative of whole new dimensions of Third System activity.

In the liberal democracies, where citizens' rights are formally protected,the idea of a Nuremberg Obligation to resist crimes of state is crucial. If individuals in sufficient number manifest this kind of higher loyalty, then a powerful movement against endowing governments with the option of discretionary violence and war-making will begin to take shape.

CONCLUSION

We need to monitor developments in the world from a demilitarising perspective. This requires a sophisticated frame of reference, alive to struggles against domestic tyranny and injustice and against forms of imperialism, as well as preoccupied with the avoidance of warfare, especially beyond the nuclear threshold. The tactics of demilitarisation cannot normally – beyond the issue of nuclear weapons threat or use – be expressed in too universalistic terms. Finally, the First System seems generally implicated in the ongoing dynamics of militarisation, the Second System seems stalemated by a tension between its impotence and its mandate, and the Third System, alone at present, seems able to sustain normative initiatives of consequence that move in a demilitarising direction but not without a certain ambiguity, especially when its goals involve the seizure of political power, often entailing a new cycle of militarisation.

NOTES

1. A fundamental distinction needs to be drawn between the United Nations Organisation *as political actor* and the United Nations Charter *as political vision*. Only the Charter is consistently premised on world order values, and its vision has not been consistently or fully implemented in the life of the Organisation, although the degree of realisation has varied through time. For more on this see Falk, *A Global Approach to National Policy* (Cambridge, Mass.: Harvard University Press, 1975), Chapter 10.
2. In some formulations, for instance that of the International Foundation for Development Alternatives (IFDA), the Second System is associated with the market and market forces such as corporations and banks, while all governmental institutions, including intergovernmental mechanisms – for instance, the United Nations – are assimilated into the First System. For world order purposes, however, the tripartite division of systems, as presented in the text, seems better adapted for inquiry and analysis.
3. As for instance, advocated by Robert C. Johansen and Saul H. Mendlovitz, 'The Role of Enforcement of Law on the Establishment of a New International Order: A Proposal for a Transnational Police Force', *Alternatives* VI, 2 (1980), pp. 307–37.

4. For a fuller statement of this position, see Ali Mazrui, *The African Condition* (Cambridge: Cambridge University Press, 1980).
5. *Disarmament for a Just World: Declaration of Principles, Proposal for a Treaty, and Call for Action*, issued on the occasion of the International Workshop on Disarmament, 27–31 March 1978, New Delhi. For text, see *Alternatives* IV, 1 (1978), pp. 155–60.
6. *Declaration for a Just World: The Failure of Non-Proliferation*. Draft prepared by a group of concerned scholars to be presented at the Lisbon Conference of the World Order Models Project, 13–20 July 1980. The final text appears in *Alternatives*, VI, 3, (1980), pp. 491–6.
7. For text of Rajgir Declaration, see *Alternatives* VIII, 2 (1982).

10 Towards Security for the People

To consider alternative forms of security in international affairs is to pose immediately the question: alternative to what? In the boldest sense, the reply might be: 'alternative to the reliance on highly militarised structures of official authority operating at the level of sovereign states'. In effect, alternative security implies the displacement of 'the war system' as the ultimate arbiter of international conflict.

Yet such a response is not entirely satisfactory. It posits a future free from militarism, but it tells us nothing about the current and intervening quest for security, given the multiplicity of states and their remarkably diverse circumstances. When we inquire about security in our world, we find ourselves on slippery, uneven ground. In essence, we normally consider security as specified by governments, with or without the backing of their citizens. Security implies both a state of mind (feeling secure) and a spectrum of capabilities (assessing ability to handle threats to state interests). The psychological dimension of security is further stressed by reliance on threats of retaliation as a way of avoiding the burdens of actual defence.

The clearest meaning of security involves the perceived and actual capacity of a government to defend its territory and formal independence against foreign enemies. This central concern is inseparable from attention to political developments in bordering areas, especially the emergence or displacement of hostile leadership. This meaning of security is expanded in various directions by imperial states to encompass the defence of values, ideology, interests, allies, access to resources and markets and geopolitical positions (for example, secure borders, sea-lanes).

In its international usage, security also implies for many a sharp dividing-line between 'inner' and 'outer', but this is exceedingly misleading. If the essence of security is the perceived capacity to defend the governing process and its leadership, then 'internal security' becomes an important dimension. Contemporary militarism is often centred on the protection of the governing process against popular forces and revolutionary challenges. Governments in many peripheral states receive military assistance from foreign states, as do, to a lesser extent, opposition movements. Internal conflict becomes internationalised, and warfare goes on within the borders of one state, while often the main antagonists are other, rival states.

What ensures security, then, is a question which must be examined within a given context. It may relate directly to the fears and ambitions of a particular political leadership and its people in a specific situation. Dangerous forms of warfare often arise out of inconsistent definitions and perceptions of security requirements by governments and coalitions of governments in competition with one another.

The chapter is written in a critical spirit, depicting the rising costs and dangers of security as specified by governments. At the extreme, this governmental idea of security has produced a nuclear arms race that is a threat to human survival. Yet even without the apocalyptic menace, the workings of the war system in the modern world exact an enormous, avoidable toll in human suffering, or put differently, in precluding the realisation of human potential. In addition, the orthodox orientation towards security impairs the quality of political life in all societies. Even liberal democracies are anti-democratic in crucial respects when it comes to 'national security' under modern conditions. Militarised bureaucracies in high-technology societies are permanent war machines prepared at all times to engage in an ultimate war. Whether the citizenry understands and endorses this posture, with its attendant risks, has recently been called into question by a growing anti-nuclear movement.

On quite a different level, the demands of modernisation amid mass poverty have put great pressure on Third World countries. This pressure is intensified by the various efforts of countries in the First World to retain their influence in the post-colonial period. One result is a series of tensions between state and society in those countries that have linked their future to a condition of great dependency on outside forces; another is tension in relations with outsiders for those governments that have opted for autonomous development based on mass support. Dependency encourages internal militarism to be repressive towards the domestic population, whereas breaking away generates interventionary pressures that lead to militarisation in the defence of sovereign rights. As a consequence, human rights and democracy are often sacrificed, violence occurs and various types of warfare result, while the great social challenges of poverty and development are neglected.

The case for alternative security is broad indeed, and proceeds from an entirely different outlook. Instead of security for governments, let us consider security for the peoples of the world against militarist intrusions upon their quest for individual and collective goals. What would security for the people entail in terms of military capabilities? It might imply an ethos of resistance and liberation that could, under certain conditions, even rely on certain forms of arms defence. The peoples of the world are not likely to trust declarations of peaceful intentions by their traditional enemies until effective supranational restraining structures are firmly established or some sort of non-militarist mood takes a definite hold in international life. The re-orientation of security will not proceed at the same speed or according to the same agenda in different parts of the world. Security requirements will be perceived and interpreted differently, but the redirection of energy and outlook from the government to the people seems clear enough.

Finally, security for the people may mean many new things besides ways of finding effective strategies to resist enemies and rivals – an essentially negative quest. For some peoples, for instance, those in the Sahel or southern Asia, security has a more comprehensive and positive sense that includes creating arrangements to ensure the distribution of adequate food supplies in such a way that those in need will be fed. For other peoples, security may revolve around access to energy supplies they can afford. For still others, it may mean strengthening (militarising, if you will) the governing process sufficiently to guarantee that sovereign rights and internal order are respected by external forces and that 'normal' life within society can proceed.

The basic argument here is that the appropriation of the meaning of security by governments is under increasing siege in a variety of settings. This condition of siege generates extreme forms of militarisation to offset the various populist demands being made on behalf of security for the people. In other words, the very fragility of the notion of the security of governments is a principal explanation for increasing recourse to extremism and desperation. One role of critics and advocates of security for the people is to make the links between this fragility and the resulting extremism and desperation as transparent as possible. The growing transparency in the nuclear domain has helped produce a peace movement on a world scale. A second role is to provide convincing images of how security for the people might operate to achieve a quite different set of goals, thereby demonstrating that practical alternatives to militarism exist. A final role is to explore how state power might be successfully challenged on behalf of security for the people. The circumstances vary from country to country and political system to political system. In many Third World countries, the issue is mainly one of re-orienting the governing process in the direction of mass needs and autonomous development. In Europe, with the Swiss model as one image, shifts towards non-alignment, neutrality and national resistance could be a move towards security for the people.

The diversity of tactical situations should not blind us to the underlying unity of this undertaking: a re-orientation of security for the sake of the well-being of peoples, and ultimately, of people in relation to their natural habitat, the earth. Governments would continue to organise and administer many security activities, but the orientation and instrumentalities of the effort would be different.

Among the adverse features of security for governments is the growing disjunction between the potential harm and the power of authority. The leaders of a nuclear superpower can devastate the entire planet, but cannot defend their own society, regardless of their level of armament. Leaders of smaller countries can do nothing, however neutral and pacific their inclination, to cordon off national territory from the lethal effects of nuclear madness. The technology of modern war, linked to the sovereign claims of states, makes a mockery of the traditional logic of territorial self-defence and self-help as the main basis for security in the state system.

This chapter offers no solution. The very unevenness and complexity of 'security' limits the implications of any given inquiry or set of proposals. Some wider implications of a change in our understanding of what security is about are explored. Other perspectives and emphases relative to the unceasing quest for security, reflecting variations of class, culture and region, are also needed to initiate a broad exchange of ideas on the future of security.

THE TRADITIONAL IMAGERY OF SECURITY: THE SPARTAN ILLUSION

Security in international affairs assumes the unconditional prerogatives of the sovereign state to defend itself. Under normal circumstances, the government has an uncontested right to define the content of security for a given state, and to take measures to protect the state against both internal and external threats. The international political order does not generally call into question representational links between government and state, although if the government loses its capacity to impose its will at home or if it is associated with a hostile ideology, then other governments may question its authority, by breaking off diplomatic relations or refusing to accord diplomatic recognition.

The character of international security is also shaped by the inequality of states. Powerful states often define their security in expansive terms which extend to the protection of 'friends' and allies, or are associated with upholding a balance of power within a given region or even throughout the world, and may even include control over foreign foundations of economic viability, including markets, access to resources and the assured flow of vital resources from source to destination. In other words, powerful governments perceive and act as if their security depends on discharging a broad 'managerial' role in international life. Often, the security requirements of leading states are satisfied at the expense of weaker states, for instance, within spheres of influence. Here, the strong state satisfies its security at the expense of the political independence, even the territorial integrity, of the weaker state.

The more modern idea of 'collective security' looks towards the protection of *all* states against military attacks by the concerted, but voluntary, actions of the organised international community, by way of international institutions, either regional or global. The predominance of Machiavellian patterns of statecraft, as well as ideological geopolitics, has generally prevented the formation of a political consensus, which is the precondition for the functioning of a voluntary collective security approach that lacks independent sources of funding and decision-making.

Security policy in the world political system is a complex reality. It has come to be closely connected with various manifestations of militarisation. Entrenched leadership regards security as including the removal of international threats to 'stability' and 'balance', especially extra-legal and revolutionary threats that oppose existing structures of power on fundamental grounds. Depending on the magnitude and character of these threats, the internal dynamic of militarisation may come to dominate the formation of security policy, sometimes in conjunction with a hegemonic foreign government, a circumstance that exists in many parts of the Third World, where there are strong links of collaboration and dependency between governing elites and powerful foreign governments.

In one sense, security is extended to cover the entire range of public policy, but in a fundamental respect it is military prowess that underpins the realisation of its most ambitious non-military goals. The opposing view in the political sense tends to accept a wider militarist frame of reference, and to fall back, if necessary, on the claim that its concerns will make the country stronger and the military instrument more efficient and effective. It is absolutely essential for a radical critique of current conceptions and structures of security to understand the full implications of its own analysis. Otherwise, as the German progressive thinker Rudolf Bahro asserts, 'all the problems of the present will be insoluble and every conceivable catastrophe and atrocity will turn out to be inevitable' despite the best intentions *and* a powerful popular movement.[1] Putting the issue more concretely, there is a genuine danger that certain partial demands of anti-militarist groups for enhanced security can be satisfied, while at the same time actually *stabilising* the overall structures of militarism, including 'nuclearism'. For instance, the European campaign against the deployment of Pershing II and cruise missiles, the campaigns for a freeze on nuclear weapons production and the global campaign for 'serious disarmament negotiations' can each succeed without having any radical effect on the militarist character of state power and security policy.

The dynamic of security has certainly become closely intertwined with the fact that the use of violence, especially in situations of direct conflict between states, is at the unconditional discretion of governments. Threats to security are generally projected in terms of 'enemies' who would destroy an enemy state if they could. Preventing destruction, then, has meant endowing governments with the military capacity either to discourage attack, or if it comes, to defend territory against an invasion. Security has thus, in its essence, involved a test of opposed military capabilities and wills, although the definition of *military* has been broadened in recent decades to embrace techno-industrial arrangements and the morale of the people. Such a progression naturally produced a notion of 'total war' or 'absolute war' well before the advent of nuclear weapons. It contrasts with normative and earlier cultural images of war as a delimited test of wills by specially equipped military professionals who fought each other at 'the front' (a circumscribed geographical space). Of course, this image of war was itself idealised; unrestricted wars of annihilation have been waged, at least since late neolithic times. From the point of view argued here, the critical element of continuity over time, despite changes in tactics and a series of weapons innovations, involves the dominance of the security process by the official leadership of a state. That dominance may be dispersed within a government, as when the legislative branch participates, or it may all be concentrated in the will of a king or a dictator. Elective 'checks' may also operate to influence official policy on security matters, but the central point remains that security is overwhelmingly defined by the government in situations of war and peace.

Karl von Clausewitz gave this prevalent image of unrestricted war its most influential formulation in the early nineteenth century. In his treatise, *On War*, Clausewitz sets forth these views with clarity and forcefulness, in a manner that both exemplifies the spirit of competitive politics and codifies the central reliance on violence to resolve international conflicts. The essence of the Clausewitzian view is contained in such ideas as 'whoever uses force unsparingly finds that he has the advantage over him who uses it with less vigour' and, hence, that 'as each side tries to dominate the other, there arises a reciprocal action which must escalate to an extreme' such that 'the disarming or destruction of the enemy . . . or the threat of this . . . must always be the aim of warfare'.[2] Yet even Clausewitz made recourse to war conditional upon its utility for the realisation of a political project; warfare was only appropriate if the military means could be kept proportional to the political objective.

This instrumental orientation towards war acknowledges no limits by way of norms or values, and has naturally culminated in the absolutism of modern war, characterised at the limit by a claim of state right to wage a war of extinction with nuclear weaponry. The capability underlying this ultimate threat is the outcome of two important dynamic tendencies: the modernising process of continuous and accelerating technological innovation in weaponry involving the progressive substitution of capital for labour; and the mobilisation by officialdom of the entire range of economic capabilities and moral enthusiasms of a society around a single centrally directed war effort. Both of these tendencies have helped to militarise the modern state, while simultaneously making the enemy society as a whole, including its civilian population, industrial base and natural habitat, 'legitimate' targets of belligerent action. The wider implications of these large-scale terrorist claims to destroy for the sake of state interests make a mockery of moralistic denunciations of small-scale terrorism. The huge permanent bureaucracy of the nuclear national security state, where special interest groups heavily influence the specification of defence needs and where leaders decide matters of ultimate destiny by anti-democratic procedures, is the inevitable result of this process. Furthermore, this process occurs in a setting where there is neither a defence against a major nuclear attack (whether from accident or design) nor any realistic prospect of recovery after a major nuclear exchange.[3] It also adopts, as its faceless characteristic stance, the depersonalised workings of complex computers, whose operations of threat perception and targeting may eventually decide the fate of humanity. This militarist structure has been rendered virtually immune from criticism by the depths of its bureaucratic roots, which extend to business, media, elected officials and the academic world.

The militarist consensus is ultra-stable, at the very time when the failure of military power to achieve the security goals of even the most powerful is producing a crisis of legitimacy of the modern state. This general circumstance is found in varying degrees in the very diverse range of states that currently make up the international political system. For instance, neither superpower, however much it augments its capabilities, can ever be 'secure' against devastating uses of nuclear weapons by its adversary. Further acquisitions of weapons at current high thresholds cannot alter this situation; at most, they might fool a state's own people temporarily. Weaker states would obviously not be able to maintain their societies intact in the event of a nuclear attack. That is, no government can provide high levels of security, although some can do better than others depending on their leadership, location and degree of involvement in competitive geopolitics.

The special language used by governments helps insulate security planning from any popular understanding which might lead to opposition. Some years ago Philip Green identified this discourse as 'deadly logic, namely, a mixture of Clausewitzian orientations towards war with an adversary view of international conflict, in which the foreign enemy is viewed as containable only by way of credible threats of devastation.[4] Since there is no defence against serious attack, war, should it come, either takes the form of an aggressive first strike, or is reduced to an exchange of retaliatory threats that it would never be rational or morally acceptable to carry out. Within this framework, technological innovation goes on and on, providing ever higher levels of assured destruction of the foreign society, but premised on shorter time-intervals within which to respond. The substitution of capital for labour results in action and reaction patterns increasingly independent of human intervention. Errors in computer programming or processing have come perilously close, on a number of occasions, to setting off an entirely accidental war of mutual annihilation. These conditions of fragility are making many people increasingly afraid, putting governments at odds with their own citizenry and undermining the basic claim of political leaders that they have the ability tb provide national populations with security.

The challenge of nuclearism must be given a certain priority, but is, in any event, organically linked to the other varieties of militarism that sustain conditions for all types of hegemonic exploitation, including exploitation of other classes and races. There is no way to handle the problem of contemporary 'insecurity' without a revision of the entire ethos of security, as it operates between and within sovereign states. Such a revision may be obtained, if at all, through the global nature of the pressures generated by the various interlocking forms of discontent. At this stage, the phenomenon of national revolution, with all of its diversities, does present a formidable challenge to post-colonial patterns of North/South hegemony, as well as to certain forms of internal militarisation. That is, hegemonic geopolitics in North/South settings is definitely on the defensive, although far from defeated. The 'softer' orientations of development assistance and ideological persuasion have been virtually abandoned by both superpowers in favour of undisguised projections of military power. Reliance on militarism to offset deteriorations in a political position is indicative of imperial power in its declining phase.

The encounter between interventionary geopolitics and national revolutionary activities creates serious dangers of wider, escalating warfare, especially in areas where oil is at stake and where East/West rivalries are intense. National revolution, as a political phenomenon, challenges militarism on grounds of anti-imperial nationalism and internal repressiveness. The revolutionary message is that the government is not a legitimate foundation for the exercise of popular sovereignty. Unfortunately, most victorious revolutionary movements have quickly reproduced militarism in their own approach to governance, in the name of defending the revolution against enemies within and abroad. Anti-militarism, then, succumbs to the prevailing tides of militarism, although the ideology and symbolism of alignment and repression are reversed.

National revolutionary programmes consistently emphasise a demand for autonomy in political, economic and cultural spheres. This demand is given additional stature because it has been so widely endorsed in institutional settings, even by governments, in the form of support for norms of national self-determination, sovereign equality and non-intervention. This support is contained in a variety of United Nations documents. People are fighting and dying to achieve autonomy and popular sovereignty. A strong emergent and successful movement of non-alignment exists and is tied to the complex passions of nationalism. This movement lacks a comprehensive analysis that relates particular national situations to the wider global context. It is not surprising that victories by national revolutionary movements are so rarely sustainable: new forms of hegemony emerge (a Third World state shifts its dependency pattern, but it rarely achieves sustainable autonomy); repression of the 'old' variety is displaced by new forms of repression (often justified as necessary to uphold autonomy subsequent to a successful national revolution); and internal forms of unfulfilled nationalism threaten the unity of the state (state-centred versus minority nationalisms).[5] In other words, hegemony and repression are embedded in the overall structures of the world economic, political and cultural (including information) order, and cannot be effectively overcome at the state level. For this reason, it is crucial to prospects for global transformation that social forces mobilised against imperial politics and domestic repressive regimes enlarge their interpretation to include the relevance of strategic rivalry between the superpowers.

The reverse argument holds even more strongly. The mobilisation of concern against the dangers of global warfare depends for political success on social forces confronting internal structures of domination and exploitation. Implicit in these movements, *if* their vision is bold enough, is a drastic globally conceived revision of security, based on the values and aspirations of the people as a whole. Without this drastic revision, victories for demilitarisation tend, at most, to be tactical, and what is worse (for reasons already indicated), are rarely sustainable (for example, the Limited Test Ban Treaty did stop atmospheric testing by the signatories, but underground testing was increased to a level where it equalled the total volume of pre-Treaty testing). Therefore, the arms control measure helped prevent atmospheric pollution, but it did not slow down the arms race.

The modern form of the Spartan Illusion is the conviction that an individual state can detach itself, if militarily strong and determined, from the overall structures of security operative in the world. Detachment cannot succeed without the support of a wider process of transformation, although some forms of detachment achieve more than others. Nuclearism in any form produces acute anxiety in a crisis, and poses a variety of insoluble problems associated with priorities and values. Radical anti-imperialism assuredly weakens certain patterns of hegemonic security, but it creates vulnerability to new patterns, such as shifting alignments from one super-power to another, allowing capital entry via multinational corporations, banks and international financial institutions on constraining terms, or remaining subject to alien-imposed cultural patterns that undermine indigenous morale.

Similarly, international reform strategies such as non-alignment, self-reliance, a new international economic order, promotion of human rights and arms control do not undermine the basic premises of statism, nor do they erode the militarist structures in place or challenge the persistence of a Clausewitzian ethos of war. All modes of reform that depend merely on the voluntary processes of adjustment by existing units of power are incapable of overcoming the fundamental insecurity of present global arrangements, although improvements are certainly possible. Such adjust-ments are, at best, arrangements of restraint at the margins. They arise from bargains struck with the existing leadership at the state level and necessarily incorporate the influence of militarist elements. These bargains, admittedly, may be useful, even necessary, to slow down the pace of the arms race and to discourage destabilising weapons systems (for example, anti-ballistic missiles – ABMs). It is however a mistake to suppose that a sequence of arms control arrange-ments moves governments in the direction of demilitaris-ation and disarmament. The stronger dynamic of bureau-cratic orientation, technological momentum, and statist drives to maximise military power has continued to over-whelm pressures for restraint. There is no cumulative learning experience associated with such steps, or only one which would build a case for the cynicism of political leaders. The cost here of emphasising arms control goals is to confuse and mystify the public by suggesting that mana-gerial impulses to stabilise military dimensions of rivalry may justify continuing trust in the capabilities of govern-ment in relation to security policy. Our emphasis, in contrast, is on the importance of a public awakening as to the urgency of rethinking security from the perspective of the people, in relation to their individual lives and the persistence and growth of their collective existence.

Only a holistic perspective based on the reality of human unity can provide a wholly adequate political and moral foundation for a new vision of security. Such a perspective is being formed through opposition to existing security structures, as the outcome of a politics of struggle. Of course, to be an opposition movement is not sufficient, as the goals pursued may fall far short of structural change, as when a revolutionary leadership constructs its own militarist structures, despite an initial commitment to human rights and democracy. Such a recreation of militarism, we argue, arises from the properties of the global system to a far greater extent than it does from the hypocritical qualities of opposition leaders who feel themselves forced to defend their gains by 'reinventing' militarist tactics and structures of their own; within their operative frame of reference, such defensive moves may be imperative for survival. In fact, the militarist framework dominates the political consciousness of even its opponents, and as a result they oppose militarism by militarist means. If leaders refuse to adopt such means, they often seem ill-equipped to lead the struggles of the oppressed.

Those who ignore these wider structures of militarism at work in the world perish as a consequence, and arguably augment human suffering, despite heroic intentions. However, a further point is that defensive militarism may partially or totally sacrifice, for the sake of survival, the liberating vision that animated the revolution in the first instance. There is thus a definite need for a global vision of revolution that sees the struggle against the various forms of militarism as essential. This could produce new leaders receptive to the world order agenda, as well as to the specific imperatives of national revolution and anti-imperialism.[6]

Our special concern here is with images of security provided through the mechanisms of popular sovereignty operating on the basis of the best available information. Unless political life is able to absorb such image-making the political system is virtually 'closed' to the idea of transforming security. In these respects, withholding and manipulating information deliberately impairs the capacity of citizens to establish a security policy responsive to *their* will.

The main dangers to world peace arise from four complementary structures of militarism that set the security agenda for the governments of the world:

the strategic arms race (East/West rivalry and predominance);

the closely associated managerial dynamics of arms sales, hegemonic geopolitics on a global scale and intervention in the internal affairs of weak states (North/South; East/West; East/East; South/South);

the peripheral war system of proxy war, state-building conflict, and regional rivalry (South/South; East/West; North/South);

the internally repressive tendencies of the militarised state (systemic in scope).[7]

The purpose of Table 10.1 is to summarise the overall perspective. At present, the security function is dominated

Table 10.1   The demilitarisation process

Militarism	→ Demilitarisation	→ Genuine security
I. Strategic arms race	→ Stabilisation, détente, defensive postures	→ Disarmament, peacekeeping, resistance training
II. Hegemonic geopolitics	→ Respect for sovereign rights (including self-determination)	→ World community of diverse peoples
III. Peripheral war system	→ Procedures for peaceful settlement	→ Regional communities of diverse peoples
IV. Internal militarism	→ Human rights; civilian rule; reduced defence sector	→ Humane governance

by the four types of militarism that expose the connections

between geopolitical and imperial elements in world politics, as well as between external war-making and internal
repression. The position of a state within the world political
system may make it more conscious of certain forms of
militarism than others, but the four varieties are in some
real sense pervasive.

Briefly put, the strategic arms race contains the risk of
catastrophic nuclear war. As such, it both constrains and
shifts militarist energies to other arenas, including intervening in struggles for political alignment in the Third
World. This same dynamic underlies peripheral wars where
the antagonists are Third World countries, but the terms of
the conflict are influenced by First World patterns of arms
supply and prior dominance. The three forms of war-fighting
militarism dispose the internal politics that relate the state
of the society to adopt a war-like character, partly because
the military sector assumes control over the wider governing
process and partly because an orientation towards security
for the government generates real antagonisms with security
for the people.

The 'process' imagery is diagrammed to suggest distinct
demilitarising paths. In each instance, the immediate
horizon is specified by the outer limits of reformist logic for
a world essentially constituted by sovereign states. Demilitarisation implies a re-orientation of government identity,
where the content of security is provided by popular will
rather than by the calculations of interests and the protection of privileges set forth on behalf of elites. Whether such
an interim programme of reform is more or less difficult
to achieve than the transformed structural environment of
'genuine security' is a matter of conjecture. What is clear,
however, is the need to combine a series of tangible
reformist steps guided by the comprehensive spirit of demilitarisation with the vision of genuine security based on a
post-state framework of world order. Table 10.1 is deceptive
to the extent that it portrays a sequence of stages (militarism
→ demilitarisation → genuine security). Our thinking is
more 'three dimensional'. Both a long-range vision and a
commitment to tangible steps are necessary and must be
mutually reinforcing from the outset. The presentation is

linear as a convenience. In any event, the experience of the future is sure to be far more complex than any schematic portrayal.

Achieving genuine security means finding the practical means to initiate a process of demilitarisation along each of these four dimensions.[8] This possibility implies a popular social movement, emerging social forces with a definite programme and vision of radical change. The obstacles to demilitarisation can be lessened, but not overcome, within the present political framework of social attitudes, economic privilege and rulership; a movement dedicated to demilitarisation requires an appropriate vision of a transformed structure of governance and it also depends upon a programme of transition that takes specific account of the here and now in various settings around the world.

In this chapter we explore the broad contours of the imagery of security generated by existing structures of militarism, and contrast that imagery with a vision of security suitable for a demilitarising and demilitarised world. Needless to say, the main intellectual challenge, at this stage, is to be bold enough to be responsive to the unprecedented structural scale of challenge, without being utopian in the negative sense of breaking credible links between the means proposed and the ends pursued. One measure of our tragic situation has been the inability, as yet, to fashion non-utopian imagery of transformed security. As a consequence, popular dissatisfaction is tempered by accommodation (e.g. arms control) or becomes demoralised (e.g. passively waiting for the bomb), cynical (e.g. 'it's no use') and susceptible to the simplistic nostrum of fundamentalist appeals.[9]

This tragic circumstance has been especially characteristic of the dynamics of the war system, including its peripheral war and nuclear dimensions. Possibilities of achieving autonomy in relation to North/South militarism and of achieving humane governance in relation to statist militarism are credibly present in the dynamics of national revolution. At the same time, the strategic arms race imposes serious, largely 'invisible', constraints on prospects for other types of demilitarisation.[10] Understanding the interlocking character of these four types of militarism can help to establish the necessary global context for a new image of security. It is also important to realise the extent to which militarism is itself a product of the wider organisational and ideological framework of statism, with its implications of sovereign rights and denial of a global and human community, and its resultant sub-species identity. This framework itself would need to be superseded in the course of finding the grounds on which to oppose militarism.[11]

SECURITY FOR THE PEOPLE: THE AFFIRMATIVE QUEST

A starting-point may be that, in the centres of power, warfare as a central mode of statecraft has largely lost its justification, even from a Clausewitzian/Machiavellian perspective. War, to be an instrument of rational political behaviour, has to be coherent in a means/ends sense. Their endorsement of absolutism was based on the idea that victory on the battlefield was meaningful and that defence of society was possible. When that rationality is lost, war is reduced to a blind, mutually destructive fury. Deterrence is a desperate, largely unsuccessful, effort to distract attention from the irrationality of the overall enterprise by relying on ultra-rational forms of strategic discourse. If deterrence could have been stabilised at minimum levels, with a central objective of mutual reassurance, then perhaps the Clausewitzian/Machiavellian framework would have remained relatively convincing. But the outbreak of a nuclear arms race that is wasteful and dangerous and a set of geopolitical stances ambiguous in their relationship to nuclear war suggest a breakdown of the Clausewitzian/Machiavellian rationale for the war system. The prevalence of peripheral war is partly a reflection of the fact that the manifestly destructive consequences convince leaders of the central militarist state systems that their survival depends on confining war-related phenomena to arenas of indirect encounter.

The basic approach taken here is to suggest that security for the people can be achieved through demilitarisation along each of the four dimensions of militarisation depicted in Table 10.1. Of course, political reality is extremely complex in many respects. Anti-hegemonic demilitarisation may, for instance, contribute in specific instances to the outbreak of a peripheral war. The post-colonial circumstances of Indo-China, the Middle East and the Indian subcontinent are illustrative. There is, alas, no simple blueprint for the promotion of demilitarisation. Positive action depends on the possibilities implicit in a particular setting of international relations. The meaning of 'positive' in this regard can be assessed by reference to world order values (peace, economic well-being, social and political justice, ecological balance and – an overall catchall – humane governance at various levels of social organisation).

These values cannot be effectively promoted within the framework of statist conceptions of security. These conceptions presuppose that security is the province of governmental actors relying mainly on military and diplomatic capabilities (and other resources of strength). Although the language of politicians claims to work on behalf of national interests and the well-being of the whole society, the realities of state power suggest much more particularistic orientations, in terms of class and bureaucratic caste. In effect, large-scale economic interests and entrenched elites shape the definition of public good that gives contours to the idea of security. The revolt against monarchism implicit in the American and French Revolutions was in part a reaction to autocratic war-making and eventually gave rise to popular demands for democratisation of security policy and to governing processes that avoided the creation of permanent military establishments.

Despite these developments, leaders of all states adhered, more or less, to Machiavellian conceptions of statecraft that viewed international society as essentially a species of anarchy. War was implicit in this orientation, and prudent preparations for war were seen as the principal ground for maintaining peace. As state power expanded and as war-making appropriated the latest technological innovations in the art of destruction, notions of restraint receded and the basic distinction between war and peace became blurred.

This process culminated in the introduction of weapons of mass destruction into the calculus of statecraft at a time of ideological and geopolitical rivalry (Cold War) between the two main poles of power in the world. It also coincided with the turmoil created by the widespread efforts of non-Western peoples to achieve autonomy. This turmoil persists, despite the virtual completion of decolonisation, in part because the economic and cultural aspects of Western dominance were not eliminated by the achievement of political independence. As a result, national revolutionary and counter-revolutionary violence and peripheral war persist in the present era of global politics. The combination of these elements creates an increasing risk of general war, a risk that is accentuated by the declining fortunes of both superpowers. Declining empires tend to provoke great wars.

Given this setting, leaders of governments are caught in a maelstrom of forces that they cannot control or shape. Their mode of perception (including that of 'loyal oppositions') is established by the Machiavellian world picture, and their instruments for response are established by militarised bureaucracies.[12] In nuclear settings, this pattern results in a strategic arms race of increasing expense and risk in order to achieve a psychological upper hand in relation to the geopolitical struggles. In non-nuclear settings, or settings where the risk of escalation is perceived as minimal, the overall situation produces a continuous cycle of warfare, resulting in great loss of life and suffering for peoples engulfed by the dual consequences of state-building and peripheral status. More than 140 wars since 1945 have taken an estimated 10–15 million lives. Moderating proposals and gestures are overwhelmed by the bureaucratic/technological dynamic of modern statism.

Perhaps an illustration can clarify this. The popular film *E.T.* describes two modes of encountering a benign extraterrestrial being: the humane innocence of a child's sensibility, which creates mutual trust; and the high-technology methodology of the militarised state, which is predisposed to regard the visitor as a threat which must be dealt with coercively. Those who act for the state are not malicious, but perform roles specified by larger frameworks of paramilitary and technocratic sensibility that define the spectrum of choice. They are virtually helpless, as individuals, to halt the horrifying momentum of state power operating to uphold its version of the public good (protecting the earth by elaborate procedures of quarantine and isolating the extraterrestrial specimen for scientific observation and study). There is no capacity for the statist approach to succeed, given contemporary circumstances, although it could fail in more or less dramatic ways. As *E.T.* makes brilliantly clear, to seek humane, or even prudent, responses from the state to the challenge of an extraterrestrial visit is simply to embrace futility.

Such is our central contention with respect to security. The state cannot respond except within bureaucratic technological frameworks that are themselves the essence of the problem, generating incoherence, false priorities and betrayed values, conceiving of otherness as hostile in design. Table 10.2 expresses this assessment in analytical terms. By discussing system-diminishing, system-maintaining and system-reforming perspectives, it is argued that certain moderating steps can be taken despite structural constraints; that a given government can minimise, to some extent, its degree of involvement in the overall workings of militarisation; and that individuals in positions of authority can engage in responsible action. A sub-argument is that far-reaching system-reforming objectives may, somewhat paradoxically, be more difficult to realise than more ambitious system-transforming goals. Reformism does not have a sufficiently potent social force to challenge entrenched forms of militarism, and can only achieve tactical gains through a bargaining process, carried on within the existing techno-military framework of state power. Such a process has been visible throughout the quest for arms control, each step in the direction of reform being compensated for or cancelled out. For instance, offering a 'no first-use' pledge for nuclear weapons can only be considered if there is a corresponding build-up of conventional weaponry; a mutual freeze can only be established after a prior weapons build-up. System transformation can draw upon populist forces of rising

Table 10.2 Militarisation and Demilitarisation Policies

Dimension of militarism / Policy posture and world order values	Strategic arms race	Hegemonic geopolitics	Peripheral war system	Internal militarism
System-diminishing	Accelerated arms race; first-strike doctrine and systems; East/West antagonism	Interventionary diplomacy; support for Third World militarism	Arms sales with restraints; absence of regional and global peaceful settlement procedures; blatant superpower involvements	Accelerated tendency towards military rule; gross violations of human rights; declining popular sovereignty and democratic participation
System-maintaining	Moderate-paced arms race; flexible targeting; mixed East/West relations	Selective low-profile interventionary diplomacy, within spheres of influence; indirect support for political status quo via international financial institutions	Moderated arms sales; regional procedures; constrained super-power involvement	Countervailing tendencies towards militarisation and democratisation on domestic level; support for ideals of democracy, human rights, and civilian rule

Table 10.2 Continued

Policy posture and world order values	Dimension of militarism			
	Strategic arms race	Hegemonic geopolitics	Peripheral war system	Internal militarism
System-reforming	Minimum deterrence; stablised defence spending; mutual reassurance; freeze; no first use; détente; East/West trade and cultural exchange	Non-interventionary foreign policy with support for new international economic order and North/South global negotiations	Regional resistance to strategic geopolitics; nuclear free zones; elimination of foreign bases, troops, and alliances	Increasing potency of popular movements in support of democracy, human rights, and civilian rule; declining legitimacy of internal militarist forms of governance
System-transforming	Disarming process; renunciation of war; holistic orientation towards foreign policy; human rights and peace	Displacement of state-centric international politics; popular sovereignty on a regional and global, as well as national, basis	Effective regionalism; intra-regional disarming process and peaceful settlement machinery	Humane governance relying on limited coercive procedures within strict constitutional frameworks of due process; leaders accountable for adherence to standards of democracy, human rights, and civilisation

discontent, as well as upon a different set of concerns and identities.

Underlying a system-transforming perspective is a different framework for evaluating reality, danger, otherness: a framework called here a 'holistic world picture'. One property of this holistic world picture is to feel and act upon human identity as a basis for choice that is grounded in contemporary reality alongside varieties of national identity that help clarify choice for adherents of the Machiavellian world picture. The more encompassing holistic framework does not repudiate national identity at all, but expresses this identity in a more holistic spirit. Table 10.2 portrays the overall content of a demilitarising orientation, although in a schematic form and without any 'politics'.

There are several 'fronts' in the struggle (movements opposed to organisations or bureaucracies) against the war system:

> the anti-nuclear movement centred in Europe, Japan and North America, but supported by many non-Western governments and leading citizens;
> the anti-hegemonic struggles of Third World peoples against control of their national, economic, social and cultural destinies;
> movements in support of human rights and democracy, often linked to anti-hegemonic struggles, and drawing support from non-governmental organisations and private citizens.

These movements cover three dimensions of militarism, but do not challenge the peripheral war system; nor do they focus, as yet, on war as such. Such a circumstance is understandable as peripheral wars are, in many respects, derivative from the three other types of militarism; and to challenge peripheral war-making capability would seem to imply, at this stage, assault on the full sovereignty of Third World countries, an implication contained, without doubt, in the First World stress on non-proliferation. It is worth noting that the two great triumphs of revolutionary non-violence in our century (Gandhi against British imperialism, Khomeini against the Pahlavi monarchy) both 'normalised' their movements through participation in militarist frameworks, India more moderately than Iran, but nevertheless in a standard, anti-Gandhian manner. Also, these movements are quite distinct from one another and have no clear image of their longer-range goals, often focusing local political energies on very immediate grievances or anxieties.

Movements against militarism require a greater awareness of the links that stem from the nature of the modern state and from rivalries among states. These links provide the ground for cohesiveness, which in turn could generate a stronger challenge to militarism. Without transforming state/society relations into more democratising forms and without gradually displacing the Machiavellian world picture, it will seem impossible to overcome either the technological momentum of the arms race or to disrupt the basic policy-forming framework.

Furthermore, it is important to explore alternative orientations towards security. Blueprints of centralised peacekeeping in a disarmed world are easy to contrive, but they are not helpful; reality cannot be reduced convincingly to mechanism, and when the attempt is made, most alert readers reject the effort as naive or a mere projection onto the global landscape of home-grown, inapplicable patterns of governance.[13]

What is needed is a clearer feeling of an alternative direction, based on ideas of security implanted to some extent in the experience of societies. Moreover, despite the importance of a more unified critical analysis of militarism, it is important, when it comes to positive security, to make an inquiry based on the specific situation of a given country.

The task of overcoming alienation sufficiently to achieve results on all four planes of the anti-militarist struggle requires, above all else, an understanding of the global context. It is not at all a matter of sentimental or utopian pleas for human solidarity. It is rather an analysis of the nature of oppressive structures sufficiently rigorous to reveal the basis for their genuine elimination, even if the process of elimination takes a long time and proceeds by stages. As we have argued, revolutionary nationalism and anti-imperialism derive support from opposition to mainstream geopolitics in the First World. Similarly, anti-nuclearism and anti-imperialism in the First World reinforce pressures generated by revolutionary nationalism and anti-imperialism. Of course, the short-term impact often seems to move in the opposite direction – Third World challenges intensify First World militarism. Yet this intensification is what exposes the incoherence, distorted priorities and betrayed values of militarism as a source of security even for the citizenry of the powerful. This exposure is what generates an opposition movement, but towards what end?

Several generalisations indicate a sense of direction:

(1) *Struggle of the oppressed.* The starting-point for a revision of security is the awareness of the oppressive character of the rulers' security, as well as the realisation that alternatives are possible and depend on struggle and a persuasive image or images of an alternative, called here people's security.

(2) *Withdrawal of consent and cooperation.* As Gandhi and others have emphasised, and demonstrated, the simple withdrawal of consent and cooperation is a powerful instrument of struggle, especially if guided by a tactically sensitive leader. In Gandhi's words, spoken in 1920, 'the problem before us, therefore, is one of opposing our will to the will of the Government'. Struggle does not necessarily imply violence, and, in fact, where the focus of effort is opposition to militarism, struggle may generally (except possibly *in extremis*) imply a renunciation of violence as a means.

(3) *Empowerment.* The struggle context establishes the 'realism' of the necessary path and its formidable obstacles. The withdrawal of consent demonstrates the power and competence of a mobilised population, and is essential to overcome widespread popular passivity, especially when it comes to challenging the security prerogatives of the state, with an understanding of freedom and responsibility.

Part of empowerment is the 'rediscovery' of competence at the popular level, and the simultaneous exposure of incompetence at official levels. In many separate settings, political leadership at the grassroots level concentrates on making people feel their own competence to proceed as if the government (and its inhibiting capital-intensive assumptions about competence, that is, 'modernisation') did not exist. Mobilising resources at the disposal of ordinary people – no matter how impoverished and uneducated – including their freedom and responsibility to create a future, can be empowering, and contagiously so.[14] This type of empowerment overcomes attitudes of dependence upon which the internal exploitative structures of statism finally rest.

Empowerment can also occur at the collective level, even, to a certain extent, through the medium of government action. Questioning alliance relationships and dependencies can move political leaders and their publics in the direction of self-reliance, which may have the effect of localising militarist structures, but also of confining their role to defensive missions (the Swiss model). Certain forms of self-reliance could be system-diminishing in effect, as, for instance, the widespread acquisition of nuclear weapons by additional states, often portrayed as the most probable consequence of loosening alliance relations. Here too, perhaps, it becomes clear that 'adjustments' at any level of international society that do not include an attack on militarism and war are likely to be absorbed into the Machiavellian frame, possibly even weakening certain stabilising features of the present system that derive from the 'managerial' side of geopolitics.

(4) *Identity: We are all oppressed.* The struggle against militarised security potentially includes the entire human race, including current leaders. These leaders are now exposing their own families, including their direct descendants, to the prospect of a nuclear holocaust. In this sense, militarist identity is never complete, and can be broken down, or at least deeply compromised, eroding the will to oppress. The process of building an awareness of oppression, already well advanced in relation to hegemonic and internal militarism, is begin-

ning to take shape with respect to geostrategic militarism, especially with regard to its most frightening nuclear dimension. Religious leaders are beginning to speak clearly to those in power on these issues, setting up the grounds for withdrawing consent, and even of imposing procedures of accountability by which to assess the behaviour of leaders. Professional groups are beginning to undermine public confidence in the competence of existing structures to provide security; anti-nuclear doctors have been especially effective in this regard, by emphasising their inability to cope with post-attack environments; without the possibility of health care there can be no security.

(5) *Concrete objectives.* It is difficult to mobilise, at this stage, around general security goals. More specific objectives that seem attainable within a short time provide a sense of purpose and build confidence. Thus, opposition to provocative or wasteful weapons systems, to certain patterns of deployment, to first-strike and limited war doctrines, and to the expansion of militarism ('the freeze') have emerged. Of course, it becomes critical to convince those who are active in such movements that their real goals are more ambitious, and that the concrete objectives that now seem attainable are way stations on the path to genuine security.

(6) *Imagery of people's security.* The basic undertaking of security is to promote and sustain varieties of well-being: health, economic and ecological viability; sense of community; trust in leadership; political participation; liberation of human energies and the human spirit. Yet in a world of unequal and antagonistic polities, often with overlapping nationalities and adversary ideologies, some notion of 'defence' remains central to security. A first step would be a new configuration of military capabilities and consciousness based on strictly construed defensive missions; a second, the development of confidence in non-military forms of resistance against attack, the extension of the ethos of non-cooperation and grassroots competence to the situation of resisting occupation and conquest. A third step would

be an increasing reliance on what Thomas Jefferson once called 'an energetic citizenry' rather than a professional military caste to provide the community with security and a fourth, a post-Machiavellian global framework suitable for the interplay of diverse polities, stressing shared destiny and identity.

These dimensions of security for the people provide an orientation. The specific tactics and imagery will be evolved by participants as the struggle of the oppressed against militarism in all its forms proceeds. We do know that to succeed this struggle requires unprecedented resolve and perseverance, which implies having a clear idea of what is necessary. The transparency of this dependence of ends upon sufficiency of means is crucial.

NOTES

1. Rudolph Bahro, 'The SPD and the Peace Movement', *New Left Review* No. 131 (Jan.–Feb. 1982): 21.
2. From W. B. Gallie, *Philosophers of Peace and War* (Cambridge: Cambridge University Press, 1978), p. 49.
3. Well depicted in Jonathan Schell, *The Fate of the Earth* (New York: Knopf, 1982), esp. pp. 3–96; Ruth Adams and Susan Cullen, (eds), *The Final Epidemic: Physicians and Scientists on Nuclear War* (Chicago, Ill.: Education Foundation for Nuclear Science, 1981); Louis René Beres, *Apocalypse: Nuclear Catastrophe in World Politics* (Chicago, Ill.: University of Chicago Press, 1980).
4. Philip Green, *Deadly Logic: The Theory of Nuclear Deterrence* (Columbus, Ohio: Ohio State University Press, 1966).
5. Nationalism should not necessarily be identified with statism, although statists often mobilise popular support for foreign policy by appeals to nationalist sentiments. Nationalism can be anti-statist, as when a minority people seeks 'autonomy' within the state or 'secession' from the state, or when national identity embraces more than one state.
6. See Robert C. Tucker, *Politics as Leadership* (Columbia, Mo.: University of Missouri Press, 1981), esp. Chapter 4, pp. 114–57.
7. For elaboration see Richard Falk, 'A World Order Perspective on Authoritarian Tendencies', New York, Institute for World Order, World Order Models Project. Working Paper No. 9 (1980); Richard Falk, 'Nuclear Weapons and the End of Democracy', *International Foundation for Development Alternatives Dossier* 28 (1982): 55–64.

8. Explored in more detail in Richard Falk and Yoshikazu Sakamoto, 'Demilitarization I and II', Special Issues, *Alternatives*, Vol. 6, Nos. 1 and 2 (1980).

9. Cf. discussion of fundamentalism in Robert Jay Lifton's section of Lifton and Falk, *Indefensible Weapons* (New York: Basic Books, 1982).

10. For instance, the international arms race generally works against tendencies towards democratisation or redemocratisation. See Chapter 5 above.

11. For explorations along these lines see Richard Falk, Samuel S. Kim and Saul H. Mendlovitz, (eds.), *Toward a Just World Order* (Boulder, Col.: Westview Press, 1982); see also Richard Falk and Samuel S. Kim, 'An Approach to World Order Studies and the World System', New York, Institute for World Order, World Order Models Project, Working Paper No. 22, 1982.

12. Cf. discussion in Falk section of Lifton and Falk, *Indefensible Weapons*.

13. For critiques of globalist solutions along these lines see F. H. Hinsley, *Power and the Pursuit of Peace* (Cambridge: Cambridge University Press, 1963); and Walter Schiffer, *The Legal Community of Mankind* (New York: Columbia University Press, 1956).

14. For discussion along these lines see Paulo Freire, *Pedagogy of the Oppressed* (New York: Herder and Herder, 1972); *Pedagogy in Process: The Letters to Guinea-Bissau* (New York: Seabury, 1978); see also Rajni Kothari, 'Toward a Just World', New York: Institute for World Order, World Order Models Project, Working Paper No. 11, 1980.

11   The Future of World Order*

Perhaps more profoundly than any international lawyer of our time, Wolfgang Friedmann combined a deep humanistic commitment to an improved system of world order with a lively awareness that proposals for global reform must first pass tests of political feasibility to warrant serious attention. It is a great tribute, I think, to the strength of Professor Friedmann's vision that he could accept the harsh realities of international relations, especially given the persistence and intensification of the war system, without over the years growing either sentimental or cynical, that is, without succumbing to the easy advocacy of either instant world government or the facile endorsement of what was once called *realpolitik*, but which might now be more easily recognised if identified as Kissingerism or for that matter, Brzezinskiism.

It is within this intermediate zone of what I would call practical idealism that Friedmann's many notable contributions were made. He saw clearly, and far earlier than most of his colleagues, that the mixture of nuclear weapons technology, demographic and ecological pressure, and massive poverty were overwhelming the problem-solving capacity of a fragmented system of sovereign states. In this sense, his pioneering work in the 1960s on a series of functional issues anticipated the current emphasis on 'the management of interdependence'.[1] Having ruled out both

---

* A portion of this essay was initially delivered as a part of the Yencken Lectures at Australian National University on 10–11 September 1974.

utopian blueprints of a new world order and dysutopian visions of decay, Friedmann believed that the best hope for genuine, substantial progress in world affairs arose from the functional logic of international cooperation based on mutual advantage in the many areas of proliferating interaction. This hope rested on the conviction that governments would become more cooperative with one another as they came to realise that territorial interests could be protected in an interdependent world only by entering into an ever-expanding web of cooperative international arrangements.

In this spirit, the future of the oceans was an appropriate test case of the reformist potentiality of the state system. Wolfgang Friedmann, characteristically, sensed ahead of most the pivotal significance of the rush to exploit the mineral wealth of the oceans for the future of world order.[2] As was also characteristic he tried to lend support to as progressive a legal solution as was consistent with the political framework of the state system, perhaps pushing expectations slightly beyond the horizon of what others deemed realistic but still analysing options in terms that were sufficiently politically relevant to influence serious debate.

It is alarming, but not surprising, that Wolfgang Friedmann's death left an intellectual vacuum in international legal studies that has not been filled. Friedmann's particular brand of functionalism-searching for areas of convergent state interest as the building blocks of a burgeoning international law of cooperation – is peculiarly relevant in this period of resource diplomacy and of a broad call for 'a new international economic order'.

This chapter does not even pretend to fill this vacuum left by Friedmann's departure in the slightest, but it does draw inspiration from his abiding concern with understanding what opportunities for creative human action existed within a given set of political constraints. Friedmann was very aware of the tension between freedom and necessity in relation to the work of global reform. His emphasis was upon the opportunities for action once the elements of necessity – that is, the practical constraints – are taken into account. Friedmann's work and life are a ringing testimonial to the reality of freedom, and hence, the responsibility it entails:

The first and most fundamental principle is the moral necessity to accept freedom of choice and a sense of individual responsibility in the future of mankind. The historian may well regard political developments as conditioned by laws of growth and decline, or record helplessness in the face of circumstances. But the essential factor in such development has always been human behaviour, and only the conviction that we are enchained by the events of the past can compel us to believe in the inevitability of developments in our own time.[3]

In the spirit of this affirmation, I seek to clarify the way students of world order might think about the prospects for global reform. Implicit in this inquiry is my belief that existing frameworks are partially outmoded because the premises of the state system have been eroded to a large extent. In view of this situation it is difficult to take the traditional framework for granted in considering what kinds of incremental changes are feasible and desirable. As Wolfgang Friedmann clearly understood, it is the structure itself that is changing, and yet elements of continuity persist. My effort, then, is to identify a framework appropriate for a period of structural transition.

Alfred North Whitehead suggests that it is the mixture of blind historical forces and powerful moral visions that combine to destroy old modes of order and create new ones. For the European society of this time, it was steam and democracy that had displaced the old order of privilege and status, whereas looking backwards in the history of the West it was the barbarians and Christianity that mounted their successful assault upon the Roman Empire. Whitehead observes that:

The well-marked transition from one age to another can always be traced to some analogues to Steam and Democracy, or – if you prefer it – to some analogues to Barbarians and Christians. Senseless agencies and formulated aspirations cooperate in the work of driving mankind from its old anchorage. Sometimes the period of change is an age of hope, sometimes it is an age of despair.[4]

I believe that human society is now undergoing such a transition from one age to another, but not on the level of an empire or civilisation – such as Rome or the West – but a transition of greater magnitude, encompassing the planet and the entire human species. To grasp this unprecedented process of transition it is initially necessary to depict both the 'senseless agencies' and the 'formulated aspirations' that are driving the human species beyond its separated condition of fragmentation and deadly sub-species rivalry.[5]

It is also necessary to consider whether grounds for hope exist. Whitehead's dichotomy of hope and despair in an age of transition would, as of the moment, lead most of us to identify ours as one of despair. Whitehead observed that: 'When mankind has slipped its cables, sometimes it is bent on the discovery of a New World, and sometimes it is haunted by the dim sound of the breakers dashing on the rocks ahead.'[6] The connections between constructive and destructive energies seem more dialectical than Whitehead's comments suggest. That is, it is 'the dim sound of the breakers dashing on the rocks ahead' that may summon the vital forces needed to embark on the perilous journey to 'a New World'; it is the challenge of the future that summons the response in the present.

Proceeding from this orientation I propose to consider the political life of the human species in relation to its impending transition to a form of order beyond the state system, and to the unresolved character of the order that awaits. Within this indeterminate future lies forever locked beyond full disclosure the answer as to whether it is plausible to be hopeful about the future of the planet.

The mood of despair rises out of an interpretation of basic international trends, and interpretation that was discredited as alarmist as recently as five years ago but is now almost an ingredient of conventional wisdom on the part of almost all informed observers who are not government officials. This despair results from the realisation that 'the senseless agencies' are posing grave threats to the stability of political relations, and even to the survival and well-being of the human species and the habitability of the planet. Nuclear hazard, resource depletion, population pressure are the barbarians at the gates. The search for equity, the spreading awareness of deprivation and exclusion, and intense demands for justice and redistribution of wealth and influence constitute 'the formulated aspirations' of the age, often blandly described as 'rising expectations', 'revolutionary energies', or 'the development imperative'. Put simply, the planet is too crowded, its resource base too constrained, its social structure too hierarchical, and its political structure fragmented and overly responsive to the concerns and interests of dominant groups to allow for an easy transition to a global community where the needs of the species for survival with dignity could be satisfied. As such, the pressures are mounted against mechanisms ill-conceived for such global integration, and the options narrow to various frantic efforts to stave off disintegration by refusing to heed the formulated aspirations of peoples. Can this holding operation of the state system succeed? Do we as citizens for a given time and place and members of a species want such a strategy to work during our lifetime? Are there alternatives for the future that transform world order without breaking it asunder?

Despite 'the dim sound of the breakers dashing on the rocks ahead' the statist logic proceeds more rigorously than ever. No organised society has yet seriously proposed a new basis of organisation for human affairs. Political leaders seem particularly obtuse about planning for the future; they seem occupationally committed to projecting an attitude of hope, especially when the case for despair is overwhelming. Why is this the case? Because the legitimacy of government rests, even in non-democratic societies, on its capacity to cope adequately with the basic problems of its peoples. But suppose these problems cannot be solved. Then it is tempting in the extreme to deny their existence, or more plausibly, to underestimate their seriousness. As matters now stand, the great challenges facing humankind are approached, if at all, with the most effusive tact whenever national sovereignty is in issue. Why is this? The answer is relatively simple. The constructive forces trying to fashion some kind of world order response to the dangers posed by these senseless agencies are trying to devise some way to entice governments to tiptoe up to the edge. So like luring to the water a child who cannot yet swim, the need to offer national leaders constant reassurance is intense. Hence, those who work with or for bureaucracies on these problems are caught up in a terrible dilemma – either governments will do nothing at all or they must be told that nothing will encroach upon their traditional prerogatives if they display the good faith to consider them. Therefore, sovereignty, at once, the root enabling and disabling attribute of the world order system, must be uncritically reaffirmed in the very context in which its traditions are incompatible with reaching real solutions.[7] Good illustrations of this prevailing mood were the statements made in the summer of 1974 at the opening session of the UN World Population Conference held at Bucharest. Even relative optimists about international prospects, such as John P. Lewis, consider recent population growth as 'inexorably ominous', a 'clearly non-sustainable' surge.[8] Overcoming this situation by a continuing reliance upon the traditional *laissez-faire* approach in which governments are asked to do no more than to celebrate the dire conditions that exist in the world seems totally unrealistic. But it is precisely this sanctimonious tone of concern without any movement towards accountability that was struck at Bucharest, which was, indeed, the unavoidable price of holding a meeting of governments on world population policy at this time. The 1974 meeting in Bucharest on population policy could be held because governments were reassured that they would not be asked to cede their sovereign control over the subject-matter, nor even expected to abandon pro-natalist postures toward the future.[9] Note that it is not being argued here that the state system is incompatible with a responsible world population policy, but only with a Hegelian view of sovereign prerogative, a view that was dangerous and romantic in the worst sense even at the moment of its utterance.

The Hegelian view of state sovereignty was endorsed at Bucharest. Nicolae Ceausescu of Romania, leader of the host country, assured the delegates in his welcoming remarks that every country 'has the sovereign right to promote that demographic policy . . . that it considers most suitable, consonant with its national interests, without any outside interference.' Even the Secretary-General of the United Nations, Kurt Waldheim, felt obliged to say that whatever action is proposed at Bucharest 'emphatically recognises the prerogatives of national sovereignty.'[10]

In the background, of course, are countries like Brazil, Argentina, Czechoslovakia, and many others which pursue avowedly or operatively pro-natalist or *laissez-faire* policies. Indeed, the Brazilian government announced only weeks before sending its delegation to Bucharest that it seeks a doubling of its present population by the end of the century so that it might cross the 200 million threshold by the year 2000.[11] Her leaders, probably correctly, regard population size as one critical credential for access to superpower status. Even further in the background, is the deteriorating world food situation, the deepening pockets of starvation, and the growing belief that mass famines in the Indian subcontient and elsewhere in Asia, Africa and Latin America are virtually inevitable in the years ahead.[12] World food reserves have been steadily falling over the past decade or so. The most trusted indices of food security are the per cent of reserves as a share of annual grain consumption and the number of days at present consumption levels that the reserves would hold out. The figures in 1961 were 26 per cent and 95, whereas the estimates for 1974 are 7 per cent and 27 days; even in absolute quantities deterioration is evident – the reserve stock in 1961 was 154 million metric tons, whereas the estimated figure for 1974 is 89 million.[13] Taken in conjunction with the increases in world population, the decline in the stock of food reserves indicates a dangerous vulnerability to mass starvation for the world as a whole.

Also in 1974 the Executive Board of UNICEF issued a Declaration of Emergency because of the dangerous situation confronting 400–500 million children in Asia, Africa and Latin America. In the words of the Declaration, 'The Board concludes that an emergency situation faces many of those children and believes that it is the Board's duty to call this danger to the attention of the world community.'[14] The tragic situation in the Sahel is already familiar, afflicting some 25 million people with the danger, now fortunately somewhat alleviated, of starvation. A tribe in northern Chad, suffering through eight years of drought, all its cattle dead and most of its camels gone, was faced by an outbreak of diptheria among its undernourished children who were too weak to resist its effects. When Morse Pensah, an FAO administrator for West Africa offered to send drugs, the tribal leaders begged him not to do so. 'Starvation, they told him, would be too slow a death. Let diphtheria rage.'[15]

If the dangers posed were to other sectors of world society than to those Fouad Ajami has referred to as 'those who do not matter', to 'the marginals' as the more neo-Darwinian commentators often put it, then we would also share the UNICEF atmosphere of emergency.[16] These problems will remain abstract, as do all questions of justice, until the victims pose threats that are perceived as dangerous and credible by those with the power to change the situation. It remains uncertain whether the hungry masses will allow us to forget them, whether they will die politely and quietly, or will strike back in some way at the cruelty of their destiny.

At a gathering in the United States not long ago, the novelist Bernard Malamud reacted to this kind of question: 'If it's true what you're saying, then what do we do about it. I don't want to live in a world where 400 million children are in danger of either dying from starvation or growing up deformed by malnutrition.' In a sense Malamud is saying that the moral question is prior to the political question – that even if millions will starve in peace it is not in our interest as human beings to let this happen. Can we prevent this? Whose decision shall it be? It is, of course, true that the task of formulating a common world population policy to be uniformly applied is vastly complicated by the unevenness of national situations and their official perception. Thus, some governments sense different priorities about the relative importance of inhibiting population growth, have different ideas and traditions about the normative costs of doing so, have different views as to why population growth is a menace and, therefore, what to do about it. This condition of unevenness is so fundamental that it virtually precludes the formation, even in years ahead, of a global consensus on what should be done at national levels. The most that can be expected, as the bad effects of continued population growth become more widely appreciated, is that governments might try to strike a world order bargain of the sort that is being attempted at present with respect to ocean resources. Here, too, unevenness of situation and perceptions preclude a consensus; hence, to reach agreement it is necessary to strike a bargain through compromise and tradeoff. Even if governments negotiate an agreement that commands wide assent it would not be assured that it could be implemented in a context of rapidly shifting perceptions as to what is reasonable and fair.

The American Secretary of Agriculture, Earl Butz, has spoken of food as power, and so it is. Food experts report that 'North America today' controls 'a larger share of the world's exportable surplus of grains than the Middle East does of current world oil exports.'[17] Because of geopolitics Egypt will receive large grain exports from the United States, because of geoeconomics other Middle Eastern countries will also receive preferential treatment. Lester Brown said, at Bucharest, because of physical factors such as drought and climate changes cutting into North American food output, the United States 'might soon become the arbiter in decisions as to which nations starve and which survive' as 'American surpluses, if any, will be insufficient to feed all those demanding food.'[18]

It is significant that Brown's comments were made at a non-governmental forum organised at Bucharest to compensate for the insufficiency of governmental perspectives. It was the same at the UN Conference on the Human Environment held at Stockholm. To find out what is needed to be and should be done about the environment it was necessary to attend non-governmental counter-conferences and heed voices like those of Barry Commoner, Paul Ehrlich, Dai Dong, and the Oi Committee; but to find out, alas, what could be done it was necessary to attend the desultory and ritualistic intergovernmental sessions.[19]

But even this distinction is not without difficulties. After Lester Brown spoke at Bucharest he was challenged by an African delegate in the audience: 'You in the developed countries have the paper, and we have to read what you put on it. You want us to go back to our villages and take your pills. You over-intellectualised everything. Why don't you listen to us for a change?' In reporting the incident Malcolm Browne tells us that 'She was applauded as she stalked out of the hall.'[20] There are no wise men from the rich, white, dominant part of the world who have any moral authority with the poor and weak of the world. And reverting for a moment to Lewis's analysis of population pressure we should recall that he linked it to 'widening international income disparities' and regarded both tendencies as 'even more inexorably ominous than the appearance of worldwide wars, the invention of nuclear weapons, or the galloping hegemony of the automobiles'.[21] There are two points here: first, the need to listen to spokespeople from the victim societies and secondly, the insufficiency of the sort of technocratic quick fixes that appealed even to genuinely concerned individuals and governments in the favoured portions of the world. In this crucial sense, current world order challenges are overwhelmingly political and moral. What changes are needed in social, economic, and political organisations at the national and global levels to deal with world poverty? How can such changes be brought about?

In the quite different context of energy policy the results of pressure on the state system are the same: namely, not less, but more statism. The United States under Richard Nixon initiated Project Independence to assure the country of national self-sufficiency in energy supplies by the 1980s. Gerald Ford in his first major speech as President told a joint session of Congress: 'We must not let last winter's energy crisis happen again. I will push Project Independence for our own good and the good of others.'[22] Side-effects of Project Independence represent a boost for the nuclear power industry, a further relaxation of safety standards, and a growing unwillingness to impede resource development for reasons of environmental protection. Similarly, the main response to the new wealth of the oceans and to the problems of fisheries from overfishing and pollution is to increase, not decrease, the role of sovereign prerogatives.

Instead of international management for human benefit, the probable new line of development is a carving up of the most valuable portions of the oceans into quasi-sovereign coastal zones of 200 miles or more.

The same story is evident with regard to the multinational corporation. The principal response to its great power and penetration capacity is not what we might have expected or hoped for, namely, the creation of an effective framework of international regulation of business to serve the general welfare, but rather an enhancement of the economic role of national governments so as to enable a greater statist capability to strike a better national bargain.[23]

We find the same pattern evident elsewhere. The protection of the world environment provides yet another illustration of the pattern, a poignant one because of the extent to which the planetary coherence of the biosphere is the most fundamental expression of the inability of artificially demarcated political actors to cope with ecological decay.[24]

Perhaps, the most telling context of all is the evolution of the war system in the 32 years since the Hiroshima explosion. Increasingly, we find an abandonment by the superpowers of any commitment to disarmament or even denuclearisation. Arms control goals increasingly do little more than place high ceilings on arms spending that justify increasing defence budgets rather than the reverse. Indeed, we find an opposite tendency. Superpower status and respect do seem to follow from the acquisition of nuclear weapons. China understood this, India's nuclear explosion was a further testimony to this wisdom. Brazil seems to grasp the relevance of nuclear status to its superpower aspirations, a natural complement to its unabashed pronatalism. And Richard Nixon, in perhaps his most dubious diplomatic initiative, promised nuclear power plants to several governments in the Middle East during his visit in the spring of 1974; the Soviet Union has, in the meantime, stepped forward with its own offers of nuclear generosity. Instead of gilded bird cages or sculptured ivories imperial ceremonies of ingratiation involve the bequest of nuclear reactors, which bring the recipient to the very edge of a nuclear weapons capability. With increased oil prices raising import costs the pressure on several key governments to earn foreign exchange by arms sales is greater than ever before. Several key industrial countries are virtually locked into a major arms sales programme – in 1973 estimated at $8.5 billion for the United States alone – to avoid economic collapses. In the Western press India was lectured about its irresponsible decision to walk across the nuclear tripwire at the very time Richard Nixon was engaged in his Middle Eastern nuclear diplomacy. Again, the impulse towards collective self-destruction is evident: instead of initiating a process of denuclearisation through, for instance, a formal declaration of no first use of nuclear weapons, the strong and powerful nuclear actors pointlessly censure and even punish the weak and poor for their failure to impose on themselves a regime of nuclear self-denial.[25] The irony of the posture is not lost, but neither are the dangers of accelerated proliferation abated.

This double standard of nuclear powers is resented especially by states with the potential to acquire nuclear status, and it parallels the more diffuse anger felt by poorer countries when told to limit *their* populations for the sake of humanity. This resentment was effectively expressed by M. Anandakrishnan, an India diplomat:

In the last few weeks there have been reports of seven nuclear explosions (only two underground), each several times more powerful than India's. The Nuclear Non-proliferation Treaty provided unlimited license for a handful of nuclear-weapons countries to proliferate their weapons while tying the hands of other countries even on research for peaceful uses. India would not sign such a discriminatory treaty.[26]

On such an issue of reciprocity and equity the governments are more restrained than their peoples. According to a poll conducted among highly educated Indians some weeks after this explosion, two-thirds of the respondents wanted India to make the bomb despite Indira Gandhi's repeated pledges to the contrary.[27]

Even reactionary, pro-Western governments acknowledge the impropriety of the industrial rich telling the developing poor to exercise self-restraint for the sake of the planet. Aranjo Castro, Brazil's Ambassador to the United

States, put the point as follows, in a letter to the *New York Times*:

> I have never seen in your editorial policies any sign or any inkling of a suggestion to the effect of the non-desirability of further expansion of the US economy, although this nation has attained unheard of levels of development and industralisation. . . . And we are likewise puzzled by the fact that those who propose some 'limits to growth' fail to propose any rational limit to underdevelopment and poverty.[28]

Of course, there is a double irony present, because whereas Ambassador Castro is absolutely correct in his indictment, it applies even more directly to his own government, which has subordinated the claims of its poor so as to further satisfy the greed of its native rich.[29] Besides, the foreign investor and multinational corporation, that is, the rich sector of world society, has been a main benefactor of Brazil's refusal to heed 'the limits to growth'. These comments on current developments exhibit a mixture of genuine concern and deliberate confusion that is emanating from the dominant portions of world society, those that are at once somewhat attentive to 'the breakers dashing on the rocks ahead' and often responsible for sustaining the dangerous situation.

The case of India is, perhaps, the most ominous. The size and population of India, the commitment of its leaders to building a decent society, the relative absence of repression, the major effort by the government to deal with population growth, and food shortages, the strength of Gandhian ideas of non-violence and the recent nuclear explosion combine to make India a critical arena, one that is very discouraging at the moment.[30] The celebration of Independence Day on 15 August 1974 was the grimmest in the 27 years since India regained political independence. Indira Gandhi could tell her people nothing better than that 'Losing courage has never helped. . . . The people of India have never been crushed under any burden.' An economist, Prem Shankar Jha, writing in *The Times of India*, observed that 'After a quarter century of effort, the goals the country set for itself seem actually to have receded from view.' Mrs Gandhi finished her speech at Red Fort by assuring her people that 'the shortages are not of an extent as to make them unbearable.' She told her audience that 'We may have to modify our habits, change traditional ways and we may also have to suffer a bit.' But she concluded 'To believe that nothing is getting done or can be done, and to get utterly dismayed would be truly a dangerous thing.'[31] Such an assurance was set forth at a time when at least 200 million Indians are reliably reported living below the very low poverty line of $40 earnings per year. Mrs Gandhi was right to fear the political consequences of a sense of hopelessness – it sharpens the prospects into a choice between undesirable extremes: repressive violence from the elite or the mass. Put differently, such conditions invite the choice between the Brazilian solution and the Chinese solution to the challenge of development in a context of misery and inequity. The resurgence of Naxalite terror in Calcutta and the nuclear explosion in Rajasthan are among the indications that India, as now constituted, is moving in the direction of adopting drastic strategies. What possible bargain could be struck on a global level that could allow India to find a way out that did not presuppose repression at home and danger abroad? And what governments would have any incentive to reach such a bargain?

Bitter struggles in many parts of the world suggest a human willingness in situations where deprivation is acutely sensed to resort to the politics of desperation. The pervasive threat posed by terrorism is part of the critical context of danger. Governments unable to meet the needs of their people and unwilling to embark on the difficult kind of reforms that might change the situation are also unable and unwilling to abide by the dynamics of political self-determination. A dreadful cycle of violence ensues, the terror of insurgent factions being abetted by the repressive regime of incumbent governments. In a transnational setting, the desperation of militant Palestinians is suggestive, as well, of the extent to which the politics of desperation is not curtailed by a 'law and order' calculus of the relation among forces. The killings of Israeli athletes at the Munich Olympics in 1972 and the Maalot massacre of Israeli schoolchildren in 1974 bears grim witness, not so much to the fanatical acts themselves or to the depravity of the perpetrators, as to their effectiveness in piercing the veil of public indifference. The point here is that various forms of terror arising from situations of extreme discontent provide a pretext and rationale for militarised civic life throughout the world, an atmosphere that is antagonistic to all efforts to unfreeze the status quo, even efforts that are designed to conserve what is most valuable about it.

What I am saying by way of diagnosis, then, is suggestive of what that archetypal American soldier said of a destroyed South Vietnamese village: 'we have had to destroy the village in order to save it.' Put into the rhetoric of world order – 'our leaders are destroying the state system in order to save it.' In neither context is it mindless destruction – it is just a matter of carrying a serviceable logic in one historical setting into a new setting where it becomes unserviceable. As Erik Erikson observed, 'the facts are getting out of hand.' Or reverting to Whitehead, the senseless agencies are not being neutralised by the formulated aspirations and so, indeed, the sound of the breakers dashing on the rocks ahead seems closer, more ominous. It is in this historical situation that I think we need to face questions about whether we can construct a system of world order capable of sustaining life on earth in a manner that does not violate our elemental sense of decency. I think these questions need to be posed with all the seriousness at our disposal, by citizens in all parts of the world, and not just by those with paper enough to write books. New sparks of political consciousness must be struck if we are going to be able to effectuate a world order solution that serves the interests of the human species as a whole; the only viable moral premise for politics in the ecological age is an anthropological one.

The confusion now current may be a prelude to clarity. The biblical parable of the Tower of Babel is acquiring an uncomfortable aptness; the Lord said: 'Come let us go down, and there confuse their language, that they may not understand one another's speech . . . and they left off building the city.' Part of our deficiency concerns the knowledge at our disposal, especially for those of us interested in global reform. In this sense, it is necessary to find a means to transcend the confrontation between a food expert like Lester Brown and an angered African delegate who wants to hear about solutions, not problems. Obviously, knowledge tempered by humility is needed; obviously, also a holistic outlook that is integrative in stance is called for to overcome the angle of vision appropriate for a world organised into sovereign parts. My central proposition is that for better or for worse, for richer and for poorer, the world will be organised as a whole. It is a matter of making the most of the free play that still exists within such a constrained prospect. Before advancing a positive perspective of my own, I would like to consider briefly the mainstream dialogue on the direction of global reform.

Not so long ago Hedley Bull has described 'the construction of a viable international order' as 'the central issue of international relations in our times'. To achieve this result it will be necessary, Professor Bull tells us, to form a consensus among 'the deeply divided groups of which world society today is composed'. And Professor Bull warns, and I agree, that 'No consensus is possible that does not take account of the demands of African and Asian countries for political, economic and racial justice, and these cannot be satisfied without drastic change in some of the traditional attitudes of the Western powers.'[32]

In a sense, Professor Bull's call for consensus is conceptually, but not normatively, equivalent to a similar call that has been voiced from time to time by Henry Kissinger. But the equivalence is deceptive. What Kissinger seems to have in mind is moderating Great Power relations and ignoring, or at most placating, Third World demands for a more equitable internal order. It is a consensus, if at all, only among a few critical actors and it seeks to achieve order without first satisfying justice demands.[33] Professor Bull's solution looks towards what is, in effect, a new social contract of global scope whereby governments cooperate over time in creating a reasonably fair and equitable world system where the stake in stability is high all around.[34] The political foundation for such a new order appears to derive, in part, from an appeal to self-interest (without such a consensus 'the centre cannot hold' and 'the blood-dimmed tide of anarchy' will result) and, in part, from our sense of decency (many people do care about the sufferings of others enough to help with their elimination especially if the alternative is to face a hostile, dangerous challenge).[35]

It is a momentous question to ask whether the governments of the world are, under any set of conditions, capable of achieving and acting upon the enlightened awareness presupposed by such a consensus, as well as to determine with as much precision as possible the extent of dislocation that would be required to give it effect. Before the realities of resource scarcity, and the wider constraints, embodied in the phrase 'the limits to growth', were assimilated, there existed a widely shared and politically convenient conviction that the proliferation of dynamic growth models from the rich industrial countries could gradually cut the shackles of world poverty without requiring painful adjustments or sacrifices by rich and powerful countries; on the contrary, such self-serving Western pundits as Herman Kahn argued that the greater the growth of the rich the quicker would the plight of the poor be alleviated. But now, as the world teeters on the brink of mass famine and economic collapse, there is also a growing realisation that growth dynamics are unlikely to provide the material basis for an equitable international order. Indeed, the stark realisations caused by the 1973–74 world crisis, with its sharply higher oil prices, has brought poorer countries (and even advanced industrial states such as Italy) closer than ever to a condition of chronic bankruptcy. The hopes of just a few years ago kindled by foreign aid, developmental economics and 'the green revolution' have faded, and it now seems that a combination of economic and physical factors will make it increasingly difficult to keep the world food supply growing fast enough even to meet highly inadequate current per capita consumption standards.

It is within this setting that my disagreements with Secretary Kissinger on the one side and Professor Bull on the other take shape. These disagreements can be formulated in a simple way:

it may be possible, but it is highly undesirable to achieve

the kind of solution that Secretary Kissinger appears to favour:

it would be desirable, but it seems virtually impossible to achieve the sort of solution that Professor Bull proposes.

Such an assessment follows from the discussion of the global setting that has already been made. For the Kissinger type of consensus to take hold requires an agreement on moderation among the main centres of state power that presently exist in international relations; the cement for such an agreement would be mutual respect for a favourable status quo, the need for coordinated efforts to maintain political order and economic viability, and a shared renunciation of any serious effort to gain position or power at the expense of other governmental participants in this directorate of the rich and powerful. Implicit in this scheme is a large role for the multinational corporation (and its socialist equivalent) which inclines both politics and economics in a regressive direction, but not necessarily rightwards. What the multinational corporation requires is order and predictability. Therefore, it is not surprising that big businessmen return home to America enthusiastic whether they have been to Peking or Rio de Janeiro. Either China or Brazil is a positive model as they share in common a capacity to provide domestic order. What is intolerable is uncertainty, especially of a sort associated with popular discontent. Therefore, Argentina is a disfavoured economic setting, not because its government is antagonistic to business enterprise, but because the leaders and police have not yet preempted all the political space and succeeded in suppressing political dissent, terrorism and kidnapping. What I am suggesting is that the multinational corporation perspective is, or at least pretends to be, increasingly non-ideological, demanding from host governments only a high degree of order with respect to its economic operations. To achieve such order is almost certain to entail coercion, and such coercion will be needed through time if no social transformation at the bottom is involved.

Thus the China and Brazilian models are not really equivalent at all either in effect or in the mind's eye of the multinational corporate elite. China, by means of a long revolution, reconstituted state power to promote a new economic order for its people, eliminating the widest income disparities and, seemingly, dealing with poverty, although not without inflicting hardships on a significant portion of its population. Brazil, in contrast, has experienced a counter-revolution dominated by a conservative military elite, its economy has been organised around considerations of GNP and profitability, with very little of benefit accruing to the bottom 75 per cent of its population. A continuing brutal programme of repression has been institutionalised without even the compensating benefits of social transformation. This Brazilian strategy is centred on development under the aegis of the multinational corporation, which by the nature of its operation is heavily focused on servicing the top layers of a mass economy – that is, electric appliances, cars, middle-class luxuries, rather than clothes, schools, medical facilities. Until recently it could at least be said that the Brazilian model was easier to shake off than the kind of bureaucratic socialism associated with the communist world. But I am afraid this is no longer the case. Advances in the art of counter-insurgency politics have included the development of bureaucratic and para-military efficacy that make it exceedingly difficult, if not impossible, to organise an effective opposition even if mass discontent exists.

Given the extent of world poverty and the degree of dissatisfaction with inequities, such a Kissingerian consensus at the top would not succeed in sustaining order and stability at the bottom without brute force and efficient bureaucracy, especially depending on authority being delegated out to repressive intermediate regimes. In essence, the implication of the Kissinger approach, it hardly matters whether the goal is witting or not, is to vie for a post-Allende Chile solution or, what is the same, but in a less spectacular mode, the Brazil solution, i.e. alliances with highly repressive governments that rule and impose their will without either soliciting the consent or meeting the needs of the governed. And more than just alliances. Disclosures show a pattern of CIA interventions to help tip the balance of domestic forces so as to allow Brazilian solutions to prevail in the domestic play of forces. The militarisation of politics already is accepted as normal within the Soviet bloc and therefore its extension to non-communist poor countries would not create any serious ethical problems for political managers in Moscow. Quite the contrary. Whether this solution would be stable would depend very much on the extent to which the mutual respect and perceived shared interests at the top were sufficient to generate the central guidance procedures needed to manage the complex interdependencies of the world economy and of the global ecosystems.[36] It would also depend on sustaining the counter-insurgency postures of many governments over a long period of time. For reasons that I have already suggested this stability model is likely in the future to require more comprehensive and harsh methods and to spread its tentacles to many additional societies. In the United States we are still, despite the Nixon demise, wrestling with the structural problems of what has come to be called 'the imperial presidency', which involves in its most extreme manifestations the adoption by the government of a counterinsurgency stance toward the American citizenry, although fortunately, still of a mild variety. In several other liberal democracies in Europe and Asia polarising moods are unfolding as the mounting inability of moderate, consensual government to solve a lengthening agenda of problems grows manifest. Rather than a reversal of international traditions of selfishness so far as the needs of others are concerned, I notice mainly gathering neo-Darwinian storm clouds in which scarcity on many sides (oil, food, money, space, clean air and water) makes the choice between 'us' and 'them' even easier than in the past to make on purely selfish grounds. Liberal ideology, supported by the industrial revolution and the credibility of an idea of progress, was premised on evading or overcoming the neo-Darwinian issue altogether by saying 'us' first and then 'them' with enough for 'all' in due course. The United States has been and, I suppose, remains the principal testing ground for this ideology, and hence, Kissinger's repudiation of its ethical premise of human solidarity is especially significant at a time when such a premise no longer seems sustainable. I would emphasise not only Kissinger's repudiation of the politics of empathy but the extent to which his diplomatic stance seems widely admired even by foreign statesmen.

I am led to the pessimistic conclusion that Kissinger's solution – the so-called structure of peace – might work for the world in the same perverse sense that South Africa's or Soviet Russia's structure of peace has 'worked'. It is this form of 'peace' that is being plotted on the geopolitical drawing-boards of the powerful, perhaps not in the conspiratorial spirit these words imply, but as a natural expression of convergent assessments as to what is desirable and what is possible by leaders in the critical states of the world.

In opposition to this kind of imposed world order Professor Bull proposes a consensus that is wide enough to satisfy the minimal needs, at least, of voices of discontent. Such a proposal, especially, coming as it does from such an influential and realistic student of international relations as Hedley Bull, deserves our most careful and sympathetic attention. Of course, Professor Bull, so far as I know, has not yet spelled out what he has in mind, what kinds of adjustments would be appropriate and necessary to strike that historic social contract which would be the vital expression of a new international order. In my view, governments cannot hope to effectuate such a consensus without prior social and economic transformations on a national level – the domestic disparities are too great, the scarcities too pronounced, the capital surplus too restricted, the capacities for disruption too dispersed and potent, the erosion of economic viability too evident, and the energies of the entrenched elites too formidable to reach any kind of workable consensus among governments as to what is fair and just in the world. Furthermore, the proliferation of centres of national decision make it impractical to establish the central guidance mechanisms that are needed to cope satisfactorily with the growing challenges of economic and ecological interdependence, challenges that range from assuring that currency transactions do not upset the delicate balance of the world economy to gaining confidence that increases in world population do not overwhelm the material and social basis of decency in human relations. On this general level of analysis, then, I am making two kinds of contentions: first, the evidence available suggests a monumental absence of *will* on the part of leadership groups to achieve a redistributive consensus that is premised on justice for all sectors of global society; secondly, to the extent that such a redistributive consensus could be reached as to goals, it could not be successfully implemented by the state system.

I am suggesting in this second contention that Professor Bull does not express the crisis in broad enough terms to capture economic and ecological factors and, therefore, the kind of solution proposed, at most, keeps conflict within bounds of moderation and makes satisfactory progress toward the elimination of mass poverty and foreign economic exploitation from the international scene.

I believe, along with Professor Bull, that we need at this stage of history to shape a consensus about the character of global reform. However, I do not think that governments are now in a position to shape such a consensus, but are concentrating upon the task of providing reassurances of their capacities to deal with national problems. In its most extreme form, this reassurance involves the unwillingness of governments to face unpleasant facts. For instance, recently several African governments have been reported reluctant to acknowledge even domestic starvation because of an evident fear that it would reflect unfavourably on their governing capacities. But such an extreme instance is but a grotesque caricature of a general situation of unacknowledged ineptitude. Whether the preferred figure is Nero fiddling while Rome burns, the discovery that an emperor has no clothes, or the sovereign pomp and circumstance of the world population conference, the underlying message is the same – a refusal by governments to face the prime challenges of our world in realistic terms. Therefore, I would argue that the future of world order is too important to leave to the wisdom and action of governments.

At the same time, the process of global reform is a moral and political one, an awakening of consciousness and mobilisation of effective energies. In this respect that anonymous African woman at Bucharest is correct to deplore the tendency of Westerners to over-intellectualise their proposals, exhibiting the biggest fallacy of the Enlightenment. Any person's particular situation in space and time represents a provincial perspective, whatever the rhetoric, and is incapable of providing an ideal solution for the whole.

My own experience suggests that the most positive development at the moment is that a global multilogue of these issues of the future of world order is beginning to take place. No undertaking seems more worthwhile at present than the exchange of views with creative non-official representativies of the main cultural and political traditions of our world, not for the sake of discussion, but to build the foundation for a social movement dedicated to the creation of a peaceful and just system of world order. I have devoted most of my professional time over the past several years to an exercise of this kind, known as the World Order Models Project.[37] It is itself a non-trivial social fact that such an undertaking is conceived and carried forward at this historical moment. The impact of such consciousness-raising is disappointing on the level of action. There is no immediate authentic response to the sort of question posed by Bernard Malamud – that is, what should I do if I don't want to live in a world of malnourished and starving children.

At the most, by evolving a globalist paradigm we can interpret more fully and accurately what is happening and what we can do about it than is possible by relying on the internationalist paradigm.[38]

In my view, a different set of historical forces are at work and underlie the deepening international crisis. These forces are inclining the world system towards the emergence of a form of central guidance or scheme of global integration that is superseding the state system. This integrative momentum is undergirded by the scale and administrative capacities of business enterprise, especially the multinational corporation. While the sun may occasionally have set on the Union Jack even during the apogee of the British Empire, the same may not be said of the Hertz banner or the Pepsi billboard.[39] The interaction of territorial sovereign states is increasingly at variance with the *functional logic* of planning, guidance, and budgeting that are needed for a planet that has less and less surplus capacity and is more often faced with the realities of scarcity.[40] Put in different terms, to achieve stable solutions for the future, if possible at all, presupposes *a new system of world order* including as an essential structural element *a system of non-territorial central guidance*. By emphasising non-territoriality we are ruling out a territorial world state (even on a federal or confederal model) as a world order solution that is either desirable or necessary. I believe there are several plausible variants of non-territorial central guidance, the most plausible of which would be highly regressive and unpleasant even as compared to the inadequacies of the present international order. For purposes of abbreviation and clarity I shall refer to the state system as S^1 and to the prospect of a new superseding system as S_2. I will also distinguish between positive or desirable world order systems by putting a plus $(+)$ sign before the S, to negative or undesirable systems by putting a minus $(-)$ sign before the S, and to mixed results by combining signs $(\pm)$. Thus, Professor Bull's solution is an instance of $+S_1$, Kissinger's an instance of $-S_1$, and of my own proposals an instance of $+S_2$.[41] Part of my argument is that the future belongs to S_2, although the variant of S_2 that will prevail is far from clear.

Let me evolve this perspective a step further. I identify the present moment in history as situated relatively late in the life of S_1 and identify it as S_0, in the following schematic terms: In such a context I place emphasis on the options available in the interval of uncertain duration that separates S_0 from S_2 (see Table 11.1). It is this interval that I identify as the period of Transition (i.e., $S_0 \rightarrow S_2 = T$) which in turn is subdivided into three parts: T1, T2, T3 = T = $S_0 \rightarrow S_2$.[42] My own view of Transition to $+S_2$ is based on three sets of developments correlated with the three stages of Transition (see Table 11.2):

T1 = Consciousness-raising in National Arenas
T2 = Mobilisation in Transnational Arenas
T3 = Transformation in Global Arenas and Construction of Non-Territorial Central Guidance Mechanism.

Table 11.1 System Change and Historical Process

S_2	S_1	S_1	S_2	S_3	S_4
			$+S_2$		
			$\pm S_2$		
			$-S_2$		
		$S_1(EU) \rightarrow S_1$ (1974)			
		S_0 or S_1 (1974)			

World order values

V_1 = Peacefulness
V_2 = Economic well-being
V_3 = Social and political justice
V_4 = Ecological quality

$S_1(EU)$ = European regional state system
$S_1(EU) \rightarrow S_1$ = transition from a regional to a global state system

T(t)ransition

$T = S_0 \rightarrow S_2$
$T1$ = Consciousness
$T2$ = Mobilisation
$T3$ = Transformation
$t = S_0 \rightarrow S_1$ (next phase, e.g., 1815, 1918, 1945)

Positive futures

$+S_2$ = Survival
$+S_3$ = Development
$+S_4$ = Transcendence

Negative futures

$-S_2$ = Repression
$-S_3$ = Dehumanisation
$-S_4$ = Subhumanisation

Table 11.2   Transition Path to $+S_2$

T1 =	Domestic Arenas change in Consciousness; pre-eminence of V_1, V_2, V_3, V_4 as basis for response to S_1 world order crisis and adoption of $+S_2$ as desirable outcome.
T2 =	Transnational Arenas dominate process of mobilisation to implement changes of consciousness achieved in T1.
T3 =	Global Arenas dominate process of transformation to actualise in authority structures a new constitutional order (non-territorial centre guidance) and a new social contract based on the postulates of $+S_2$.

The gist of my argument is that S_1 is doomed by the need to manage interdependencies, amid scarcity, although the energies of nationalism remain dominant, and if anything, are leading to further patterns of assertion at the present time.[43] As a result the immediate prospect is for a highly coercive and reactionary S_1 arrangement, a $-S_1$ that seeks to stem the tide of disintegration by manipulation, if possible, by brute force to the extent necessary. My overall conclusion can be formulated as a hypothesis consisting of three principal parts:

1. There is no way to sustain a contractual relationship between the people and the government at the state level without protracted reliance on repressive force so long as S_1 persists;
2. To achieve a social contract on the state level based on some notion of consensual rule it will be simultaneously necessary to reach a social contract on a global level;
3. A global social contract presupposes a successful process of transition to a condition of $+S_2$ which is organised around the emergence of non-territorial central guidance capabilities as well as drastic redistribution of power, wealthy and influence.

Given such an interpretation of world order prospects, two questions seem paramount:

Can this favourable outcome be brought about?

What is the most beneficial way for individuals and groups to work toward this result?

These questions bear on the politics of transition, and we lack traditions of speculation that might offer guidance. In essence, the quest is for the sort of outlook that one associates with Wolfgang Friedmann's work, an outlook that is visionary without being utopian. It is *visionary* in the crucial sense of transcending the constraints of present arrangements of power. But it is *anti-utopian* in the equally crucial sense of providing a politics of transition to link the present with a preferred future.[44]

NOTES

1. See especially W. Friedmann, *The Changing Structure of International Law* (1964); Friedmann, 'General Course in Public International Law', 127 Academie de Droit International, *Recueil des Cours* 39 (1969).
2. W. Friedmann, *The Future of the Oceans* (1971).
3. W. Friedmann, *An Introduction to World Politics* 21 (5th ed. 1965).
4. A. N. Whitehead, *Adventures of Ideas* 7 (1933) (hereinafter cited as Whitehead).
5. This formulation with references to Freud by Erik Erikson at a session of the Wellfleet Discussions of Psychohistory held in August 1974.
6. Whitehead, at 7.
7. This observation applies mainly to the post-industrial sector of world society. For less economically evolved societies the stress on sovereignty may have mainly positive effects. There is great unevenness of position in the international system among states with respect to problem-solving and, hence, it is not possible to make satisfactory system-wide generalisations.
8. Lewis, 'Oil, Other Scarcities, and the Poor Countries', 27 *World Politics* 63, 64 (1974) (hereinafter cited as Lewis).
9. Some observers, nevertheless, regard such a conference as valuable because delegates are educated to an appreciation of the magnitude of the problems posed and transmit their appreciation to national leaders. In effect, beneath the conference polemics a real learning experience occurs.
10. As quoted in *New York Times*, 20 August 1974, at 9, col 1.
11. The open question is whether Brazil will have 400 million in 2025. The present fertility pattern virtually assures 200 million Brazilians by the year 2000.
12. See Brown and Eckholm, 'Food: Growing Global Insecurity', in *The United States and the Developing World: Agenda for Action 1974*, at 66 (J. Howe ed., 1974) (hereinafter cited as Brown & Eckholm).

13. These figures are taken from tables compiled in ibid., at 74; also, in 1962 the United States had the equivalent of 81 million metric tons of idle cropland, whereas in 1974 it has none.
14. U.N. Doc E/ICEF/CRP/74–21, 21 May 1974.
15. Quoted *New York Times*, 24 February, 1974, s. 4 at 2, col. 3.
16. Well expressed by Fouad Ajami, 'The Global Populists – Third World Nations and World Order Crises', Princeton University Center of International Studies, Research monograph No. 41, May 1974.
17. Brown & Eckholm, at 75.
18. *New York Times*, 21 August 1974, at 2, col. 4.
19. T. Artin, *Earth Talk: Independent Voices in the Environment* (1973).
20. *New York Times*, 21 August 1974, at 2, col. 2.
21. Lewis, at 64.
22. Quoted *New York Times*, 13 August 1974, at 20, col. 5.
23. See Gilpin, 'The Politics of Transnational Economic Relations', in *Transnational Relations and World Politics* 48 (J. Nye and R. Keohane (eds.), 1973): also R. Barnet and R. Muller, *Global Reach: The Power of the Multinational Corporations* (1975) (hereinafter citied as Barnet & Muller).
24. Recent disclosures of the extent to which SST technology, aerosol spray chemicals, and atmospheric nuclear explosions may be depleting the ozone shield that protects earth from the lethal rays of the sun illustrates both the problem and the unresponsiveness of principal institutions of authority to considerations of planetary well-being.
25. See K. Subrahmanyam, 'The Indian Nuclear Test in a Global Perspective', India International Centre, 1 August 1974; R. V. R., Chandrasekhara Rao, 'Proliferation and the Indian Test', 26 *Survival* 210 (1974).
26. Letter (dated 17 July, 1974) from M. Anandakrishan to the Editor, *New York Times*, 24 July 1974, at 40, col. 3.
27. Reported *New York Times*, 3 August 1974, at 2.
28. Letter (dated 13 August 1974) from A. Castro to the Editor, *New York Times*, 19 August 1974, at 24, col. 5.
29. For a range of serious assessments of the Brazilian experience since the *coup* of 1964, see *Authoritarian Brazil* (A. Stepan (ed.), 1974).
30. For a probing depiction of the Indian failure see Morris, 'India: Ripe for Revolution', 10 *WIN* 4, 17 (1974).
31. Reported *New York Times*, 16 August 1974, at 6, col. 3.
32. Hedley Bull, 'Australia's Perceptions of our Role in the World' 14 (July 1974) (mimeographed text).
33. Even Kissinger seems recently aware of the precariousness of his own vision of world order. In a long interview with James Reston, Kissinger revealed this new concern: 'I would like to leave at least the beginning of a perception of a structure that goes beyond these centres of power and moves toward a global conception. There is no question in my mind that by the end of the century this will be the dominant reality of our time. I believe we have to move toward it

now.' See 'Secretary Kissinger Interviewed for New York Times', 71 *Dep't State Bull.* 629, 638 (1974).

34. Various ideas leading in the direction of a global social contract are gaining currency recently. See Gardner, 'Report of the Seminar' and 'A Postscript', in *The World Food and Energy Crises: The Role of International Organisations* 49 (Conference at Institute of Man and Science, Rensselaerville, N.Y., May 1974).

35. A very perceptive discussion of these tendencies and their practical limits can be found in Stone, 'Approaches to the Notion of International Justice ', in *The Future of the International Legal Order* 372 (C. E. Black & R. A. Falk (eds), 1969).

36. For elaboration of what sort of central guidance procedures are needed and possible see R. A. Falk, *A Study of Future Worlds*, ch. IV (1975).

37. For an account of the World Order Models Project, see General Introduction by Professor Saul H. Mendlovitz, its primary architect, in ibid. at *xvii*.

38. This is the main theme of lectures given at Yale Law School in March 1974. Falk, 'A New Paradigm for International Legal Studies: Prospects and Proposals', 84 *Yale L.J.* 969 (1975).

39. Point borrowed from Barnet & Miller.

40. See W. Ophuls, 'The Scarcity Society', *Harpers*, April 1974, at 47.

41. There are an array of positive $(+)S_2$ models possible. Some are depicted in Chapter III of my book, *A Study of Future Worlds* (1975) and others are more fully and adequately depicted in the various perspectives embodied in the World Order Models Project. See *On Creating a Just World Order* (S. H. Mendlovitz (ed.), 1975).

42. In $+S_1$ conceptions of global reform, the changes are by definition of an intra-systemic character. For one compelling analysis along these lines, see S. Brown, *New Forces in World Politics* 185–215 especially (1974).

43. These patterns of assertion are associated with the resource diplomacy of the industrial countries and the redistributive strategies of the Third World.

44. A very thoughtful book on these issues is B. Moore, Jr, *Reflections on the Causes of Human Misery* (1972).

12 Technology and Politics: Shifting Balances

The complex connections between technology and politics are at the heart of the cultural crisis we are experiencing. It is indicative of the special character of this crisis that the issue of the relationship between technology and pessimism is selected as the focus for inquiry. It would have been quite inconceivable three or four decades ago to approach the subject of technology in this spirit, or if conceivable, then only at the initiative of very marginal or alienated individuals and groups. There has been ever since the Industrial Revolution an artistic undercurrent of thought that viewed the impact of technology on society as largely negative in its consequence. However, only recently has a pessimistic view of technology penetrated our sensibilities in a culturally significant way.

To describe the character of this significance is complex. As a matter of background, it seems helpful to begin with several general assertions that suggest a context for more specific inquiry. Perhaps the most important of these is my conviction that both the leaders and citizenry of the dominant countries of the world are increasingly aware that the old models for solving the problems of society are no longer working. The reference here is to such fundamental and characteristic problems as those of security, energy and economic well-being. These are each premised on a set of relationships between the state and society that are increasingly seen as in a condition of dangerous disarray, producing a situation in which the various authority systems of our civilisation can, at best, do no more than neutralise the dangers and challenges being posed, that is, stave off the worst. Implicit here is the absence of confidence in the possibility of a better future. At the centre of this realisation that the old models are not working is an appreciation, often unstated, that the state, the structure of the state embodied in governing institutions, is simultaneously too big and too small.

The state is too big to deal with human problems on a humane scale and, as a consequence, is inevitably expressive of, through the sheer degree of bureaucratic complexity and impersonal forms of decision-making, the existence of an unbridgeable gap between rulers and ruled. This gap is only barely being disguised by traditional methods of politics. The current disenchantment, for example, with governing processes here in the United States goes far beyond the legacies of Vietnam and Watergate. It is a more funda-mental structural disenchantment and has to do with the inability of economic, ecological or security frameworks of policy-making to provide genuine reassurance and hope for the peoples of advanced industrial societies.

At the same time, the state is too small with respect to the functional reach of underlying problems. Whether concern be concentrated upon building a framework for international security, or for peace, for the maintenance of ecological quality, or for the distribution and production of resources and the conservation of these resources, the situation is the same: any of these problems requires a political capability truly planetary in scope. There is a growing awareness, both associated with various forms of interdependence and a keen sense of our vulnerability to disruption in reaction to external events, that we are, and shall remain, dependent for our well-being, and possibly our survival, upon the prudence, self-restraint and rationality of actors, often with adversary intentions beyond our control. This vulnerability is in a fundamental respect an inevitable consequence of the fragmentation of political authority among sovereign states, each of which enjoys territorial dominion and many of which have at their disposal an increasingly modern military establishment capable of inflicting distant harm whose use remains largely discretionary.

Beyond the central reality of the state being too big and too small there is no prospect of an adequate political framework, alternative to the state system, that can be seen realistically emerging in the next few decades. Indeed, we are living in a period of intensifying nationalism around the world, and the intensification of statism is among the most important political developments of our time. The movement of decolonisation has led to the emergence, for the first time in history, of a state system that is genuinely global in character and in which all major cultures participate actively and much more autonomously than they ever did in the past. This statist structure is superseding the hegemonic patterns of international order in which a few imperial actors managed the system from the top.

At the very moment, in other words, when the interdependence of international life suggests the needs for supranationalism and for political integration, we are experiencing a further intensification of political fragmentation. Moreover, most of the world regards this decentralising of authority and power as a positive development. The movement towards decolonisation is a principal reason why so many individuals in the poorest parts of the world are, by and large, optimistic. In the course of their lifetimes these peoples have experienced a shift from humiliating types of formal dependency to a political reality of much greater independence and freedom – at least freedom on that formal sovereign level. This kind of freedom as collective self-determination is a very real achievement for many societies and peoples in the world. And this statist tendency does not necessarily end with the achievement of political independence. The tendency subsequently shifts its energy to struggles on the economic and cultural planes, often more fundamental in character (as one Indian intellectual put it some years ago, 'It will be easier to get rid of the British than of Coca Cola'), struggles that explain the attractiveness throughout the Third World of such ideas and movements as 'non-alignment', 'self-reliance', and 'delinking'. Neocolonialism, the replacement of the formal colonial structures by more informal ones that are dominated by a collaboration between ruling elites, multinational corporations, and the new international financial institutions loosely associated with the United Nations – institutions like the IMF and World Bank – have been playing intrusive and domineering roles in the lives of the societies of Asia, Latin America and Africa.

In this broad international context, technology is perceived by many Third World progressives as playing an ambiguous and confusing role at present. From the point of view of non-Western societies, technology is presented as the bearer of the promise of liberation from mass misery and poverty, as the enabler of genuine participation in world society on the basis of equality – at least equality on the level of development. It is in this spirit that Third World elites have generally adopted the ideology of modernisation which includes acceptance of the idea that Western technology applied and introduced into their society in a major way will provide not only stability but will contribute rapidly to social welfare. More recently, this automatic promise of technology has been increasingly challenged. This challenge has not meant, by and large, an anti-technological reaction; it has meant, rather, a more conditional view of technological promise. Thus, at the same historical period when the technology of the West is looked upon as the great hope for liberating these impoverished societies of the world from their burdens of mass misery, there is also in the world, among leaders of oppressed peoples, a growing sense that their oppression is a consequence of an international system of domination undergirded by technology, that, in the postcolonial era, technology is a kind of alien missionary offering them Western values and interests.

Typical of this more recent defiant spirit is a declaration issued at Poona, India, by intellectual activists sensitive to Third World concerns and dedicated to a radical programme of global reform:

With the Third World political, bureaucratic, military, academic, and communications elites accepting the superiority of Western-style modernisation and the role of science and technology in it, there has emerged a global system of control, hegemony, exploitation and repression, all in the name of modernity and the theory of progress, all in the name of science and technology.

The declaration goes on:

The compelling drive to sell products made possible by modern technology, regardless of whether they serve any real social need, necessitates the colonisation of the mind itself. High-powered advertising is used to hook some of the most deprived peoples of the world on senseless consumer goods so that the head of a family may spend a large portion of his earnings on Coca Cola while his children starve.

In this world of fragmentation on a state level and of conflict between the developed North and the much less developed South, technology acts simultaneously as an instrument of domination and as a strategy of liberation. It therefore plays a confusing role, a role that varies from context to context depending on the capacity of a particular leadership to relate its reliance on technology to a broader and more humane conception of development. It is especially important for Westerners to understand these ambiguities associated with the transfer of technology from North to South. In the West there persists a general preconception that the transfer of modern technology to less developed countries is almost necessarily a positive good. Of course, some Western analysts appreciated the destabilising impacts of technology transfer if accomplished too rapidly. Such an appreciation has been popularised by the rapid fall of the Shah during 1978, a moderniser whose collapse has been partly attributed by his former supporters to a pace and form of modernisation (that is, by a central effort to introduce modern technology) that was both too rapid and ill-suited to Iran. As a consequence, traditional sources of stability in Iran were disrupted without anything emerging in their place.

In my view, such lines of interpretation of the Iranian Revolution are seriously misleading. It is contended that the Iranian Revolution is a regressive development because it allegedly intends to 'turn back the clock', that is, to deny to Iran the kinds of high-technology industries that have been associated with the period when the country was run as a Western-style developing country under the leadership of the Shah. It is still impossible for American policy-makers to acknowledge that modernisation and humane development might be in conflict under certain conditions. It seems evident that many poor people in Iran overwhelmingly rejected *their* experience of modernisation because they accepted the charges of their religious leaders that the corruption of their indigenous culture and religion was an effect.

The leaders of the Iranian Revolution are a diverse lot, but they are not against technology as such, and indeed many of them point out that Ayatollah Khomeini's revolution was itself waged with the benefits of Xerox machines, cassettes and telephones. There is a widespread belief that the Shah's modernisation schemes brought the wrong kinds of technology to Iran and that what benefits occurred were not shared nearly widely enough. The new leadership is determined to avoid technologies which require outside experts to make them work or which are geared to production priorities that make the people and society of Iran a dependent cog in a world economic structure. To the extent that modern technology perpetuates dependence on the West it is necessarily regressive and hostile to the healthy development of Iran as a society. The Iranian Revolution may fail for many reasons other than its rejection of modernisation as the key to development. In the event that the movement to build an Islamic republic collapses, the failure is likely to be blamed by many in large part on the refusal to rely on the role of modern technology to facilitate and sustain economic growth. But such an explanation, should it be offered, is likely to be far too facile, missing more than it encompasses. Reducing dependence on technology that cannot be absorbed by the skill level that exists in a given country is closely associated with the quest for cultural self-determination in the Third World, an aspect of the wider process of self-determination that is a vital element in the phenomenon of nationalism, which, in turn, is defining the contours of politics in so many countries around the world at this time. As such, the rejection of a technology which does not grow out of the culture and capabilities of particular national societies manifests the spirit of legitimate governance.

At a minimum, then, I think it important to acknowledge that we in the West do not have a universal, superior technology to provide the rest of the world. It is not necessarily a blessing and a benefit to transfer Western technology to other societies or to encourage its adoption through a collaboration with the elites running the governments of many of these countries in ways that exploit their own people. One of the characteristic features of this kind of technological relationship is that the elites of Third World countries are often more aligned to the values and interests of the elites of the North than they are with the people of their own society. Part of the transnational bargain among elites is to introduce a high technology kind of development process that benefits a small proportion of the less developed society, disrupts its connections with its own cultural traditions and with its own dynamic of self-determination, and establishes a profitable climate for foreign capital and multinational corporations. The argument which flows from this line of reasoning is that the state system is likely to persist, that technology is both a critical dimension of hierarchy in the state system and a set of capabilities tending to cut disparities between the weak and strong in international society.

It also seems useful to emphasise that in a period when the old models are not working and there is no consensus behind an alternative framework for dealing with the challenges confronting our civilisation, there is a tendency to respond to failures by accentuating the characteristics of the failing system. That is, the main decision-makers know no other way of responding to challenges than by way of intensification of old methods. In effect, as things get worse there is a tendency to do more of the worst things, even if the probable consequences are harmful. Let me illustrate. As the world runs out of cheap energy the compulsion to obtain additional energy vindicates even reliance on such a desperate technology as nuclear power. As governing groups find themselves unable to provide security to defend their society from military attack, they engage in the most expensive and fruitless arms race ever to occur in human history. This dangerous and wasteful arms race occurs even though it is virtually impossible to translate strategic military advantages into political and economic goals. Nuclear war is the extreme case. Under no circumstances can it be supposed that a government would gain enough to make it rational at the strategic level to initiate general warfare. This generalisation holds regardless of the relative balance of military capabilities at a particular time between the two superpowers. It is eschatological adventurism to suppose that geopolitical stakes of whatever kind can create a calculus by which it is worth taking a risk of nuclear exchange. It is only as a result of a tacit agreement by leading governments to treat strategic superiorities as if meaningful, pretending that security is endangered when the other side gets the edge, that some kind of justification and rationalisation for a continuation of current levels of defence spending and deployment can be maintained by the superpowers and their respective allies.

Such reason-defying patterns of conduct are bewildering at one level. Why do intelligent, well-intentioned men (and an occasional woman) persist in behavioural traits long after their utility has been manifestly exhausted? To accentuate the old is easier and more politically acceptable than to experiment with the new, which will always threaten, if not actually displace, entrenched interests. The place of technology in our cultural experience is illustrative. For many decades Western technology was filled with promise, largely vindicated by performance. Then, more recently, a variety of technological directions of effort produced socially frightening results – some of which far outweighed expected benefits. A call came for 'technology assessment', for more discrimination in the application of technological solutions to our problems. This call did not quell the pessimistic drift of popular reaction. The champions of relentless technological innovation were also the assessors, and nowhere was there moral energy sufficient to define and protect the public interest. Technological momentum seemed itself a runaway engine that was carrying the vessel of civilisation towards a precipice. It is against this background that our inquiry proceeds.

One way to interpret the current mood of pessimism in the West is as a gigantic, deferred backlash against generations of optimism. The recently tarnished myth of progress had rested on the conviction that a science-based technology could provide more and more goods and services for more and more people. Those who retain this optimistic outlook increasingly sound less like true believers, from a cultural point of view, than like salesmen bound to a position that interest or habit makes necessary to defend. In other words, those who still believe that technology is our best hope for societal advance lack the cultural underpinnings of genuine support that were formerly sustained by a consensus that technology was the bridge between problems and expectations.

Now why, we must ask, has the bright dream of Western technology turned into a nightmare in so many respects? Of course, the gains associated with technological innovation were never without attendant costs and risks. But in the past these costs and risks were largely borne by the poor, especially by marginalised workers, and to some degree by the poorer sectors of the world. What has happened in the last several decades is that the technology of destruction, especially mass destruction epitomised by nuclear weapons, has meant that we are *all* living now under a constant indefinite threat of virtual extinction; and this threat occurs in a setting of conflicting ideologies and ambitions where different societies maintain antagonistic scenarios of how to organise the world in the future.

In addition, there has been a sudden ecological awakening to the reality that industrial progress beyond a certain threshold also means pollution, depletion of accessible resources, and most important politically, a deepening vulnerability of all societies to the most environmentally irresponsible actors, often located beyond the reach of national jurisdiction. We are all endangered by oil spills from unseaworthy tankers, by the dilution of the ozone layer, and by atmospheric nuclear weapons tests. These dangers are attributable to the policies of specific states whose actions reflect a reading by their governments (often themselves unrepresentative of their own populations) of national interests. The prevailing world order system has virtually no capabilities to uphold global interests. The United Nations and its specialised agencies are constrained by the dominance of states and by the acceptance of state sovereignty as a basic organising principle. Our social institutions and even our cultural mores are maladapted to defending the planet against decentralised fragmented destructive behaviour. We are organised around principles of individualism at all levels of social organisation, from what we do privately, to what we do corporately and societally and civilisationally. In all these settings, we seek to maximise private gain as defined by the particular actor.

Deference to the public interest is extremely weak. Altruism, although real, has never been a strong characteristic of the human species. To the extent that the wellbeing of others and of the planet in general and of future generations is dependent on altruism, it is dependent on something so fragile and feeble as to be irrelevant. The future seems almost certainly, as matters now stand, to be shaped as a consequence of the interplay of various selfish tendencies. This prospect, given the inequalities, antagonisms and capabilities at the disposal of various actors, induces pessimism on the part of anyone concerned about the quality of the whole (planet, species), and about human destiny.

For a long period of human history, this decentralisation of self-centred individual and collective behaviour made no essential difference to the quality and stability of the whole. The world was big enough to accommodate, with only marginal disruption, the interplay of these various self-centred quests. The growth of scale in both the organisation of economic existence and in the complexity of technological capacity have built a new series of thresholds in human history. These have been crossed. As a result, capabilities for upholding the general interest and future seem increasingly necessary, and their absence is more keenly felt.

The situation has been aggravated in complex ways by the international character and development of the sovereign state. The state, which purports to be the custodian of public interests, has increasingly and evidently become both the captive of private and special interests, as well as the promoter of technological innovation. The governing process does not stand apart in a detached way to assess and protect. It is committed to a certain direction of development, often for corrupt reasons associated with pressures from interest groups, but also because it remains convinced that political stability requires continuous expansion of the productive bases.

This adversary identity of the modern state is most dangerous and apparent in relation to war-making potential. Here the mutual reinforcement between government and armaments has produced a phenomenon new even for liberal democratic societies – the so-called national security state permanently prepared to wage general war. This governmental reality consists of a military-industrial-academic complex which stimulates the dynamics of national security under all sets of international circumstances. Entrenched here are sets of very powerful vested interests and obsolescent attitudes that shut out other views, thereby reinforcing the dangerous dogmatic notion that national security can only be upheld through military competition.

The nature of security, given the technology of destruction and delivery, has deeply altered the character of the state itself. Deterrence as the fundamental premise of security in the nuclear age involves reliance on mass terror to inhibit foreign leaders. There is a deep moral cost exacted by the credible willingness to kill millions of innocent inhabitants of a foreign society so as to discourage its leaders from provoking us. And of course the situation is reversed with regard to the way in which our principal rival government in the Soviet Union threatens American society. Indeed, deterrence as a foundation for national security, however dubious its moral claims, is preferable to those war-fighting conceptions of nuclear weaponry that are increasingly favoured by the military establishment. Such conceptions rest on the near normalcy of nuclear weapons, as well as on the possibility of tactical uses, battlefield roles, on the distinction between military and civilian targets, and on the capacity to keep limited nuclear wars from escalating. Such hyper-rational departures from the balance of terror are not to be trusted, especially to the extent that nuclear war becomes not only thinkable but palatable for reasons of statecraft.

What we call security rests on a morality of mass terror. When the guardians of order and justice, the authority figures, found the security of the state on these premises, then those that seek change, those who are oppressed, those who are weak, are also likely to subscribe to an ethos of terror. One of the most frightening things introduced into the contemporary framework and very much associated, it seems to me, with the technological power-base of modern society, is the centrality of terror to the politics of order and the politics of change. To limit the notion of terrorism to those who hijack planes and kidnap executives and diplomats is to subscribe to a very pernicious and peculiar ideology which exempts those who work to implement the secret policies of the most 'civilised states of the world'. It excludes from the circle of terrorism those who engage in assassination plots overseas, design weapons of mass destruction and propose doctrines for their use, and draw up contingency plans for nuclear wars. Terror pervades the international order of our times, and embraces the governing processes of the states which seem most 'civilised'.

More serious than this moral situation is the direct influence of military technology on the character of civil order. Instantaneous delivery systems able to bring devastation to any place in the world in a matter of minutes restructure society in several respects. First, such weaponry means that no level of armament can provide any kind of defence against a determined attack. In addition, a government has to remain at all times in a pre-war state of readiness. There is no such thing as a condition of peace in the nuclear age because there is no time to get ready. The United States has in the past been protected by two oceans. It now must at all times be ready to fight major wars at less than an hour's notice.

One consequence is that the professional military establishment exerts great influence on national policy. For this reason alone there is a continuous tendency to bias the political process in militarist directions. At the present time, it is very difficult for the President of the USA to do anything in any major area of foreign policy without the endorsement of the Joint Chiefs of Staff. These military leaders possess an internal veto that severely constrains the discretion of civilian political leadership in almost any sphere of state policy, whether it be negotiating an arrangement over the future of the Panama Canal or reaching out for some kind of meaningful arms control or arms reduction arrangement. In the entire sphere of international relations there is no easy way to diminish the influence of the military on our national policy-makers. Both political parties accept this role for the military establishment, and it seems almost impossible for an anti-militarist to gain nomination for high office, even at the Congressional level. Perhaps a President willing to confront his own bureaucracy and special interests could take the issue to the people. However, such a President would have to undergo 'a conversion' in office, since at present he or she would not be electable if an anti-militarist stand was clear from the outset. Perhaps a third party committed to radical goals of this character could introduce new images of security into political discourse. Quite possibly, also, some international breakdown in the years ahead, especially if it involved the use of nuclear weapons, would create a far greater receptivity to anti-militarist politics. But at the moment a very rigid international political situation exists in which dominant states are increasingly militarised in relation to their domestic governing processes. Third World countries are also – and this is a comparatively recent development – increasingly militarised. This new horizontal extension of militarism is partly a result of an upsurge of arms sales. Armaments are a growth industry capable of diminishing balance of payments deficits in the rich oil-importing countries. More and more countries are capable of fighting modern destructive wars on the scale of World War II within their respective regions. Moreover, governments in every major region in the world possess, or are close to possessing, nuclear weapons. In terms of our theme, the technology of violence has been globally disseminated, creating a more homogenous planetary reality, but hardly a more reassuring one. Under these circumstances, the best that our more enlightened leaders can do is hope to muddle through for yet another period of years, but muddling through is neither inspiring as politics, nor can it set aside the pessimistic mood that has taken shape in a world in which dangerous trends seem out of control.

Shaping personal responses to this situation seems to me difficult, but crucial. I think the beginning of a response is to acknowledge that only a miracle will get us out of the present trap. Such an outlook underscores the insufficiency of a rational, secular kind of problem-solving orientation – the sort of orientation we are accustomed to rely upon. To rest our hopes on a miracle means, it seems to me, most essentially, that we believe in the credible rebirth of some kind of religious civilisation in our midst. This rebirth would have to transform the relationship between self, society and Nature in a direction that transcends the materialist consensus long dominating our value-system. In considering such a radical possibility, literally a cultural revolution, it is necessary to examine the ironic connections between technology and governments as they bear on comprehending how change might come about.

I want to suggest this ironic character by reference to a recent science fiction film called *The Meteor*. Despite its mediocre character, the movie is exceedingly useful for my purposes. The plot involves a comet which hits a huge meteor in the asteroid belt and sends a meteor hurtling towards earth, posing a grave threat of enormous catastrophe because the meteor upon impact was expected to cause a fifty-mile wide belt of absolute destruction. In addition, the meteor was accompanied by large fragments that themselves caused avalanches, tidal waves and produced minor disasters around the world. It turned out that in this situation the only hope of saving the earth from the main catastrophe rested on the fact that the United States had developed, through its space programme, a secret and illicit weapons system poised for attack from outer space on the Soviet Union. And, conveniently, the Soviet Union had developed an identical secret illegal system that was in position poised for attack on the United States. The only means of saving the earth was to arrange for the collaboration of both systems (Project Hercules and Peter the Great – the code names appropriately given to these two weapons systems). The collaboration was required because either missile system alone lacked the sufficiency of megatonnage needed to intercept the meteor. Only a coordinated strike could produce that result. To achieve this coordination required both political agreement and technical implementation. It was necessary that the firing of the realigned missiles would be so coordinated that they would strike the meteor at the same moment.

The political dynamic of this situation was more difficult than the technical one. In both societies it was necessary to overcome the resistance of military leaders who remained preoccupied with Cold War calculations despite the immediacy of the threat to the planet as a whole. A reasonably enlightened President and head of the Politburo managed eventually to prevail and save the situation at the last instant.

Part of what is interesting here is that, at the first level of interpretation it was an enormous blessing that not one superpower but both had the malevolent wisdom to engage in massive secret exploitation of the most sinister technology of destruction that one can imagine. (Incidentally, this was an illustration of space cooperation that worked; the missiles did indeed intercept the meteor, and the earth was relieved from this interlude of fantastic danger.) Within the context of the film, we should be grateful for the paranoid sensibilities of our military guardians as they were unwittingly projecting salvational plans we, as citizens, are never told about. Of course, *The Meteor* is a romantic film in the sense that this covert malevolence works out for our collective salvation. In actual fact, such a working-out is not plausible.

At a second level of interpretation, there is the sublime realisation embodied in this story that even the development and deployment of nuclear weapons turned out to be a disguised blessing for the human species. If nuclear weapons

had never been developed, there would have been no possibility of protecting the planet against this falling meteor.
That is, in a pre-nuclear historical situation the earth would
have been genuinely devastated by this bit of galactic
turbulence.

At a third level of interpretation, though, we need to
acknowledge that this scenario is simply science fiction. It
is not very likely that a meteor of such size would be directed
towards earth or that an accidental convergence of illegal
weapons deployments could be used to avoid catastrophe.
What is credible, however, is the degree to which national
security and danger are shrouded in an official web of
secrecy and deception. What is most starkly realistic about
the plot is the extent to which our personal and collective
destinies are being guided by those who have a rigid and
inappropriately militarist approach to the future. This film
accents the degree to which we who seem so powerful from
one perspective, are fundamentally helpless and adrift
because we live in societies managed by very technocrat-
ically-oriented elites. It makes no difference from this point
of view – from this larger metaphysical point of view –
whether we happen to be in the United States or the Soviet
Union. This kind of destructive technological orientation
has no ideological bias. It is acceptable on either side of the
geopolitical dividing-line in world conflict. The logic of state
power has become linked to the mega-death technologies
of the war system. And, to borrow a phrase from symposium
respondent John Broomfield, the human species is a
mistake-prone species. At present, also, there is no counter-
logic at work within the political processes dominant in the
world, and hence, no humanistic or religious resistance is
being mounted against the dangers of following the materialist and technological mind-set all the way to the end of
the road, ultimately to oblivion. This apparent impasse
evolved out of earlier interactions between science and politics. These earlier interactions are the necessary ground on
which to fashion a new type of interaction which better
serves human purpose.

The relationship between technology and state power has
so far passed through three stages in Western civilisation.

There was first of all the stage of religious primacy where religion essentially restricted scientific inquiry to the extent that it collided with revealed truths. From the beginning of recorded history, the deepest wisdom of our civilisation generated warnings about the dangerous consequences of unrestricted scientific inquiry. The forbidden fruit of the Garden of Eden was, of course, the tree of knowledge. The Greek gods were angry at Prometheus for stealing fire and for making the prospect of technological innovation freely available to human society. Daedalus who tried to fly plunged to the sea when his waxen wings melted in his encounter with the stronger forces of the sun's power. The epitome and culmination of religious primacy in relation to science was expressed by the forcing of Galileo in the early seventeenth century to back down from his defence of Copernican convictions that the sun, rather than the earth, was the centre of the solar system.

The second principal stage featured the reign of scientific autonomy, a period which witnessed the emergence of Protestantism, the rise of capitalism, and the belief in reason. A new secular humanism took shape that embodied positive ideas about social development and enlightenment. In essence, the new orientation stressed human freedom and responsibility, and dispensed with all forms of religious dependence. No limits were placed upon the endeavours of men and women. Steadily increasing productivity of capital generated a large surplus that enabled both rich and poor to feel they had a stake in facilitating this modernising dynamic. Not all was bright in this period. Marxist and other critical ideas emerged to suggest that beneath the rhetoric of humanism was a reality of class struggle and exploitation; but capitalism proved fairly resilient, managing, despite cyclical declines, to reconcile profitability with an improving standard of living for the poor. Besides, on the issue of science and society, Marxism did not question the notion of scientific autonomy. Its contention was that it was necessary to reconstitute the state in such a way as to allow the dynamism of technology to improve the lives of society as a whole rather than the priviledged elite who controlled the means of production.

This second stage has been succeeded by the present period of cultural doubt. This doubt is not shared, or at least not acknowledged, by the leadership or the main elites of the society. It is a widely diffused latent doubt in the capacity of science and technology to provide the basis of a positive future. Many of us feel we are being victimised by a runaway technology, a feeling compounded, as suggested earlier, by the fact that the state and all other representative institutions are both incapable of and unwilling to protect the public interest even on a national scale, much less on a global scale where there exists no credible authority and enforcement capability in being or on the horizon. In other words, at present, we lack the political basis for translating our doubts about technology into an institutional and organisational form that could overcome the autonomy of technology on behalf of long-term human values. Without such an effective apparatus committed to technological curtailment there is no realistic basis for hope. As it is, there exists some doubt as to whether at this stage, even if the political will existed, which it does not, it would be possible to protect planetary, long-term interests. It may be too late. To what extent is technological momentum reversible? There are certain symbolic battlefields where grassroots doubts are challenging the technocratic priorities of entrenched interests. The future of nuclear power is being challenged in this spirit throughout the industralised world in anti-state political action. Regardless of the outcome with respect to such an issue of high salience, the grounds for reconstruction, the relationship between science and society, must be reconstituted on a spiritual foundation.

In this situation where the stage two notions of autonomy are encountering the stage three mood of doubt, we desperately need a fourth stage – a new covenant between the state and society that will reconcile science and technology with the well-being of the individual, of society, and of the planet as a whole. The discovery and acceptance of this new covenant may be the central political quest of our time. We cannot, as citizens, wait around too much longer. It is not helpful to be passive, awaiting catastrophe or miracle.

Although it will take a miracle, we act responsibly only if we try to make that miracle happen.

A short film about an anti-nuclear activist, called *Paul Jacobs and the Nuclear Gang*, documented the degree to which official cover-ups of nuclear danger have occurred over the years, especially in Nevada and Colorado, causing terrible damage to the health of exposed citizens falsely reassured. I took part in a discussion about the film immediately after it was shown in which a man stood up and said, 'We can't be polite any longer, these bastards are trying to kill us.' The great social struggles of the world against the visible forms of oppression embodied in colonialism started with similar realisations by those who previously resigned themselves fatalistically to their status as victims. The much less visible but equally dangerous forms of oppression associated with runaway technology harboured in large-scale, non-accountable bureaucratic institutions requires a response organised around values and attitudes of resistance that associate the well-being and positive destiny of the planet with the possibility of breaking out of cycles of violence and terror.

Such a political deliverance has to proceed from bold premises. These premises can be suggested by some provocative remarks that intend to be suggestive rather than conclusive. An adequate posture towards technology will require, first of all, nothing less than an abolitionist attitude toward the institution of war itself, an attitude towards war and violence that is comparable in its clarity to the attitude taken several centuries ago towards slavery as a social institution. The early abolitionists also confronted a societal consensus that declared slavery to be unavoidable and, hence, inevitable. Sensible people were urged to clean slavery up, to make it less brutal, to make it more humane, but to refrain from futile efforts to eliminate slavery altogether. Such reformist gestures take for granted the structure that generates the social evil, and as a result, they are morally compromised. Also, the prudential feeling about practicality rarely is able to mobilise effective support. The movement against slavery required the abolitionist perspective that demanded, without conditions, its elimination.

With such an unconditional perspective creating pressure, compromises can sometimes be struck because the defenders of the status quo feel threatened. The same reasoning applies at this time to the relationship between the state and society on a whole range of issues, including the interlocked connections between war and technology.

In sum, unless we approach the structures of our own invisible oppression in an abolitionist spirit, we shall not be able to establish a credible foundation for optimism or hope in the future. We will not be able to bring technology back into line with human aspiration, nor assure ourselves that the technology can help achieve a positive human future. Rabelais said it well a long time ago – 'science without conscience is but the ruin of the soul.'

A social movement which seeks to encourage a new political environment for the technological future will need to ground itself in a new appreciation of the sacred relationship that exists between humanity and the cosmos. This is a matter of properly locating personal destiny within oneself, as well as at the centre of our relationship to nature and to other sentient beings. Without a spiritual base, no movement for transformation can succeed in the face of the many existing obstacles. Spirituality is needed to mobilise support, to strengthen the will of aspirants, and to assure the perseverance required for this impending struggle of the future, a struggle to recreate society through a new religious covenant that will enable humanity to once again look towards the future in a spirit of hope.

13 The Spirit of Thoreau in the Age of Trident

I

Henry David Thoreau went to jail in 1842 rather than pay a poll tax whose revenues were used, in part, to pay for President Polk's colonialist war against Mexico. That long ago Thoreau insisted that a citizen had a civic responsibility to oppose an unjust war: 'The soldier is applauded who refuses to serve in an unjust war by those who do not refuse to sustain the unjust government which makes the war.' His more general counsel was to '[l]et your life be a counter-friction to stop the machine. What I have to do is to see, at any rate, that I do not lend myself to the wrong which I condemn.'

These days, rarely noticed except when prison sentences are announced, there are a growing number of Americans who are dedicating their lives to stopping the machine. Now the machine has become nuclearised and threatens, at least in our imagination, the ultimate human crime of omnicide, not an idle threat, given the validating findings of several groups of scientists about the prospects for 'nuclear winter' in the aftermath of nuclear war. Unlike Thoreau who lives on in our tradition for his single night in a comfortable Concord jail (a friend paid his outstanding tax to obtain his release), these unsung Americans, our contemporaries, some of whom have received long prison sentences and others have served time repeatedly for their status as career criminals-of-conscience, are remaining for years behind bars away from family, freedom and work. Many are returning over and over again to put their bodies in the way of the machine. Their lives have become haunted by the darkest shadows of nuclearism.

A particular focus of these resistance activities has been 'first-strike' weapons systems. It is important to understand why. As moralists, legalists and strategists have argued ever since Hiroshima, with nuclear weapons in existence, it is impossible to disinvent them or to be sure that if we renounce them we shall not tempt others to engage in nuclear blackmail, or even surprise attack. Whether deterrence or disarmament is safer, saner or more moral is arguable in a world of hostile states and widespread conflict. Most radical peace activists tend to respect this tragic circumstance, although their definite preference is to take the risk of vulnerability connected with disarmament.

What they refuse to tolerate, however, is the use of nuclear weapons, not for war-avoidance roles (deterrence), but for geopolitical power plays. The construction of first-strike weapons systems is so objectionable because it strips away the masks of inevitability from the so-called nuclear dilemma, and makes it clear that our leaders have become hypocrites of the most fundamental kind. In essence, a first-strike weapons system is one that is designed to be used to attack, not retaliate – for instance, submarines with many nuclear warheads on their missiles having high degrees of accuracy, yet relatively vulnerable to attack by others, or cruise missiles that are easy to destroy while still on the ground, but hard to stop once launched because their low trajectory eludes radar. If retaliation were the purpose of these systems, then weapons designers would emphasise survivability of their missiles above all. As well, strategic doctrine would be clear that the only mission of nuclear weapons was to deter others from using them.

Resisters have been persuaded that the United States government is building first-strike weapons systems at the present time. Robert Aldridge, a former Lockeed engineer, has been important in confirming these suspicions. He had been in charge of the Lockeed unit charged with designing the Trident submarine. He resigned from an important job and gave up a successful career because he became convinced that the United States was building weapons for a possible war of aggression in the future that might rely on the system he was designing. Aldridge has written a careful book entitled *First-Strike: The Pentagon's Strategy for Nuclear War* that summarises the technical arguments for so regarding the Trident Submarines.[1] He has also lectured widely and given his entire life over to informing people about these developments. Aldridge is not a political person in the classical sense. He is a devout Catholic, a family man of quiet ways, and someone who conveys the utmost integrity and credibility. To those already concerned about the menace of nuclear weapons, and their role in our foreign policy, the life and testimony of Robert Aldridge provides powerful professional confirmation of their worst suspicions, as well as of their moral intuitions.

Those who have been especially activated seem, especially, participants in Christian faith communities with a special concern for bringing justice into the world on a personal and daily basis. They regard the Gospels as a call to action, and view Jesus as a divine person who gladly gave his life rather than submit to unjust authority. There are many variations on tactics and outlook, but two clusters of tendencies stand out. One can be associated with Seattle near where the naval base for the Trident submarine is located, but it has had a widening arc of ripple effects. The resolve to resist is centred on Ground Zero (the name given to the place of maximum blast effect at the time of a nuclear explosion), a small group of devoutly religious persons whose efforts are known more widely as a result of their excellent newsletter, sympathetic media coverage in the area, a supportive Catholic archbishop, and the writings and inspiration of James Douglass, Shelley Douglass and Jean Clark. Their tactics have been non-violent, influenced by Martin Luther King, Jr's civil rights movement and even more, by the theory and practice of *satyagraha* in India under the guidance of Gandhi. They have organised blockades of sailing boats to prevent the entry into port at the Bangor base of the first Trident class submarines and they have on six or more occasions blocked the 'white train' that carries the missiles and warheads for Trident submarines from their place of assembly at a Pantex plant in Amarillo, Texas. A monitoring and solidarity network has grown up along the route of the train suggesting the birth of a movement at the grassroots. For instance, two years ago a half dozen residents of Fort Collins, Colorado blocked the white train as it passed through their city. They were dragged by police from the tracks and charged with criminal trespass, but in the end considerable community support and policy divisions in the local DA's office led to the case being dropped.

These activities are continuing, although the government has tried to take counter-measures by painting the train a neutral colour and sending it as discretely as possible by a variety of alternative routes. By now several dozen resisters have been arrested, prosecuted, convicted on various occasions, and have returned to repeat their 'crime'. There are also physical risks undertaken. The drivers on the train are apparently under orders not to stop even if the tracks are obstructed. This means that if the police fail to remove the protesters from the tracks they could be crushed. So far, no incident of this sort has occurred. Perhaps the drivers have secret orders, or themselves harbour a grain of disobedience, and would brake the train at the last instant. Yet, from the protesters' perspective they are putting their bodies directly in the way of the machine. They are expressing a commitment unto death. That is, of the utmost seriousness.

It is not generally appreciated that Thoreau linked his defence of civil disobedience with his retreat to the rustic simplicity of Walden Pond from emerging industrial society in nineteenth-century New England. Towards the end of *Walden* there is a passage that expresses Thoreau's attitude towards law and governmental authority; the great aesthetic naturalist there insists that, above all else, an individual is 'to maintain himself in whatever attitude he finds himself through obedience to the laws of his being, which will never be one of opposition to a just government, if he should chance to meet with such.' Remember that given Thoreau's scepticism about government, to posit a just government was to enchant the mind with a kind of political oxymoron. The proper citizen, then, is the morally activated individual assuming some sort of oppositional stance. Such a credo has many resonances in the American experience including the rags-to-riches saga of Horatio Alger, the often lethal glory of pioneers and cowboys who pushed the frontier into the wilderness, and the dark metaphysical journey of Ahab and Ishmael into the lawless watery wilds.

Thoreau's specific originality was to turn his grasp of this heroic side of American character into a moral questioning of the state, and then to act accordingly. In this regard, Thoreau gives conscience priority in his arrangement of virtues: 'I think we should be men first, and subjects afterward. It is not desirable to cultivate a respect for law, so much as for right.' In the end of this seminal essay Thoreau asserts, 'There never will be a really free and enlightened State, until the State comes to recognise the individual as a higher and independent power, from which all its own power and authority are derived . . .'

Along with the Mexican War, Thoreau was also deeply troubled by the persistence of slavery as a legitimate social institution. His insistence on a moral course was uncompromising: 'This people must cease to hold slaves, and to make war on Mexico, though it cost them their existence as a people.' He thought these failures of the republic serious enough to warrant revolution: 'I think that it is not too soon for honest men to rebel and revolutionise.' This kind of clarity about what the citizen should demand from his government contrasts with the mainstream criteria of victory and wealth: To win is to be vindicated, to lose is to be condemned. Politicians in the United States have received and acted on this message from civil society almost from the beginning. The Vietnam experience reinforced this central understanding. On a more intellectual plane, apologists have rationalised the pursuit of national interests in world affairs by a biblical invocation of the fallen condition of humankind, a kind of tarnished golden rule, that overlooks the evil done unto others because it is the only alternative to their doing it unto us.

Similarly, in the eastern states of the United States there are comparable activities similarly motivated. These activities, because of the character of the operations located in the region, are directed at the weapons themselves rather than at their deployment. The most prominent of these protesters are the Berrigan brothers, Daniel and Philip, who with close associates, including Elizabeth McAlister, Molly Rush and Anne Montgomery, have engaged in a series of Plowshares activities, such as entering a GE plant in King of Prussia, Pennsylvania, where the Mark 12-A missile is assembled and Griffiss Air Force Base in upstate New York where B-52s are being retrofitted for cruise missiles, done some damage to the missiles themselves, sang religious songs at the site of their trespass, and waited until the police came to arrest them. Others have gone to the submarine base at Groton, Connecticut or to defence plants in the region, such as AVCO and Electric Boat Company, to enter and do some physical damage, 'disarmament' as they call it, to the weapons themselves. Again there are serious risks taken whenever citizens enter top-secret defence-related facilities without authorisation. Furthermore, when property is destroyed, especially if it relates to 'national security', judges tend to become harsh, even vindictive. Sentences of more than five years in jail are common in such cases, and there are a few recent cases where terms of more than ten years have been imposed. These activists are making exceedingly difficult sacrifices in their lives to awaken the rest of us to the full meaning of resting our security on this weaponry of ultimate destruction.

II

'No truer American exists than Thoreau,' Emerson said of his friend in the course of a eulogy. It remains to this day a puzzling tribute to someone most renowned for his stubborn defiance of authority. For most, to be a true American is to be obedient to the laws and deferential to the government. Patriotism is associated in the popular mind with supporting the foreign adventures of the state, dying for the sake of the flag no matter what moralists and the weak-kneed might say about the cause at stake.

Yet, surely Emerson knew what he was saying. There has

been another idea of America all along, one that is expressive of a different vision of national destiny and another conception of perfect citizenship. This is an America that started out, above all, as the end-point of pilgrimage, a place of sanctuary for the individual conscience. This is also the country that reveres the natural and innocent as qualities that had made America appear as a promised land.

At the same time, there was an underlying political forbearance in Thoreau's stance. He seemed concerned, in the end, more with the significance of moral purity to fulfill the individual life than with activating a collective process that might overcome the injustice or transform the governing process in directions more to his liking. The essence of what Thoreau demands of a citizen is this: 'What I have to do is to see, at any rate, that I do not lend myself to the wrong which I condemn!' To be sure, there is attached to this injunction a kind of absurd confidence in the social consequences of a symbolic act of disobedience:

I know this well, that if one thousand, if one hundred, if ten men whom I could name, – if ten *honest* men only, – aye, if one HONEST man, in this State of Massachusetts, *ceasing to hold slaves*, were actually to withdraw from copartnership, and be locked up in the country jail therefor, it would be the abolition of slavery in America.

Underneath this rhetorical extravagance is an all too American individualism, a wish to be left alone to retreat from society, come what may with respect to slavery.

Of course, also, it is not possible, or useful, to conjecture how Thoreau might have altered his position if trainloads of Trident missiles were passing through his beloved Concord. What continues to matter to us today is that learning to say 'No' to the state seems decisively relevant to our prospects as a people.

III

Thoreau in his famous essay on civil disobedience centres his concern on the militarism of the organised state:

'Government is at best but an expedient; but most governments are usually, and all governments are sometimes, inexpedient. The objections which have been brought against a standing army, and they are many and weighty, and deserve to prevail, may also at last be brought against a standing government.' If Thoreau thought so in 1946, one wonders what drastic response he might advocate and undertake in the 1980s when billions and billions of dollars are devoted to a terrifying array of weaponry, when military might is used at the sole discretion of the President to impose America's arbitrary will on the political destiny of small impoverished Caribbean and Central American countries, when American military power is deployed throughout the entire globe and American strategists and officials talk grotesquely, but solemnly, about *prevailing* in nuclear war, and prepare in surreal spirit for 'victory' and 'recovery'.

The situation today is, of course, far, far more extreme than anything in Thoreau's reality, so much so that it exceeds our imaginative capacities to compare the circumstances. Since Thoreau's time history has lost its moorings, making all of human society ridiculously dependent on the whims and wisdom of its main rulers. In the TV docudrama, 'The Day After', the likely severity of nuclear war had to be understated to make it even possible to present it as a potential reality, and even then, war thinkers such as Henry Kissinger complained about scaring the American people into a posture of submission by presenting the future in such horrific terms. Power-wielders don't want the reality of our situation to get in their way, no matter what the eventual costs.

Prophetically, Thoreau raised the question of citizen responsibility to oppose an unjust war. The minimum obligation of citizenship in a free society is to separate oneself from supporting those aspects of state power that are destructive and exploitative. Thoreau demands nothing necessarily more, but also nothing less.

But many continue to say, however implausibly, it is not necessary to resist, but merely to register disapproval, to vote, to petition representatives in Congress, to write letters, and to trust that the procedures of constitutional government, especially the electoral process, will give rise to the needed adjustments and produce the necessary reforms. Thoreau gave an answer to these disciples of normalcy that is more apt than ever: 'As for adopting the ways which the State has provided for remedying the evil, I know not of such ways.' When our conscience is appalled, then some response by way of non-violent defiant action is required as a message, an appeal, a warning. It is also a weapon available to society in its struggle to preserve the honour and integrity of its traditions against the menace of the state.

It is interesting to realise that Thoreau called his essay, originally given as an oration at the Concord Lyceum, 'Resistance to Civil Government', not 'On the Duty of Civil Disobedience', a title later invented by the editors of Thoreau's collected works. The distinction between 'resistance' and 'disobedience' is subtle, yet profound. Disobedience, as a stance, acknowledges the authority of the state and submits to the logic of imprisonment, while resistance raises the question, it seems to me, of who it is that belongs in prison, the officials who are acting on behalf of the state or those who resist.

True, Thoreau's resistance was based on conscience, not law. Courts have the obligation to enforce the law, and cannot bend the law to accede quixotically to the subjective prescriptions of dissenting citizens. But even here, the situation has always been confused, especially in the setting of criminal law. The underlying idea of trial by jury was to bring the conscience of the community to bear upon the application of the law. Thus, when the conscience of citizens is the essence of an alleged crime, there is a role for what is called 'jury nullification', nullifying the law and acceding to claims of conscience. Our courts have generally tried to shut down this function of the jury, and to tie jurors' hands by legalistic instructions by judges that disallow conscience to be taken into account, even in situations of symbolic criminality where the actions of those accused of lawlessness are motivated by citizen fervour for a better society.

In the anti-nuclear context, even the 'law' is in doubt and, further, the role of community conscience seems plain enough for even the most legalistic sensibility to grasp, but judges find their primary identity as officers of the state as well as men of the law, and seem more likely to serve as guardians of the state than as intermediaries between mandates of the state and challenges from the citizenry. Perhaps, in the end Thoreau is *only* a literary figure. His political acts were so puny and episodic compared to the gravity of the evils addressed. What lives is the rhetoric and the posture, and a vague understanding that Thoreau was willing to become an outlaw to underline his point. No one credits Thoreau with doing anything significant to stop the Mexican War or slavery, or even with persevering. A single night in jail is hardly a struggle to the end. In this sense, too, Thoreau seems very American, honoured as a great rebel in our tradition without having really done too much to deserve the status. Yet the honouring achieved something inspirational for others – for instance, Tolstoy, Gandhi, Martin Luther King – it has lent legitimacy to their defiance, and established the importance of the non-violent path.

IV

There have been some significant changes since the mid-nineteenth century in the legal relationship between citizens and the state. After World War II the victorious powers, led by the United States, established a judicial framework to assess the criminal liability of the defeated leaders of Germany and Japan. The most important of these trials were those held at Nuremberg upholding the basic idea that in the war/peace area leaders of governments were individually responsible for violations of international law even if they were themselves carrying out the policies of superior officials. At Nuremberg 'the supreme crime' was held by the tribunal to be planning or waging 'aggressive war' (that is, war as an active instrument of foreign policy beyond the circumstances of self-defence).

Ever since the Nuremberg proceedings there have been discussions about its quality as a legal precedent. The main criticisms have been associated with its character as victors' justice. In relation to the conduct of the war, the victorious powers engaged in behaviour that appeared 'criminal' from the perspective of the laws of war. For instance, the strategic bombing of cities in Germany and Japan, the use of atomic bombs, and the wholesale murder of European prisoners of war by their Soviet captors.

At the time, the prosecuting governments, especially the United States, emphasised that the effort at Nuremberg was to build a legal structure of accountability for the future. The American prosecutor, Robert Jackson, who took a leave from the US Supreme Court to play his historic part at Nuremberg, stated with eloquence that the principles used to assess the responsibility of the German defendants would serve as a basis to judge the victors in the future. Steps were taken to implement this conception of building a reliable legal order. At the United Nations General Assembly the essence of what was achieved at these proceedings, the Nuremberg Principles, were adopted at its very first session in 1946 by a unanimous vote of the states then members of the organisation in the form of General Assembly Resolution 95(1). Later on, in 1950, these Nuremberg Principles were reformulated in authoritative form by the International Law Commission, a UN body of legal experts that enjoys prestige because it has operated at a technical level without getting drawn into the East–West ideological struggles of the postwar world.

Throughout this process, it was the United States government that was the most ardent champion of the effort to extend the Nuremberg concept from the context of World War II to serve the international community permanently as a framework. Most international law specialists regard the Nuremberg Principles as forming a part of international law that is automatically binding on all governments.

Without attaching weight to the observation, it seems probable that Thoreau would have been disturbed by the hypocrisy of Nuremberg, but would have applauded the determined effort to make governmental leaders personally accountable for initiating and waging war, as well as for gross abuses towards people under their control (what was called at Nuremberg 'crimes against humanity'). It is also probable that Thoreau would not have expected too much to come from Nuremberg, given the way governments behave towards one another and their tendency to impose their will on the weak. He would not have been wrong. Each of the governments that sat in judgment at Nuremberg has subsequently engaged in one or more instance of aggressive warfare. There have been no subsequent prosecutions. In retrospect, it would seem that from a governmental perspective Nuremberg was 'victors' justice', nothing more.

Yet, from a citizen's perspective something new was added to political reality, something not intended by the architects of Nuremberg. The Nuremberg Principles provide a valid set of yardsticks by which to appraise the legality of governmental conduct on the most vital aspects of human affairs. What is more, the Nuremberg Principles set standards that are designed to guide and determine individual conduct. The underlying idea is that each person in whatever societal position is called upon to avoid complicity in the crimes punished at Nuremberg even if it means violating normal domestic laws. This wider pattern of responsibility has been called the 'Nuremberg Obligation'.

One thing all the anti-nuclear protesters have in common is an awareness and acceptance of the Nuremberg Obligation. Over and over again in trials across the country, the defendants explain, and seek to justify, their conduct by claiming its validation under the Nuremberg Obligation. Here again, the link with first-strike weapons systems, such as Trident is alleged to be, is quite central. The essence of this first-strike identity is to be shaped for the initation of nuclear war, and hence, the construction of such submarines is itself 'criminal' as it contemplates waging the most destructive aggressive war in all of history. And it relies upon weapons of mass destruction to carry out these aggressive designs, which seem invalid as weapons of warfare and violations of the laws of war, the second category of Nuremberg crimes.

These legal arguments have not been accepted by domestic courts in the United States, although there has been some acknowledgement of their relevance. Experts have often been allowed to testify about the Nuremberg Principles despite vigorous objection by the prosecutor.

Juries have evidently been impressed by the line of reasoning, but have generally been instructed in such a constraining way by the presiding judge as to feel that they had no option other than a verdict of guilty.

Yet, the overall effect of the Nuremberg Obligation is to change the character of the action from Thoreau's symbolic refusal to pay the poll tax. For Thoreau his stand was rooted in conscience, and the moral responsibility of an individual to act on this basis. Thoreau accepted 'law' as an expression of the state to be resisted, as necessary, by 'morality'. As a result, an opposition between law and morality will inevitably arise whenever a government acts unjustly.

For the Trident protesters the priority of morality is also central to their stand, and is their starting-point. At the same time, by invoking Nuremberg, the protesters are claiming that law, properly applied, is on their side. In fact, that upholding the Nuremberg Obligation is the paramount legal duty in the context, and that the true lawbreakers are those leaders of government who are building Trident submarines with first-strike missions in mind.

From this outlook, then, it is the institutions that are tainted, not the law. What is more, to oppose the results reached by these tainted institutions is not really 'civil disobedience' in Thoreau's sense. It is rather an insistence that citizens have become law enforcement agents in relation to the government. My guess is that Thoreau would have approved, although he might not have been out there on the tracks.

Thoreau, as we have said, was a supreme individualist. He was in retreat from the clamouring demands of modern life. He wanted, above all, to be left alone to grow intimate with his natural habitat, to explore the countryside and know its ways. As Emerson gently notes, 'I think the severity of his ideal interfered to deprive him of healthy sufficiency of human society.'

The Trident protesters are not so deprived. Their strength comes from community rather than individuality. Their prophetic witness is directed towards others in the spirit of love, not judgement. In this sense, their action is not symbolic as a gesture is symbolic. They are, as actors, closer to Gandhi than Thoreau. Their search is for symbolic actions that will mobilise others to join them on the tracks or in 'disarmament' actions at defence plants.

Beyond opposing nuclearism their strongest commitment is to renounce violence. Under no conditions will they act violently against another person. Their principled non-violence draws on early Christianity, as well as the call of Jesus not to resist evil. It also follows from Gandhi's and King's success in building movements of opposition. The Trident protesters are in the world to change the world.

V

It is important, as these particular defendants propose, to give the courts and juries an opportunity to fulfill the Nuremberg Obligation, but it would be foolish and naive to expect dramatic results, although not nearly as foolish as a few years ago. In addition to expanding resistance from below, there are important defections from nuclearism at high levels of political leadership, and there exist important statements presenting an emerging societal consensus on nuclearism, statements such as the Bishops' *Pastoral Letter on War and Peace* and the legal analysis of the Lawyer Committee on Nuclear Policy. These formulations definitely validate the reasonableness of non-violent, symbolic resistance which points to governmental illegality and immorality, as well as the emergency hazards posed by the latest phases of the arms race.

These interpretations are strengthened by the paralysis of representative institutions and elective procedures when it comes to the fundamentals of national security policy. The situation has regressed from the time of Thoreau's complaint that conscience cannot wait on the rhythms of constitutional government. Today, we are faced with something far more menacing than the encroachment on democracy caused by 'a standing army', which was the specific object of the anxiety of anti-militarists in the early life of the republic. Today, our society has become permanently galvanised to carry out an ultimate war at a few minutes' notice.

Furthermore, the global stance of the United States calls for wide-ranging interventionary capabilities and campaigns to be mounted on the sole basis of a general Presidential mandate, often undisclosed, enacted through so-called 'covert operations'. The procedures of representative democracy have been severely compromised and fundamentally inhibited. Congress has played virtually no role in questioning the moral, legal and political policies of nuclearism. The courts have been evasive and passive, and have done their best to avoid 'embarrassing' results caused by juries doubtful about their restrictive conceptions of legality. Presidential elections are a mockery when it comes to these security concerns. No major candidate can remain 'credible' with the media, and hence with the public, if he or she is seen in any way to question the national security consensus that is held by 'the state within the state', that is, by the sectors of the Federal bureaucracy associated with war/peace issues, especially the Pentagon, the State Department, and the intelligence agencies.

Representative democracy is now virtually dead when it comes to nuclear national security. Citizens conscious of the Nuremberg Obligation cannot in these circumstances rely on normal political channels. Acts of resistance must be understood, then, both as a reflection of the current failure of democratic governance and as a creative effort designed to promote the revitalisation of democracy. The political implications of the Nuremberg Obligation require, in effect, a new encounter between the citizenry and the state, resulting in a new framework of official accountability in accordance with new legal and moral guidelines, what amounts to a Magna Carta for the nuclear age. Nothing less can restore a real significance to democratic processes and give real content to the claim that the legitimacy of government rests on the consent of the governed. Citizenship and patriotism in the nuclear age must be increasingly understood as requiring participation in this struggle, to revitalise democracy and to dismantle the nuclear national security state.

With characteristic prophetic power, Leo Tolstoy commented in his old age on 'the two wars', that of the state, illustrated by the then contemporaneous Spanish-American War (1898) and that of the war against war, illustrated by the struggle of the militant and persecuted pacifist sect of the Dukoboors in Czarist Russia. It is not even enough to grow sensitive to the danger of nuclear war. War itself has become a scandal and an obscenity in a world of mass misery and fairly widespread education. The technology of non-nuclear warfare is becoming increasingly capable of levels of mass, indiscriminate destruction comparable in many of its dimensions to that wrought by nuclear weapons. Even as early as World War I the mutually destructive character of war led to widespread public questioning of the continued acceptablity of war in organised political life. Until fairly recently, the United States played a leading, if somewhat hypocritical, role in working for the prohibition of non-defensive warfare.

It is foolhardy to look to the modern state, here or elsewhere, to further the goals of the abolition of war. At the same time, such a project, however remote its prospects may seem in our militarised, wired world, is essential if we are to build a hopeful future for our children and grand-children and create a horizon of possibility that is inspired by more than current preoccupations with *mere survival*. And there are some positive signs of encouragement. Even 'realists' are beginning to affirm the abolitionist vision. Stanley Hoffmann and George Kennan have made acknowl-edgement that a secure future for human society requires the abolition of war. Kennan makes a particularly moving 'confession' of his change of heart in the introduction to his book *The Nuclear Delusions*.

What is more, we now have an ever-increasing techno-logical capacity to reliably verify a disarming process, without undue interference with sovereign rights; new infor-mation technologies, combined with sensing and monitoring capabilities, can create confidence that distrust can be reconciled with deep levels of disarmament. And finally, a wider sphere of the public is becoming convinced that 'national security' can be upheld by non-violent means, and that responsibility for its discharge needs to be reclaimed, taken away from the exclusive control of the centralised state, with its dependence on bureaucratic methods and its confidence in technology and violence.

Let me revert, in closing, to Tolstoy's war on war. He rests his optimism about the future on those who act without limits or calculations, solely on the basis of their conviction, those whom the mainstream refuses to acknowledge; in Tolstoy's words, 'no one speaks or knows of these heroes of the war against war, who are not seen and heard by anyone.' He tells, in particular, of a peasant, named Okhook, who refused military service and while being transported to jail managed to convert to his cause his guard Sereda, and whom Tolstoy quotes as saying: 'I do not want to be with the tormentors, join me to the martyrs.' Many more of us are open to this alliance, within the societal struggle at this stage.

In this sense, it is important at this time for us to question the technocratic definitions of 'useful', 'practical', and 'realistic' which the dominant culture provides. These definitions are deeply tied to the technologies of violence, to the computerisation of decisions, and even to the robot as an advance on human nature. Under much less critical circumstances, Tolstoy commented in a manner that remains illuminating:

The people of our time, especially the scholars, have become so gross that they do not understand, and in their grossness cannot even understand, the significance and the influence of spiritual force. A charge of ten thousand pounds of dynamite sent into a crowd of living men – that they understand and in that they see strength; but an idea, truth, which has been realised, has been introduced into life to the point of martyrdom, has become accessible to millions – that is to their conception not force, because it does not boom, and you do not see broken bones and puddles of blood.

I believe we are reaching the stage where honouring the Nuremberg Obligation becomes a spiritual weapon with which to fight against the violence-drenched orientations of the modern state, whether East or West. And I believe that these defendants who are facing trial these days are 'martyrs' in Tolstoy's sense: they are teaching us how to be citizens in the nuclear age.

In the end, negating nuclearism is not enough. We also require a wider vision of a human community that handles conflict non-violently, that harnesses production to human needs, and that uses far more of the resources of the planet for the benefit of all. It may seem an impossible journey, but our only solid hope as a species is to muster the courage to get on with it. As W. H. Auden once wrote, 'We who are about to die demand a miracle.' But this time the miracle will not come from without, if it comes, but from within.

NOTES

1. The idea of 'first strike' is a complex one. In essence, a combination of missiles, navigational aid, and operational plans provides war planners with the confidence that it is possible to threaten or actually initiate nuclear war in such a way as to disable, at least in large part, the capacity of the other side to retaliate. One effect of such a first-strike posture is to create a pressure on the threatened society to attack first in a period of rising tensions or crisis to avoid the adverse effects of vulnerability to a first strike. Aldridge anticipates that on the basis of present projections the United States will achieve a first-strike posture in 1988 when 18 Navstar satellites will be placed in orbit to provide in-flight guidance for missiles assuring greater accuracy for a strike aiming at Soviet 'hard targets' such as silos or command centres.

   Trident itself refers both to a new super-class of submarines and to a type of missile that can also be retro-fitted into earlier classes of nuclear submarines. By 1988 there are expected to be nine Trident submarines each carrying 24 Trident missiles, with each missile having eight 100–kiloton warheads (about eight Hiroshima equivalents), for a grand total of 1728 warheads capable of being separately targeted. It is not surprising that a Trident commander has been called 'the third most powerful man in the world'. In addition, of course, are the other classes of submarines, land-based missiles and the strategic bomber fleet. Anti-nuclear resisters regard any element of this array of weaponry to be part of the first-strike capability and a fair focus for action. Aside from the Trident submarines, a favoured target for protest is the Mark 12 or Mark 12–A warhead intended for Minuteman–3 and MX land-based missiles. The material in this note is largely drawn from Aldridge's article 'First-Strike Breakout in 1988', published in *Ground Zero*. December 1983/January 1984, pp. 1, 3.
2. The 1950 ILC text of the Nuremberg Principles follows:

As formulated by the International Law Commission, June–July 1950.

Principle I
Any person who commits an act which constitutes a crime under international law is responsible therefor and liable to punishment.

Principle II
The fact that internal law does not impose a penalty for an act which constitutes a crime under international law does not relieve the person who committed the act from responsibility under international law.

Principle III
The fact that a person who committed an act which constitutes a crime under international law acted as Head of State or responsible government official does not relieve him from responsibility under international law.

Principle IV
The fact that a person acted pursuant to order of his Government or of a superior does not relieve him from responsibility under international law, provided a moral choice was in fact possible to him.

Principle VI
The crimes hereinafter set out are punishable as crimes under international law:

a. Crimes against peace:
  (i) Planning, preparation, initiation or waging of war of aggression or a war in violation of international treaties, agreements or assurances;
  (ii) Participation in a common plan or conspiracy for the accomplishment of any of the acts mentioned under (i).

b. War crimes:
  Violations of the laws or customs of war which include, but are not limited to, murder, ill-treatment or deportation to slave-labour or for any other purpose of civilian population of or in occupied territory, murder or ill-treatment of prisoners of war or persons on the seas, killing of hostages, plunder of public or private property, wanton destruction of cities, towns, or villages, or devastation not justified by military necessity.

c. Crimes against humanity:
  Murder, extermination, enslavement, deportation and other inhuman acts done against any civilian population, or persecutions on political, racial or religious grounds, when such acts are done or such persecutions are carried out in execution of or in connexion with any crime against peace or any war crime.

Principle VII
Complicity in the commision of a crime against peace, a war crime, or a crime against humanity as set forth in Principle VI is a crime under international law.

Center of International Studies Princeton University

List of Publications

BOOKS (AVAILABLE FROM PUBLISHERS)

Gabriel A. Almond, *The Appeals of Communism* (Princeton University Press, 1954).

William W. Kaufmann (ed.), *Military Policy and National Security* (Princeton University Press, 1956).

Klaus Knorr, *The War Potential of Nations* (Princeton University Press, 1956).

Lucian W. Pye, *Guerrilla Communism in Malaya* (Princeton University Press, 1956).

Charles De Visscher, *Theory and Reality in Public International Law*, trans. by P. E. Corbett (Princeton University Press, 1957; rev. edn 1968).

Bernard C. Cohen, *The Political Process and Foreign Policy: The Making of the Japanese Peace Settlement* (Princeton University Press, 1957).

Myron Weiner, *Party Politics in India: The Development of a Multi-Party System* (Princeton University Press, 1957).

Percy E. Corbett, *Law in Diplomacy* (Princeton University Press, 1959).

Rolf Sannwald and Jacques Stohler, *Economic Integration: Theoretical Assumptions and Consequences of European Unification*, trans. by Herman Karreman (Princeton University Press, 1959).

Klaus Knorr (ed.), *NATO and American Security* (Princeton University Press, 1959).

Gabriel A. Almond and James S. Coleman (eds.), *The Politics of the Developing Areas* (Princeton University Press, 1960).

Herman Kahn, *On Thermonuclear War* (Princeton University Press, 1960).

319

Sidney Verba, *Small Groups and Political Behaviour: A Study of Leadership* (Princeton University Press, 1961).

Robert J. C. Butow, *Tojo and the Coming of the War* (Princeton University Press, 1961).

Glenn H. Snyder, *Deterrence and Defense: Toward a Theory of National Security* (Princeton University Press, 1961).

Klaus Knorr and Sidney Verba (eds.), *The International System: Theoretical Essays* (Princeton University Press, 1961).

Peter Paret and John W. Shy, *Guerrillas in the 1960's* (Praeger, 1962).

George Modelski, *A Theory of Foreign Policy* (Praeger, 1962).

Klaus Knorr and Thornton Read (eds.), *Limited Strategic War* (Praeger, 1963).

Frederick S. Dunn, *Peace-Making and the Settlement with Japan* (Princeton University Press, 1963).

Arthur L. Burns and Nina Heathcote, *Peace-Keeping by United Nations Forces* (Praeger, 1963).

Richard A. Falk, *Law, Morality, and War in the Contemporary World* (Praeger, 1963).

James N. Rosenau, *National Leadership and Foreign Policy: A Case Study in the Mobilisation of Public Support* (Princeton University Press, 1963).

Gabriel A. Almond and Sidney Verba, *The Civic Culture: Political Attitudes and Democracy in Five Nations* (Princeton University Press, 1963).

Bernard C. Cohen, *The Press and Foreign Policy* (Princeton University Press, 1963).

Richard L. Sklar, *Nigerian Political Parties: Power in an Emergent African Nation* (Princeton University Press, 1963).

Peter Paret, *French Revolutionary Warfare from Indochina to Algeria: The Analysis of a Political and Military Doctrine* (Praeger, 1964).

Harry Eckstein (ed.), *Internal War: Problems and Approaches* (Free Press, 1964).

Cyril E. Black and Thomas P. Thornton (eds.), *Communism and Revolution: The Strategic Uses of Political Violence* (Princeton University Press, 1964).

Miriam Camps, *Britain and the European Community 1955–1963* (Princeton University Press, 1964).

Thomas P. Thornton (ed.), *The Third World in Soviet Perspective: Studies by Soviet Writers on the Developing Areas* (Princeton University Press, 1964).

James N. Rosenau (ed.), *International Aspects of Civil Strife* (Princeton University Press, 1964).

Sidney I. Ploss, *Conflict and Decision-Making in Soviet Russia: A Case Study of Agricultural Policy, 1953–1963* (Princeton University Press, 1965).

Richard A. Falk and Richard J. Barnet (eds.), *Security in Disarmament* (Princeton University Press, 1965).

Karl von Vorys, *Political Development in Pakistan* (Princeton University Press, 1965).

Harold and Margaret Sprout, *The Ecological Perspective on Human Affairs, With Special Reference to International Politics* (Princeton University Press, 1965).

Klaus Knorr, *On the Uses of Military Power in the Nuclear Age* (Princeton University Press, 1966).

Harry Eckstein, *Division and Cohesion in Democracy: A Study of Norway* (Princeton University Press, 1966).

John T. McAlister, Jr, *Viet Nam: The Origins of Revolution* (Knopf, 1969).

Jean Edward Smith, *Germany Beyond the Wall: People, Politics and Prosperity* (Little, Brown, 1969).

James Barros, *Betrayal from Within: Joseph Avenol, Secretary-General of the League of Nations, 1933–1940* (Yale University Press, 1969).

Charles Hermann, *Crises in Foreign Policy: A Simulation Analysis* (Bobbs-Merrill, 1969).

Robert C. Tucker, *The Marxian Revolutionary Idea: Essays on Marxist Thought and its Impact on Radical Movements* (W. W. Norton, 1969).

Harvey Waterman, *Political Change in Contemporary France: The Politics of an Industrial Democracy* (Charles E. Merrill, 1969).

Cyril E. Black and Richard A. Falk (eds.), *The Future of the International Legal Order*. Vol. I: *Trends and Patterns* (Princeton University Press, 1969).

Ted Robert Gurr, *Why Men Rebel* (Princeton University Press, 1969).

C. Sylvester Whitaker, *The Politics of Tradition: Continuity and Change in Northern Nigeria 1946–1966* (Princeton University Press, 1970).

Richard A. Falk, *The Status of Law in International Society* (Princeton University Press, 1970).

John T. McAlister, Jr and Paul Mus, *The Vietnamese and Their Revolution* (Harper & Row, 1970).

Klaus Knorr, *Military Power and Potential* (D. C. Heath, 1970).

Cyril E. Black and Richard A. Falk (eds.), *The Future of the International Legal Order.* Vol. II: *Wealth and Resources* (Princeton University Press, 1970).

Leon Gordenker (ed.), *The United Nations in International Politics* (Princeton University Press, 1971).

Cyril E. Black and Richard A. Falk (eds.), *The Future of the International Legal Order.* Vol. III: *Conflict Management* (Princeton University Press, 1971).

Francine R. Frankel, *India's Green Revolution: Political Costs of Economic Growth* (Princeton University Press, 1971).

Harold and Margaret Sprout, *Toward a Politics of the Planet Earth* (Van Nostrand Reinhold, 1971).

Cyril E. Black and Richard A. Falk (eds.), *The Future of the International Legal Order.* Vol. IV: *The Structure of the International Environment* (Princeton University Press, 1972).

Gerald Garvey, *Energy, Ecology, Economy* (W. W. Norton, 1972).

Richard Ullman, *The Anglo-Soviet Accord* (Princeton University Press, 1973).

Klaus Knorr, *Power and Wealth: The Political Economy of International Power* (Basic Books, 1973).

Anton Bebler, *Military Role in Africa: Dahomey, Ghana, Sierra Leone, and Mali* (Praeger Publishers, 1973).

Robert C. Tucker, *Stalin as Revolutionary 1879–1929: A Study in History and Personality* (W. W. Norton, 1973).

Edward L. Morse, *Foreign Policy and Interdependence in Gaullist France* (Princeton University Press, 1973).

Henry Bienen, *Kenya: The Politics of Participation and Control* (Princeton University Press, 1974).

Gregory J. Massell, *The Surrogate Proletariat: Moslem Women and Revolutionary Strategies in Soviet Central Asia, 1919–1929* (Princeton University Press, 1974).

James N. Rosenau, *Citizenship Between Elections: An Inquiry Into the Mobilizable American* (Free Press, 1974).

Ervin Laszlo, *A Strategy For the Future: The Systems Approach to World Order* (Braziller, 1974).

John R. Vincent, *Nonintervention and International Order* (Princeton University Press, 1974).

Jan H. Kalicki, *The Pattern of Sino-American Crises: Political-Military Interactions in the 1950s* (Cambridge University Press, 1975).

Klaus Knorr, *The Power of Nations: The Political Economy of International Relations* (Basic Books Inc., 1975).

James P. Sewell, *UNESCO and World Politics: Engaging in International Relations* (Princeton University Press, 1975).

Richard A. Falk, *A Global Approach to National Policy* (Harvard University Press, 1975).

Harry Eckstein and Ted Robert Gurr, *Patterns of Authority: A Structural Basis for Political Inquiry* (John Wiley & Sons, 1975).

Cyril E. Black, Marius B. Jansen, Herbert S. Levin, Marion J. Levy, Jr, Henry Rosovsky, Gilbert Rozman, Henry D. Smith, II and S. Frederick Starr, *The Modernization of Japan and Russia* (Free Press, 1975).

Leon Gordenker, *International Aid and National Decisions: Development Programs in Malawi, Tanzania, and Zambia* (Princeton University Press, 1976).

Carl Von Clausewitz, *On War*, edited and translated by Michael Howard and Peter Paret (Princeton University Press, 1976).

Gerald Garvey and Lou Ann Garvey (eds), *International Resource Flows* (D. C. Heath, 1977).

Walter F. Murphy and Joseph Tanenhaus, *Comparative Constitutional Law Cases and Commentaries* (St Martin's Press, 1977).

Gerald Garvey, *Nuclear Power and Social Planning: The City of the Second Sun* (D. C. Heath, 1977).

Richard E. Bissell, *Apartheid and International Organisations* (Westview Press, 1977).

David P. Forsythe, *Humanitarian Politics: The International Committee of the Red Cross* (Johns Hopkins University Press, 1977).

Paul E. Sigmund, *The Overthrow of Allende and the Politics of Chile, 1964–1976* (University of Pittsburgh Press, 1977).

Henry S. Bienen, *Armies and Parties in Africa* (Holmes and Meier, 1978).

Harold and Margaret Sprout, *The Context of Environmental Politics* (The University Press of Kentucky, 1978).

Samuel S. Kim, *China, the United Nations, and World Order* (Princeton University Press, 1979).

S. Basheer Ahmed, *Nuclear Fuel and Energy Policy* (D. C. Heath, 1979).

Robert C. Johansen, *The National Interest and the Human Interest: An Analysis of U. S. Foreign Policy* (Princeton University Press, 1980).

Richard A. Falk and Samuel S. Kim (eds.), *The War System: An Interdisciplinary Approach* (Westview Press, 1980).

James H. Billington, *Fire in the Minds of Men: Origins of the Revolutionary Faith* (Basic Books Inc., 1980).

Bennett Ramberg, *Destruction of Nuclear Energy Facilities in War: The Problem and the Implications* (D. C. Heath, 1980).

Gregory T. Kruglak, *The Politics of United States Decision-Making in United Nations Specialised Agencies: The Case of the International Labour Organisation* (University Press of America, 1980).

W. P. Davison and Leon Gordenker (eds.), *Resolving Nationality Conflicts: The Role of Public Opinion Research* (Praeger Publishers, 1980).

James C. Hsiung and Samuel S. Kim (eds.), *China in the Global Community* (Praeger Publishers, 1980).

Douglas Kinnard, *The Secretary of Defense* (The University Press of Kentucky, 1980).

Richard Falk, *Human Rights and State Sovereignty* (Holmes & Meier, 1981).

James H. Mittelman, *Underdevelopment and the Transition to Socialism: Mozambique and Tanzania* (Academic Press, 1991).

Gilbert Rozman (ed.), *The Modernization of China* (The Free Press, 1981; paperback edition 1982).

Robert C. Tucker, *Politics as Leadership*. The Paul Anthony Brick Lectures. Eleventh Series (University of Missouri Press, 1981).

Robert Gilpin, *War and Change in World Politics* (Cambridge University Press, 1981).

Nicholas G. Onuf (ed.), *Law-Making in the Global Community* (Carolina Academic Press, 1982).

Ali E. Hillal Dessouki (ed.), *Islamic Resurgence in the Arab World* (Praeger Publishers, 1982).

Richard Falk, *The End of World Order* (Holmes & Meier, 1983).

Klaus Knorr (ed.), *Power, Strategy and Security* (Princeton University Press, 1983).

Finn Laursen, *Superpower At Sea* (Praeger Publishers, 1983).

Samuel S. Kim, *The Quest for a Just World Order* (Westview Press, 1984).

Gerald Garvey, *Strategy and the Defense Dilemma* (D. C. Heath and Co., 1984).

Peter R. Baehr and Leon Gordenker, *The United Nations: Reality and Ideal* (Praeger Publishers, 1984).

Joseph M. Gieco, *Between Dependency and Autonomy: India's Experience With the International Computer Industry* (University of California Press, 1984).

Jan Hallenberg, *Foreign Policy Change: United States Foreign Policy Toward the Soviet Union and the People's Republic of China, 1961–1980* (University of Stockholm, 1984).

Michael Krepon, *Strategic Stalemate: Nuclear Weapons and Arms Control in American Politics* (St Martin's Press, 1984).

Gilbert Rozman, *A Mirror for Socialism: Soviet Criticisms of China* (Princeton University Press, 1985).

Henry Bienen, *Political Conflict and Economic Change in Nigeria* (Frank Cass, 1985).

Kenneth A. Oye (ed.), *Cooperation Under Anarchy* (Princeton University Press, 1986).

Richard Falk, *Reviving the World Court* (University of Virginia Press, 1986).

Index